CIVIL WAR &
REVOLUTION ON
THE RIO GRANDE
FRONTIER

CIVIL WAR & REVOLUTION ON THE RIO GRANDE FRONTIER

A Narrative and Photographic History

JERRY THOMPSON
AND LAWRENCE T. JONES III

Texas State Historical Association
Austin

Frontispiece: Photographer Louis de Planque, ca. 1865. *Carte de visite* attributed to Eugenia de Planque. *Lawrence T. Jones III collection.*

Published by the Texas State Historical Association in cooperation with the Center for Studies in Texas History at the University of Texas at Austin.

Publication of this book was made possible by grants from the Summerfield G. Roberts Foundation of Dallas.

Book design by David Timmons

Library of Congress Cataloging-in-Publication Data

Thompson, Jerry D.
 Civil War and revolution on the Rio Grande frontier : a narrative and photographic history / Jerry Thompson and Lawrence T. Jones III.
     p.   cm.
 Includes bibliographical references.
 ISBN 0-87611-201-7 (hardcover : alk. paper)
 1. Frontier and pioneer life—Texas. 2. Frontier and pioneer life--Rio Grande Valley. 3. Texas—History—Civil War, 1861-1865. 4. Reconstruction (U.S. history, 1865–1877)—Texas. 5. Rio Grande Valley—History—19th century. 6. Mexican-American Border Region—History—19th century. 7. Texas—History—19th century—Pictorial works. 8. Rio Grande Valley—History—19th century—Pictorial works. 9. Mexican-American Border Region—History—19th century—Pictorial works. I. Jones, Lawrence T. II. Title.
 F391.T5116 2004
 973.7'13'097644—dc22
                                                                                        2004012737

5   4   3   2   1   04   05   06   07   08

ACKNOWLEDGMENTS

The genesis of this book was the result of the keen eye and historical knowledge of Bill Young, a former newspaper and television reporter in Brownsville, Texas. In 1999 a Civil War photo album was discovered in Monterrey, Mexico. The album was literally salvaged from a trash heap filled with discarded books from a recently purchased house that was being cleaned. By luck and sheer coincidence the album was shown to a friend of a friend, who brought it across the border and loaned it to a Brownsville Historical Association board member, who took the album to a board meeting, where it was shown to Bill Young, president of the association. The album was chock full of photographs, and Young immediately recognized some of the images. He also clearly understood the historical significance of the album. Under his guidance and direction the Brownsville Historical Association acquired this very rare and important piece of local history. A substantial number of the photographs included in this work are from that album.

Thanks are due Rosalinda Garza for scanning and providing digital files of everything that was asked for from the remarkable collection of the Brownsville Historical Association. Special thanks are due Dennis Keesee of Westerville, Ohio, for his supreme generosity in providing original research material relating to the rare set of hanging photographs.

We are grateful to the following for sharing their time, knowledge, and original photographs from their collections. Without their generosity, we would have no book: John Anderson, Texas State Library, Austin, Texas; Robert G. McCubbin, Santa Fe, New Mexico; Brownsville Historical Association, Brownsville, Texas; Don Beardslee, San Antonio, Texas; Martin L. Callahan, San Antonio, Texas; Laura Z. Garcia, La Retama Public Library, Corpus Christi, Texas; Homero Salinas Vera, Premont, Texas; Enrique E. Guerra, San Vicente Ranch, Linn, Texas; Rebecca Huffstutler, Curator of Archives, Witte Museum, San Antonio, Texas; Sharon Farias and Lisa A. Neely, King Ranch Archives, Kingsville, Texas; Steven F. Joseph, Brussels, Belgium; Thomas R. Kailbourn, Wellsville, New York; Philip Nathanson, Los Angeles, California; Peter E. Palmquist, Arcata, California; Mary Margaret McAllen Amberson, San Antonio, Texas; Jeremy Rowe, Mesa, Arizona; William L. Schaeffer, Chester, Connecticut; Tom Shelton, University of Texas at San Antonio, Institute of Texas Cultures; John Sickles, Merrillville, Indiana; Robin Stanford, Kingwood, Texas; Larry M. Strayer, Dayton, Ohio; Richard K. Tibbals, Berwyn, Illinois; and Patricia C. Young, Brownsville, Texas.

It should be noted that portions of Chapters I and II rely heavily on Jerry Thompson's *Sabers on the Rio Grande, Vaqueros in Blue and Gray, Mexican-Texans in the Union Army,* and *Juan Cortina and the Texas–Mexico Frontier, 1859–1877,* as well as his articles on the Civil War in South Texas, especially those relating to Santos Benavides, Juan N. Cortina, and Adrián J. Vidal.

LAWRENCE T. JONES III
JERRY THOMPSON

For Donna J. Coates,
photographic researcher *extraordinaire*

CONTENTS

CIVIL WAR & REVOLUTION ON THE RIO GRANDE FRONTIER

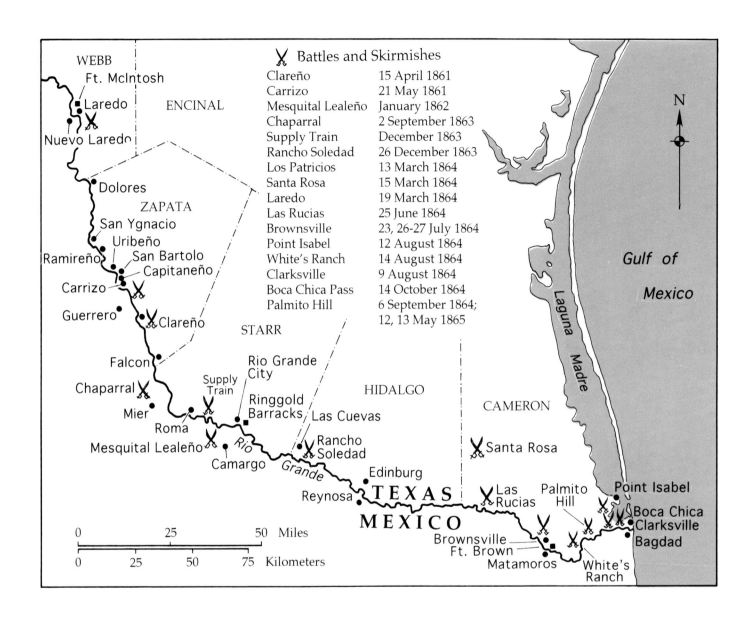

WEBB
Ft. McIntosh
Laredo
Nuevo Laredo

ENCINAL

✂ Battles and Skirmishes
Clareño   15 April 1861
Carrizo   21 May 1861
Mesquital Lealeño January 1862
Chaparral   2 September 1863
Supply Train   December 1863
Rancho Soledad   26 December 1863
Los Patricios   13 March 1864
Santa Rosa   15 March 1864
Laredo   19 March 1864
Las Rucias   25 June 1864
Brownsville   23, 26-27 July 1864
Point Isabel   12 August 1864
White's Ranch   14 August 1864
Clarksville   9 August 1864
Boca Chica Pass   14 October 1864
Palmito Hill   6 September 1864;
                   12, 13 May 1865

N

Dolores
ZAPATA
San Ygnacio
Uribeño
Ramireño
San Bartolo
Capitaneño
Carrizo
Guerrero
Clareño
STARR

Gulf of
Mexico

Falcon
Chaparral
Mier
Roma
Mesquital Lealeño
Camargo

Supply
Train
Rio Grande
City
Ringgold
Barracks
Las Cuevas
Rancho
Soledad
Rio
Grande
Edinburg
Reynosa

HIDALGO

CAMERON
Santa Rosa

Laguna Madre

TEXAS
MEXICO

Las
Rucias
Palmito
Hill

Point Isabel
Boca Chica
Clarksville
Bagdad

Brownsville
Ft. Brown
Matamoros

White's
Ranch

0   25   50   Miles
0   25   50   75   Kilometers

Introduction

THE PHOTOGRAPHERS

Only days after Confederate gunners fired on Fort Sumter in the harbor of Charleston, South Carolina, the Civil War also erupted twelve hundred miles to the west on the Rio Grande frontier in Zapata County, Texas. Four years later, more than a month after Gen. Robert E. Lee surrendered his Army of Northern Virginia at Appomattox Court House, Virginia, the battle of Palmito Ranch, just east of Brownsville, became the last land battle of the war on May 12–13, 1865. Ironically, it was a Confederate victory.

Far from the killing fields of the east, this dark corner of the Confederacy played a crucial role in the bitter war between North and South. It was here on the wild South Texas border that men from all over the western world gathered to reap the profits from a lucrative cotton trade. Avoiding the Union's ever-tightening blockade, cotton from as far away as Arkansas and Louisiana poured across the border at river villages and towns such as Eagle Pass, Laredo, Rio Grande City, and Brownsville, most of it bound for the Mexican port of Bagdad at the mouth of the Rio Grande, where ships from all over the world waited to take it to hungry textile mills in Great Britain, France, and, surprisingly, New England.

This book details the rich and often violent history of the Lower Rio Grande Valley of Texas and Mexico, particularly Brownsville and Matamoros, in the years from 1861 to 1870. While Union and Confederate forces struggled for control of the Texas bank of the Rio Grande, *Juaristas* and *Imperialistas* grappled mightily for political control of the soul of Mexico on the south bank. At one time in 1864, four armies were floundering in the

Lower Rio Grande Valley. The bloodshed that engulfed Matamoros and the border was born out of foreign intervention. With the election of Benito Juárez to the presidency in March 1861, Mexico was forced to confront a series of seemingly insurmountable problems, especially a bankrupt treasury. Mexico's European creditors began clamoring for the repayment of foreign debts the republic had incurred over decades. When Juárez declared a two-year moratorium on the payment of the country's debt, Spain, Great Britain, and France, as a show of force in hopes of collecting their claims, landed troops at Veracruz. Although the Spanish and British troops were eventually withdrawn, it became evident that Louis Napoleon Bonaparte, nephew of Napoleon I, had designs on the infant republic, and a French army began moving inland. Although defeated at Puebla on May 5—*Cinco de Mayo*—the French army eventually took the city the following year and Mexico City shortly thereafter. Supported by Mexican conservatives, Napoleon became convinced that if a monarchy was good for France, it would be good for Mexico, and in May 1864 thirty-two-year-old

Ferdinand Maximilian Joseph and twenty-four-year old Marie Charlotte Amélie Léopoldine arrived in Mexico to ascend the imperial throne of Mexico. The stage was set for a vicious war between the *Imperialistas* and the *Juaristas*.

This decisive period in the history of Texas and Mexico is illustrated through the lenses of several skilled and accomplished photographers who operated out of studios in Matamoros and Brownsville during these tempestuous years. *Civil War and Revolution on the Rio Grande Frontier* contains more than 130 of the best images taken by Louis de Planque and other photographers. The majority of these images have never been published before or even known to exist. From numerous archives and private collections, these photographs include everything from the horrendous destruction following the killer hurricane of 1867, the most powerful storm to ever hit the South Texas–Mexico coast, to gripping views of the heart-wrenching hangings of an American army deserter and three unfortunate *Cortinistas*, who were caught on the wrong side of the turbulent Rio Grande. Also included are rare scenes of Brownsville, Matamoros, and Bagdad, as well as *Juaristas, Imperialistas, Cortinistas,* Confederates, Unionists, cotton-traders, journalists, socialites, de Planque himself, the Brownsville and Matamoros merchant elite, and more than one bandit, revolutionary, and common soldier.

Photography was a relatively young enterprise at the beginning of the Civil War. From its daguerreian roots in 1839, there had been notable improvements in photographic processes by the time the photographers began operating in the early 1860s in Brownsville and Matamoros. Most of the photographs reproduced here are in the formats known as *carte de visite* and stereograph. The stereograph (commonly referred to as stereoview) is a pair of photographs mounted side by side on a card mount measuring approximately 3.25 by 6.75 inches. When viewed through a stereoscope, the two photographs appear as a single three-dimensional image. The *carte de visite* is a small single photograph mounted on card stock measuring approximately 2.5 by 4 inches. These two types of photographs were of the collodion glass plate-albumen paper-print method. This technique of producing photographs had several advantages over previous types of processes, such as the daguerreotype and ambrotype. These older processes had no negative and literally resulted in a one-of-a-kind image. The newer paper-print process was easier and much less expensive to produce. More importantly, it was reliable, and multiple copies could be reproduced from a single negative.

The commercialization of photography in the 1860s resulted in photographic materials such as paper, chemicals, cameras, and lenses being mass-produced. The wartime Federal blockade of Confederate ports created a shortage of these types of supplies in some southern locales. Such shortages were not an issue for the Brownsville and Matamoros photographers, however, because of the nearby Mexican port of Bagdad, or what the Mexicans called Boca del Rio, where practically anything and everything could be purchased.

The work of the Brownsville–Matamoros photographers is augmented by rare and previously unpublished Civil War photographs from a number of private collections. These collections consist of *carte de visite* photographs of identified Union and Confederate soldiers from specific military units. All of the men in these images either participated in combat along the lower Rio Grande or served there as occupation troops during Reconstruction. Among this group are images of soldiers who fought at Palmito Ranch, the last land battle of the Civil War.

Remote from the more familiar theaters of operations, the Rio Grande frontier has a rich history of Civil War and Reconstruction photography that has largely been ignored. Few wartime photographs of Brownsville or Matamoros have been published, but when they have been, albeit briefly, they have frequently been misidentified or misinterpreted.[1] Six of the photographs that have been published are attributed to A. G. Wedge, Matamoros, Mexico. This photographer operated in Texas during the Civil War and was in the photography business in Galveston as early as April 1861. Photographs with Wedge's Galveston imprint are quite rare. At least three of his *cartes de visite* are extant, and they show a type of Confederate first national flag as part of his imprint. All of these photographs are full-length studio portraits of Confederate officers, including Gen. John Bankhead Magruder.[2]

A photograph of General Magruder would indicate that Wedge was still operating in Galveston after January 1863, when Confederates under his leadership re-occupied the city. Wedge was probably an itinerant photographer, making him much harder to document. There is also evidence that the elusive Wedge had traveled down the Texas coast, eventually making it to Brownsville by May 1863. A previously unknown and extremely rare set of *cartes de visite* of Confederate officers was recently discovered and, when sold at auction in July 2001, literally brought world-record prices for their type of material. The *cartes de visite* were taken at Fort Brown in May and June 1863, and all have period manuscript-ink identification. There is no photographer's imprint on any of the views, but all appear to be the work of Wedge. The studio props, such as the column and curtain, appear to be the same as those Wedge used in his Galveston photographs. Furthermore, the manner in which almost all of the subjects are posed is identical to Wedge's imprinted Galveston views of General Magruder and his staff officers.

The 1863 dates on the Fort Brown views make Wedge the earliest documented Civil War photographer operating in Brownsville, although there must have been others working there at the same time or earlier. Wedge was not even the original photographer of the six Brownsville photographs with which he is credited in *The Image of War*.[3] These photographs are extant in public and private collections with the imprint of Louis de Planque. Despite the fact that Wedge's imprint appears on the photographs, it is likely that he copied or "pirated" the images and then sold them under his own imprint, a fairly common practice with nineteenth-century photographers. Wedge disappears from the photography scene after June 1863, and no further record of him has been found.

Because Matamoros was neutral as far as the warring Americans were concerned, the city and

Commission, Forwarding, Lightering and General Merchandising Business, at **BAGDAD, MEXICO.** All business entrusted to them by Matamoros and other Merchants, will be attended to with promptness. 256-6m

GALLERY OF FINE ARTS. A. Moses & Co., CASTRO HOUSE, Adjoining M. Trevino's, near Cesar St. PHOTOGRAPHS, AMBROTYPES, IVORY TYPES, MIROSCOPES, And PORCELAIN TYPES. Instantaneous Views True to Life. 217-3m

Claims against the Government of the United States. FRANK E. MACMANUS,

A. Moses and Company promoted their Matamoros photograph gallery with this display advertisement in the March 25, 1866, edition of the *Daily Ranchero. William C. and Patricia Cisneros Young collection.*

the nearby Mexican port of Bagdad were destined to attract a diverse and cosmopolitan crowd of newcomers. Fueled by the smuggling profits of the cotton trade, the geopolitical milieu there became even more complicated with competing liberal and conservative Mexican factions and the arrival of French, Belgian, and Austrian troops. In the midst of all this activity, a small number of individual commercial photographers arrived in both Brownsville and Matamoros. But, as they flocked to the border, they mainly set up shop in Matamoros, the real boomtown on the Texas–Mexican border.

Keenly aware of the economic opportunity, a

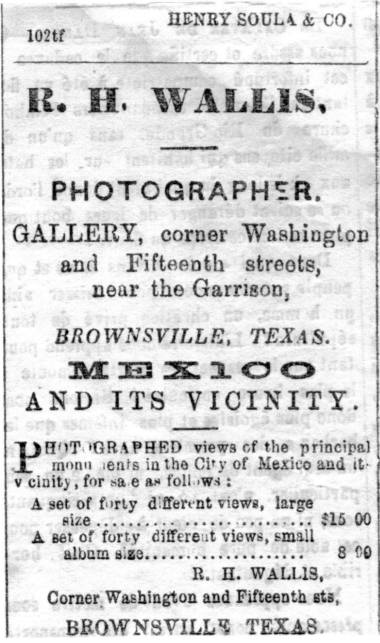

R. H. Wallis was a border photographer who advertised his services in a local newspaper. This display advertisement appeared in the *Rio Grande Courier*, June 12, 1868. *William C. and Patricia Cisneros Young collection.*

tisements. Brownsville merchants could purchase everything from plows and guns to French wines, brandies, and preserves from their New Orleans wholesalers. Prominent among the New Orleans transplants was an experienced photographer named A. Constant. Constant had lived in New Orleans since 1853 and had worked as an ambrotypist in the late 1850s at various addresses on Hospital Street. During the early years of the Civil War, Constant served as a private in Company I of the Orleans Guards, a Confederate militia unit in the Crescent City.[4] Constant had a partner in Matamoros with the surname of "Stephen." The "Constant and Stephen" imprint is exceptionally rare as compared to imprints by other Matamoros and Brownsville photographers. Although they arranged a limited amount of outdoor work, most of the extant views by this photographic duo are studio portraits. One of their more remarkable and previously unpublished photographs is a rare studio image of a group of Austrian soldiers in Matamoros.

Another New Orleans photographer who emigrated to the Lower Rio Grande Valley was A. Moses, who opened a gallery in Matamoros as "Moses and Company" at the Castro House on Bravo Street, between Iturbide and Cesar streets, the same location that was formerly the gallery for "Constant and Stephen." Like a few of the other photographers, Moses advertised in the Spanish-language edition of the *Daily Ranchero*. The advertisement refers to Moses in the plural, perhaps indicating at least two men with the same surname. "A. Moses" may be the same individual as Augustus Moses, who served with fellow photographer Bernard Moses in the Confederate army in the Twenty-first Louisiana Infantry.[5] It is not unlikely that more than one photographer with the surname "Moses" worked in Matamoros. There were six photographers with that name in New Orleans, and at least five of them were from the same family. Bernard, Edward, Gustave, and Louis Moses

few New Orleans photographers opened branch galleries in Matamoros. There had always been a strong connection between New Orleans and Brownsville, nurtured by the ceaseless traffic between the two cities, and reflected even today in some of the remaining buildings from that era. Issues of the Matamoros and Brownsville *Daily Ranchero* were often published in French and Spanish and frequently included a two-column section strictly for New Orleans business adver-

were the sons of Samuel Moses, a chemist and native of Bavaria. Complicating the matter even further is the fact that from 1867 to 1870 Louis Moses worked as a partner in a New Orleans gallery with A. Constant, the same Constant who had a gallery in Matamoros. This suggests that the Matamoros work of these men occurred prior to 1867.

At least two other photographers were working in Matamoros and Brownsville during this period. The first of these men was a Mexican photographer named "C. Yzquierdo." Yzquierdo (or Izquierdo) operated out of Monterrey, Mexico, in 1863 and 1864. It is also evident that he worked in Matamoros for a short period of time as

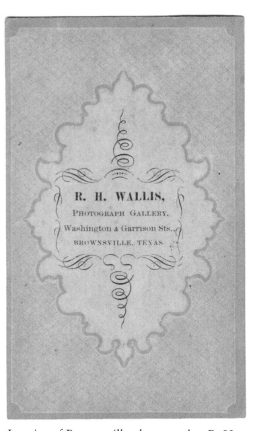

Imprint of Brownsville photographer R. H. Wallis on a *carte de visite*, ca. 1867. *Lawrence T. Jones III collection.*

evidenced by the imprint, "C. Yzquierdo, Artista Fotografo, Matamoros," which appears on a circa 1865 *carte de visite* portrait of an unidentified Mexican man. To date, this is the only known photograph with his Matamoros imprint.[6]

The second of these two photographers, L. S. Smith, is even more obscure than Yzquierdo. He appears to have been an itinerant who was in the Brownsville–Matamoros area for only a short time. None of his views are known to exist today and the only information about him comes in a brief notice in the *Brownsville Daily Ranchero* of December 4, 1866. "Mr. L. Smith, photographer, opposite the 'Ranchero' building, has laid on our table an assortment of magnificent views of the pontoon bridge, embracing, also the city front." A traveling photographer named Luke Smith shows up later in the 1870s and 1880s in Kansas, Nebraska, and California. Unfortunately, no connection has been established between him and the L. S. Smith who worked briefly in Brownsville in 1866.[7]

One of the more prolific and important photog-

raphers to arrive in the Lower Rio Grande Valley was Reuben H. Wallis (sometimes spelled Wallace). Born in England in 1828, he immigrated to the United States in 1852 and is listed in the 1861 *New Orleans City Directory* as an ambrotypist at 705 N. Levee, d[istrict] 4. By 1865 or 1866 at the latest, the thirty-eight-year-old photographer had relocated to Brownsville.[8] Wallis, who was known as "R. H.," rather than "Reuben," opened a gallery at the corner of Washington and Fifteenth streets, adjacent to the garrison grounds at Fort Brown. He was quite successful at his trade and was the only one of the Civil War–Reconstruction photographers to remain permanently in the Lower Rio Grande Valley. In his early years, when he wasn't in his gallery taking studio portraits, Wallis ventured outdoors to photograph street scenes on both sides of the Rio Grande. His extant work consists of numerous photographs of the grounds and buildings at Fort Brown. His imprint is also seen on a substantial number of *carte de visite* portraits of the soldiers who were stationed there. In June 1868 Wallis advertised views for sale of the principal monuments in Mexico City and vicinity. It is not known whether he traveled there himself and photographed in the area or if he was simply selling views taken by another photographer.[9] At this time, there appears additional confusion about the spelling of his surname and even his middle initial. In the 1880 census he is shown as "R. W. Wallace." This obviously is the same man as "R. H. Wallis" because both are shown as photographers by occupation and both were born in England in 1828. This variant spelling probably is the erroneous spelling by a census enumerator. The difference in his middle initial may be explained by the similarity of the letters "H" and "W" when inscribed and the misreading and copying thereof.

The Texas State Gazetteer and Business Directory shows him as "R. W. Wallace" for the years 1885–86, 1890–91, 1892, and 1896–97. However, in the *Brownsville Business Directory, 1898–99,* he reverts once again to "R. H. Wallis." His name always appears as "R. H. Wallis" on his photographic imprints. The confusing name-change scenario continues when "R. W. Wallace" appears in the 1900 Brownsville census.[10]

Of all the photographers in the Lower Rio Grande Valley in the 1860s, the most important was Louis de Planque, who was in the area for four years. Referred to in the *Daily Ranchero* as the "prince of photographers," the Prussian-born de Planque possessed exceptional artistic inclinations and a keen sense of history.[11] He was the only photographer in the area to operate photography galleries on both sides of the river. De Planque was a superbly talented photographic artist whose lens captured the major players involved in the history-making events of Brownsville and Matamoros. He photographed important personalities, including soldiers and politicians, as well as veteran Texas Ranger John S. "Rip" Ford, who is seen in the only known view of the Texas frontiersman in the uniform of a Confederate colonel. Other important figures de Planque photographed included Mexican patriots and military commanders such as Servando Canales, Juan Cortina, Mariano Escobedo, and Tomás Mejía. His lens also captured Henry Alonzo Maltby, the controversial editor and publisher of the *Daily Ranchero,* as well as Gen. George Getty, one of the commanders of Federal occupation forces and survivor of the 1866 cholera outbreak. Steamboat entrepreneurs and notable ranching partners Mifflin Kenedy and Richard King were also among the many promi-

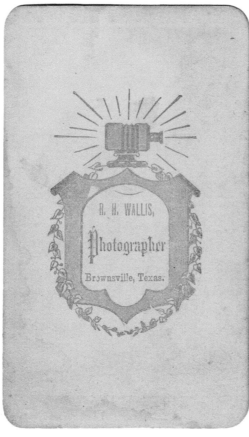

Imprint of Brownsville photographer R. H. Wallis on a *carte de visite,* ca. 1870. *Lawrence T. Jones III collection.*

nent local citizens de Planque photographed.

Born in Prussia on or about April 18, 1842, Louis de Planque did not limit himself to a life of making studio portraits.[12] He frequently took his camera equipment outdoors and became one of the earliest journalistic photographers in Texas and northern Mexico. De Planque documented the routine of daily life in a wonderful series of street scenes in both Brownsville and Matamoros. He also recorded significant activities and events. In the winter of 1866–1867 the first snowfall since 1835 swept over the area. Setting up his camera in the middle of Calle Abasolo, de Planque made a photograph showing his snowy Matamoros gallery.

After an exhausting search, nothing has been found to date a de Planque career in Europe. His name does not appear in the directories of French, Belgian, or German photographers of the period. Not one European photograph with his imprint has been located in either public or private holdings. There was a French photographer named Jules Deplanque who was active in Paris from 1863 to 1872, but no link has been established between this individual and Louis de Planque. If de Planque was a working photographer in Europe prior to coming to Mexico, it probably would have been as an apprentice or journeyman assistant.[13]

It is not known exactly when de Planque, accompanied by his wife, Eugenia, arrived in Mexico. His arrival, probably at Veracruz, appears to coincide with the introduction of French troops into the country. As he made his way north, he photographed briefly in the city of Monterrey, and at least one of those photographs is extant. No doubt he was attracted to Matamoros and Brownsville because of the cosmopolitan character of the area, brought about in part by the great number of Europeans already living there. A large percentage of the populace was fluent not only in Spanish, but in English, French, and German. De Planque appears to have fit in nicely.

By the time he arrived at Matamoros, the twenty-two-year-old de Planque was technically proficient in his vocation. He opened his first photograph gallery in Matamoros on Abasolo Street. Some of his photographic imprints show the street number as 62, and others show it as 64 Calle de Abasolo.[14] Shortly after opening his Matamoros gallery, de Planque opened a second gallery in Brownsville on Elizabeth Street. Operating two galleries at the same time obviously required at least a second photographer. Most likely, de Planque's wife, Eugenia, assisted him in taking photographs and probably did some of the gallery work herself. No Brownsville or Matamoros imprint has been found with her name, but there is no doubt that she worked later as a photographer.[15] Unfortunately, the identity of any of de Planque's assistants remains unknown. It is possible that an itinerant such as A. G. Wedge worked for de Planque at one time, which might account for some of de Planque's photographs appearing with the Wedge imprint.

Without question, de Planque was

This full-length studio portrait of photographer Louis de Planque may have been taken by his wife, Eugenia, ca. 1865. *Carte de visite* with Louis de Planque imprint. *Brownsville Historical Association.*

in Matamoros sometime in 1864. One of his earliest imprinted photographs is that of Matthew Nolan, a major in the Confederate army, who was later murdered in Corpus Christi in 1864. By October 1865 de Planque was advertising his photographic services in the *Daily Ranchero*, a pro-Confederate newspaper that was also sympathetic with the Mexican Imperialists. De Planque himself appears to have had similar political leanings. It is obvious that he knew many of the Confederate and Imperialist leaders because he was the only photographer in the area who systematically photographed them and advertised these photographs for sale to the general public. His political bent is further displayed in a self-portrait that could be interpreted as a political statement. In this rather unusual photograph, de Planque posed himself reading a copy of the *Daily Ranchero*. Another self-portrait shows de Planque dressed in a style adopted by many Imperialist army officers, especially when off duty. The French and their allies were enamored with the elite equestrian culture of the Spanish gentleman riders or *charros*. As a conceit of fashion, they sometimes adopted the elaborate costumes and *sombreros* of the Mexican *charros*, which is documented in a number of period photographs.

De Planque's photographs are quite

When Louis de Planque photographed his wife, Eugenia, he posed her much like a contemporary painter would pose his subject. This small *carte de visite*, ca. 1865, has the monumental stature of much larger paintings of the period. *Carte de visite* by Louis de Planque. *Brownsville Historical Association.*

and historian Henry Deeks. The copy now owned by the Brownsville Historical Association was not found until 1999. Additionally, a third copy is known to be extant in a private collection in the Brownsville area. Ordinarily, a photographer printed copies of some photographs for years after they were taken. The primary reason de Planque could not do this is because many of his glass-plate negatives were either damaged or destroyed during a hurricane that slammed into the South Texas coast in early October 1867. Consequently, the positive images de Planque left behind in stereograph and *carte de visite* format are the only record available of his pioneer work.

De Planque's border photography studios were prospering as late as 1867. Only the able R. H. Wallis offered any real competition with his single Brownsville gallery. By 1865 de Planque was advertising in the *Matamoros Daily Ranchero* on a regular basis. In one ad in April 1867 he offered various types of photographic merchandise, such as stereographs, along with the stereoscopes in which to view them. In addition to selling other forms of photography such as *cartes de visite* and tintypes, de Planque offered "views of residences and photographs of deceased persons taken at the dwellings." Even though the era of the ambrotype was over in North America, de Planque still had "the choicest" ambrotype cases available. Just because photographic processes changed, people did not usually discard the "old" daguerreotype and ambrotype heirloom family portraits from the 1840s and 1850s. De Planque also sold different styles of large frames, and he even hired a "first class artist" to hand color photographs in "aquarel, crayon, oil or watercolors."[16]

Just two months after de Planque's April 1867 *Daily Ranchero* advertisement, the tide of history turned against the French and their Mexican allies. De Planque's acquaintance and customer, Gen.

rare today. Although a few stereographs are extant, most of what survives is in the *carte de visite* format. How rare are de Planque images? The *carte de visite* of Col. John S. Ford in his Confederate uniform might serve as an example. This photograph wasn't even known to exist until the mid-1980s, when the first known copy was offered for sale at a Civil War show in Metairie, Louisiana, by Massachusetts photography dealer

Tomás Mejía, after being forced out of Mata-moros, was executed by a firing squad at Quere-taro on June 19, along with Gen. Miguel Miramon and Emperor Maximilian. The Imperialists surren-dered Mexico City the next day to Mexican Republican troops, and on July 19 Benito Juárez made his triumphant entry into the city.

Less than three months later, on October 7, 1867, a devastating hurricane struck the Texas–Mexican coast, causing extensive damage in Matamoros and Brownsville and as far north as Galveston. During this storm, both of de Planque's galleries sustained serious wind and flood dam-age. Regardless, de Planque saved enough equipment to photograph a good deal of the damage left in the after-math of the hurricane. He captured not only the material property damage but the human element as well. Five weeks later the *Brownsville Daily Ranchero* reported that de Planque, "the scientific photographer," had for sale "a large number of views of the tornado-wrecked cities of Matamoros and Brownsville." Reproduced for the first time, de Planque's 1867 hurricane-aftermath views are among the earliest known journalistic photographs of a single his-toric event in Texas.[17]

In the wake of the collapse of the French empire in Mexico and the subse-quent destruction of his galleries in Matamoros and Brownsville, de Planque was practically forced out of business. On March 11, 1868, he ran another advertisement in the *Daily Ranchero* notifying the public that since his gal-leries were destroyed, he had secured the services of the Pierce and Terry Book-store in Brownsville to act as his agents. Any orders for duplicates of previously taken photographs were to be left with Pierce and Terry, who were located in the post office building. However, the sudden economic downturn for de Planque must have made a new start in Brownsville impossible. Shortly after

the *Daily Ranchero* advertisement, de Planque and his wife, Eugenia, moved to Corpus Christi.[18]

It is not known if de Planque immediately opened another gallery in Corpus Christi, but by September 1869 he was operating a studio in the nearby port city of Indianola. By the spring of 1870 he had opened a gallery in Corpus Christi, and by that summer he was also working in the small town of Refugio. In addition, the enterpris-

Louis de Planque staged this studio view of himself reading the *Daily Ranchero*, ca. 1865. *Carte de visite* attributed to Eugenia de Planque with de Planque studio imprint. *Brownsville Historical Association.*

Mexican *charro* in a studio setting with his saddle and horse tack, ca. 1865. *Carte de visite* by unidentified artist. *Lawrence T. Jones III collection.*

Photographer Louis de Planque holds a *sombrero* and wears a *charro* jacket made of jaguar skin, ca. 1865. *Carte de visite* attributed to Eugenia de Planque. *Lawrence T. Jones III collection.*

On January 2, 1867, an unusual snowfall occurred in the Lower Rio Grande Valley. To record this rare event, Louis de Planque took his camera outdoors and set it up on Abasolo Street in front of his Matamoros gallery, which had a camera-shaped sign on the roof. *Carte de visite* by Louis de Planque. *Lawrence T. Jones III collection.*

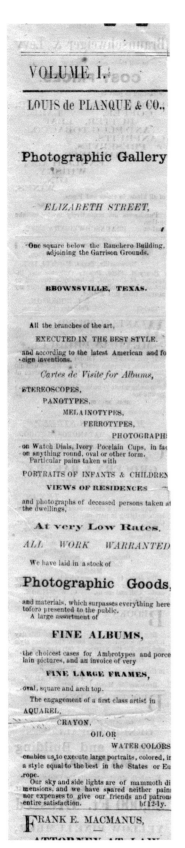

Spanish and English *carte de visite* imprint for Louis de Planque's Matamoros photograph gallery, ca. 1866. *Brownsville Historical Association.*

For his gallery on the Mexican side of the Rio Grande, Louis de Planque sometimes incorporated the national symbol of Mexico as part of his *carte de visite* imprint, ca. 1866–1867. *Brownsville Historical Association.*

Louis de Planque frequently advertised his photography business in local newspapers on both sides of the border. This display advertisement appeared in the March 10, 1867, edition of the *Weekly Ranchero. William C. and Patricia Cisneros Young collection.*

Louis de Planque produced an 1867 New Year's greeting card in an unusual *carte de visite* format. Although he probably made several of these for friends and customers, this is the only known example. It features small albumen photographs of de Planque and his wife, Eugenia. *Brownsville Historical Association.*

ing de Planque operated a traveling photography business throughout the southern part of Texas before he settled once again at Indianola in 1871. It appears that de Planque operated galleries in both Corpus Christi and Indianola at the same time. He had done so successfully with his Brownsville and Matamoros galleries, and it is likely he tried the same technique again.

In a strange coincidence, de Planque and his wife were at their Indianola gallery when the great hurricane of 1875 shattered the city. With winds estimated at 145–150 miles per hour, more than three hundred people were killed in this massive storm.[19] Much worse than the 1867 Brownsville–Matamoros storm that de Planque had experienced, this hurricane destroyed three-fourths of the buildings in Indianola. De Planque and his wife barely escaped with their lives, and no trace was left of their photography gallery and adjoining home. Once again, de Planque returned

to Corpus Christi. After raising money by presenting a lantern slide show with the only equipment he had left, he traveled to New Orleans, where he purchased new equipment and borrowed camera lenses from friends. He returned to Corpus Christi shortly thereafter and re-opened his photography gallery.[20]

There is little doubt that de Planque became the most prominent photographer in Corpus Christi, but he also operated branch galleries in Victoria, Goliad, and San Diego. He was at Victoria in 1886 when another severe hurricane struck the nearby port city of Indianola. Just as he had done in 1867 at Matamoros and Brownsville, de Planque took extensive photographs of the Indianola wreckage. He eventually settled permanently in Corpus Christi, where he operated his popular photography gallery through the 1880s and 1890s on William Street opposite the Masonic Hall. A well-known and beloved local figure, de Planque was referred to as "Don Luis." Thirty-four years after he arrived in Matamoros, Mexico, to begin his three-decade photographic adventure, de Planque died of a stroke in his adopted city on May 1, 1898. He was just two weeks past his fifty-sixth birthday when he was buried with little pageantry in Bayview Cemetery in Corpus Christi. Sadly, the grave of one of Texas's most important nineteenth-century photographers is unmarked, but its location in the cemetery was confirmed in 2003.[21]

Louis de Planque once claimed his work was equal to the best in the United States or Europe, a claim often seen in photographic advertisements of the period. With de Planque, however, this rather self-serving statement was the truth. Technically and artistically, his work was the equal of the best of his contemporaries. Unfortunately for de Planque, he operated in relative obscurity in a geographically isolated portion of

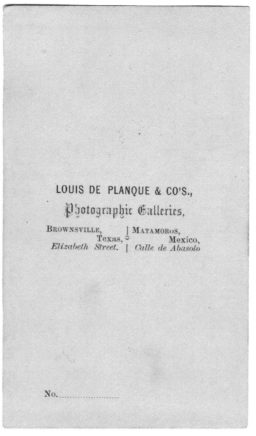

Louis de Planque and Company *carte de visite* imprint for both his Matamoros and Brownsville photograph galleries, ca. 1865. *Lawrence T. Jones III collection.*

Mexico and Texas. Although a handful of private collectors are familiar with de Planque's work, he remains overlooked and unknown to historians and the general antique photograph community.

As eyewitnesses to history, de Planque and fellow photographers Reuben H. Wallis, Constant, Stephen Augustus Moses and company, and A. G. Wedge ably captured the striking images of the people and places that made the Rio Grande frontier historically unique. Posing for the camera were Federals; Confederates; German Texan Unionists; *Juaristas*; French, Mexican, and Belgian *Imperialistas*; Contra-Guerillas; cotton traders; speculators; newspaper editors; the Brownsville and Matamoros social and merchant elite; wild border *caudillos*; and common soldiers of four frontier armies. All were part of the tumultuous history of a chaotic and tempestuous era.

MATAMOROS

With its Spanish colonial origins, Matamoros is much older than its twin city of Brownsville. The settlement began when Matías de los Santos Coy established a ranch in the vicinity in 1749 that was known as San Juan de los Esteros Hermosos. In 1774 thirteen colonists representing ten families from Camargo helped to lay out Plaza de Hidalgo, as well as a place for a cathedral on the east side of the plaza and a town hall on the west side in what was renamed Nuestra Señora del

Refugio de los Esteros (Our Lady of the Refuge of the Lake). Relatively free from yellow fever in the early years and less prone to attack from hostile Comanches and Lipan Apaches than settlements on the north bank of the Rio Grande, the community grew slowly and was renamed in 1826 for Mariano Matamoros, a Mexican insurgent and Catholic priest who had been captured and executed in the Mexican struggle for independence.

From a population of 2,320 in 1820, Matamoros grew rapidly to almost 7,000 by 1829 and 16,372 by the time of Texas independence in 1836. Carpenters, masons, and tinsmiths, along with blacksmiths and saddlers, flooded into the community. In 1824 President James Monroe established a consular post at Matamoros and by 1828 the city had a weekly postal service. The first newspaper, *Noticioso*, appeared in 1831.[1]

As the most important commercial center on the Rio Grande, the river city came to possess a colonial-inspired architecture and design similar to that of the French Quarter in New Orleans. The narrow streets and two-story brick and stucco buildings with second-story wrought-iron balconies reflected a charming Spanish and French Colonial style that can be seen today around the Plaza de Hidalgo and adjacent central parts of the city.

Despite the cholera epidemics, hurricanes, and floods that swept the city in the early nineteenth century, expanding trade brought hundreds of foreigners to the Rio Grande. This new merchant elite, mostly entrepreneurs from the United States and Europe, came to dominate the economic heartbeat of the city. Dramatic change would come with the bloody battles of Palo Alto and Resaca de la Palma and the occupation of the city in 1846 at the beginning of the Mexican War. Following the Treaty of Guadalupe Hidalgo, which ended the war in 1848, and the Mexican government's imposition of tariffs, smuggling goods into northeastern Mexico became a way of life for many of the merchants of the city.

With the Union blockade during the Civil War, Matamoros became a major trading port for northeastern Mexico and South Texas. In fact, Matamoros and the thriving and storm-battered seaside town of Bagdad at the mouth of the Rio Grande became critical ports of entry for the Confederacy. The transportation of cotton from Texas across the Rio Grande for exportation to Europe

Mexican soldiers in Matamoros stand at attention in front of their guardhouse at the Rio Grande ferry crossing opposite Brownsville. To the left of the guardhouse, carriages wait their turn for the ferry, ca. 1865–1867. *Carte de visite* by Louis de Planque. *Lawrence T. Jones III collection.*

in exchange for war materials and badly needed supplies brought a maritime boom to Matamoros that would never be equaled again.

With the booming cotton trade, men of all classes flocked into Matamoros, "most of them with a view to speculate, some to avoid service, some from mere idleness and a disposition to wander listlessly through the world."[2] By 1864, with as many as forty thousand people crowded into the city, Matamoros had become "a city of strange denizens," where "every room, every niche capable of being occupied and of holding a man was rented at a large price."[3] Everyone in the city wanted "to get rich overnight and no tradesman is satisfied with a moderate gain," a young lieutenant in Maximilian's imperialist army observed.[4] Cotton speculators, as well as "merchants, the disposers of goods, all lived in Matamoros."[5] Houses that normally rented for $10 a month were subdivided into small rooms that went for $100.[6] Living expenses escalated from $1 to $3 a day. Cotton wagons crowded the unpaved and rutted streets. As was the case in Brownsville, water was hauled from the river by *barrileros* in large forty-gallon barrels that sold for $2 each.[7] The constant chatter of Spanish, English, French, and German was common on the streets and in the taverns and brothels.

Rains often transformed the streets of the booming trade center into "unbelievable seas of mud."[8] At one time the city even contemplated converting the streets into canals similar to those in Venice, Italy. One foreign officer claimed that three horses drowned in streets that resembled small rivers, where "carriages sink up to their

Matamoros, Mexico, as seen from the Brownsville, Texas, side of the Rio Grande. The twin towers of the cathedral in the Plaza de Hidalgo are just visible on the horizon. *Carte de visite* attributed to Louis de Planque, ca. 1865. *Prints and Photographs collection, Brownsville, Texas, file, Center for American History, University of Texas at Austin, CT-0580.*

Plaza de Hidalgo in Matamoros, ca. 1865, with cathedral in background. *Carte de visite* by unidentified artist. *Lawrence T. Jones III collection.*

Matamoros: 1868–1869

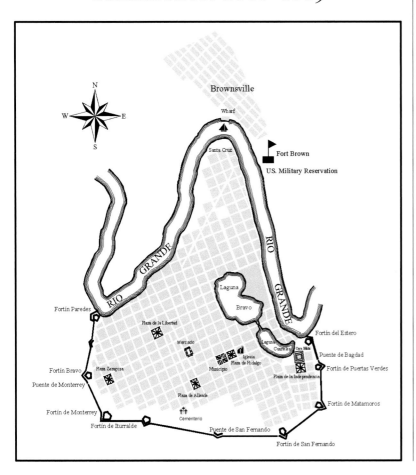

shafts and horses up to their chests."[9] To complicate matters, the rotting and stinking carcasses of dead horses and mules often were left in the city streets to decompose in the sun.

After the Imperial forces of Gen. Tomás Mejía occupied the city, fortifications were constructed encircling the city on the land side that ran from one bend in the Rio Grande to another. With the river acting as a barrier on the other side, Matamoros became the only fortified city on the Rio Grande. Eight small forts were constructed at various locations along the wall, and it was along these walls and fortifications in the summer of 1866 that some of the most brutal and bloody fighting in the city's long and often violent history erupted as Republican and Imperialist armies grappled for control of the city. With the departure of General Mejía and the *Imperialistas*, Republican generals turned on one another and the bloodshed continued unabated. It was among the turmoil of civil war and revolution that some of the most skilled photographers in both the United States and Mexico came to the Rio Grande. The visual imagery they left behind endures to this day.

The Matamoros cathedral towers were a good vantage point from which to photograph the Plaza de Hidalgo. This view shows the Mexican customs building on one side of the plaza, ca. 1865. *Carte de visite* by Constant & Stephen. *Lawrence T. Jones III collection.*

Plaza de Hidalgo in Matamoros, ca. 1865, as photographed from one of the cathedral towers. *Carte de visite* by Constant and Stephen. *Lawrence T. Jones III collection.*

Constant and Stephen were not the only Matamoros photographers to haul their cumbersome equipment to the top of a cathedral tower. Moses & Company took this *carte de visite* of the Plaza de Hidalgo from one of the cathedral towers, ca. 1865. *Lawrence T. Jones III collection.*

The Mexican customs building on the Plaza de Hidalgo also served as Gen. Tomás Mejía's headquarters in Matamoros. *Carte de visite* by Louis de Planque, ca. 1865. *Brownsville Historical Association.*

Calle de Comercia, Mata-moros, ca. 1865. The Guz-man family of San Fernan-do owned the building on the right; possibly they built it in the eighteenth century. It serves as a good example of the Spanish and French Colonial style of architec-ture in the central part of the city. *Carte de visite* by unidentified artist. *Prints and Photographs collection, Brownsville, Texas, file, Center for American Histo-ry, University of Texas at Austin. CT-0575.*

Water Carrier. Brownsville Texas

Previously misidentified as having been taken in Brownsville, this scene of a *barrilero*, or water carrier, actually was taken on Abasolo Street in Matamoros. The fence in the background was next to Louis de Planque's Mata-moros gallery, where de Planque displayed framed examples of his work for potential customers to view. The open entrance in the fence led to a small courtyard next to the gallery, where de Planque sometimes photographed large groups of people. *Carte de visite* by Louis de Planque, ca. 1865–1866. *Prints and Photographs collection, Brownsville, Texas, file, Center for American History, University of Texas at Austin, CT-0574.*

Louis de Planque was fascinated with street-vending water carriers, and he photographed them on numerous occasions as they pulled their rolling water-filled barrels down the streets of Matamoros and Brownsville. This view was taken in Matamoros. *Carte de visite* by Louis de Planque, ca. 1865. *Lawrence T. Jones III collection.*

An astute observer of nature, Louis de Planque photographed this well-groomed stallion outside a Matamoros livery stable. *Carte de visite* by Louis de Planque, ca. 1865. *Lawrence T. Jones III collection.*

Louis de Planque did not ignore the smaller creatures in the world around him. This photograph of a tarantula in Matamoros is unusual subject matter for a photographer of his era. *Carte de visite* by Louis de Planque, ca. 1866. *William L. Schaeffer collection.*

BROWNSVILLE

Across the river from Matamoros, some twenty miles inland at the southern tip of Texas, Brownsville was settled much later than Matamoros. Although the Spanish crown authorized land grants north of the Rio Grande as early as 1781, not until the arrival of the American army on the great river in March 1846 did Gen. Zachary Taylor begin the construction of Fort Texas. Built on a small exposed peninsula across the narrow waters of the Rio Grande from Matamoros, the earthen works were renamed Fort Brown in honor of Maj. Jacob Brown, who died after having been badly wounded during the Mexican bombardment of the fortifications at the beginning of the Mexican War.[1] After the Treaty of Guadalupe Hidalgo ended the war in 1848, Connecticut-born Matamoros merchant Charles Stillman and his partner, Samuel Belden, purchased a disputed title to a 4,676-acre tract of land and laid out the town of Brownsville adjacent to Fort Brown. That same year Stillman, Belden, and Simon Mussina formed the Brownsville Town Company and began selling lots for as much as $1,500 each. Stillman named the major streets in the new community for members of his family. Elizabeth Street was named for his fiancée and future bride, St. Francis Street for his father, and St. Charles Street for himself.[2]

Swollen by refugees from Matamoros and a polyglot horde of greedy forty-niners on their way to California, the town suffered a cholera epidemic in the spring of 1849 that killed nearly half the townspeople. In January 1849 Brownsville became the seat of the newly-organized Cameron County. One year later the town had a population of 519. Numerous stores sprang up when merchants from Matamoros recognized the advantage of shipping goods up the Rio Grande to Brownsville and then smuggling them across the Rio Grande to avoid paying high Mexican duties.[3]

In the years before the American Civil War, free men and women of color, carpenters, boatmen, filibustering Texas frontiersmen, rough Tejano rancheros, and schemers from as far away as Maine and New Hampshire crowded into Brownsville's newly-constructed saloons, brothels, billiard parlors, livery stables, and dingy restaurants. Daily life centered around a two-story brick market house that was constructed in 1850. Hundreds of French, Irish, English, and German immigrants, all hungry for land, cluttered the dusty streets. By April 1850 a town government, with Israel Bonaparte Bigelow as mayor, had been established.[4] Aldermen, none of whom were Mexican American despite a majority of Hispanics in the town and county, enacted laws making it illegal to shoot a pistol in town, "run a horse, mare, mule, ass, or gelding" in the streets, or ride horses or mules on the sidewalks.[5] In the increasingly cosmopolitan community, the town council also set out to regulate the area's traditionally rowdy

This Brownsville view of Levee Street looks up the Rio Grande and shows the old steamboat landing and ferry crossing, ca. 1864–1865. A similar view in the Center for American History at the University of Texas at Austin has the following accompanying information: "Over the boats is seen the top of the old John McAllen home. The old King Building, the Jerry Galvan building, King and Kenedy Saloon and Dance Hall and the two-story brick building of Gen. Pena are seen on the right." *Carte de visite* attributed to Louis de Planque. *Lawrence T. Jones III collection.*

This view looks down the Rio Grande and shows Levee Street and some of the same buildings seen in the above image, ca. 1865. *Carte de visite* attributed to Louis de Planque. *Robin Stanford collection.*

Shallow draft transport vessels line the north bank of the Rio Grande at Brownsville next to Levee Street. In the distant background, a large U.S. garrison flag can be seen flying at Fort Brown. *Carte de visite* size print used in unusual stereograph format by unidentified artist, ca. 1865–1866. *Robin Stanford collection.*

fandangos and to find enough coffins for the numerous paupers who expired weekly. By 1850 the first regular newspaper, the *Rio Grande Sentinel*, began publication.

To Capt. Randolph B. Marcy, who was stationed at Fort Brown, there was no better place than the Lower Rio Grande Valley. "Everything is beautiful now," he wrote in November 1856, "the trees are in full foliage, the grass is deep green, flowers are all in blossom and the orange trees are covered with fruit while the temperature is mild and the atmosphere balmy."[6] Brownsville could be deadly, however, as epidemics of yellow fever, cholera, malaria, and the dengue fever often plagued the town.

Although badly shaken by Juan Nepomuceno Cortina's deadly raid on the town in September 1859 and the disruption of commerce that accompanied the violence of the Cortina War, by 1860 Brownsville boasted a population of 2,734, which made it the largest settlement on the Texas bank of the Rio Grande and the fifth-largest city in the state.

The Civil War and the Confederate cotton trade brought great prosperity to Brownsville as it did to other communities on the Texas–Mexico border. In four years of war soldiers in both blue and gray, as well as cotton speculators from as far away as Arkansas and Louisiana, crowded the streets and smoke-filled bars and restaurants on Elizabeth Street. From the time Texas state troops under John S. "Rip" Ford seized Fort Brown in March 1861, to the last Federal occupation of the city in 1865 following the battle of Palmito Hill, Brownsville changed hands five times.

Although the collapse of the Confederacy dealt a temporary blow to the booming Brownsville–Matamoros economy, the Federal army set out to repair Fort Brown. By 1869 more than seventy buildings had been completed at the post. At the same time the city became a refuge from those fleeing the bloodshed south of the border. Undeniably, the years from 1861 to 1869 were some of the most eventful and historically significant in Brownsville's turbulent past.

During the period of revolutionary unrest in Matamoros, U.S. military authorities built a pontoon bridge across the Rio Grande so they could move quickly to protect U.S. property in Matamoros should the need arise. The bridge was constructed by men of the 114th U.S. Colored Troops and was called "Sedgwick's Bridge" after the regiment's commander, Col. Thomas D. Sedgwick. The buildings on Levee Street are visible on the U.S. side of the Rio Grande. Two African American soldiers stand guard near the Matamoros side of the river, ca. 1866. *William L. Schaeffer collection.*

Armed sentries of the 114th U.S. Colored Troops stand guard in this view of Sedgwick's Bridge. In the background, the business along Levee Street in Brownsville continues without interruption. *Carte de visite* attributed to Louis de Planque, ca. 1866. *Print courtesy Institute of Texan Cultures, University of Texas at Brownsville, 73-833.*

Although not readily visible in this view, Louis de Planque's Brownsville gallery was on Elizabeth Street, the most important business street then and now in Brownsville. *Carte de visite* by Louis de Planque, ca. 1865. *Lawrence T. Jones III collection.*

Looking south on Elizabeth Street in Brownsville, a group of unidentified men at left face the camera while a water carrier crosses the street. *Carte de visite* by Louis de Planque, ca. 1865. *William L. Schaeffer collection.*

Looking north on Elizabeth Street in Brownsville, the U.S. Customhouse, the Miller Hotel, and Latimer's Theater are on the right. *Carte de visite* by R. H. Wallis, ca. 1870. *Lawrence T. Jones III collection.*

Henry Miller, a German immigrant, constructed the Miller Hotel in 1848. It stood at the corner of Elizabeth and Thirteenth streets, just a block from the Matamoros ferry. With wide verandas, the two-story frame building contained a restaurant, barroom, and lodging for men only. The hotel served as a terminus for several stagecoach lines, and a small sign reading "Stage Office for Brazos" hangs from the end of the bottom veranda. To the right of the sign, a small group of unidentified men stare directly at the photographer and his camera. *Carte de visite* attributed to Louis de Planque, ca. 1865–1866. *Lawrence T. Jones III collection.*

Barratte's Restaurant set the standard for fine dining and lodging in Brownsville. It was located at Thirteenth and Elizabeth streets, just opposite the Miller Hotel, which can be seen in the background. After being severely damaged in the 1867 hurricane, Barratte's Restaurant relocated to Indianola, only to be destroyed there by a hurricane in 1875. A good portion of the tall brick building behind the Miller Hotel still stands today in Brownsville. Stereograph by Louis de Planque, ca. 1866. *Lawrence T. Jones III collection.*

Facing Twelfth Street in Brownsville, the Immaculate Concepción Cathedral was constructed from 1852 to 1856 and today is the seat of the Catholic diocese in Brownsville. The small wooden store in the center of the photograph sits at the intersection of East Adams and Twelfth Street. Most likely, this photograph was taken from the balcony of the old city market, which also fronts on Twelfth Street. The church and rectory look exactly the same today as they did when this photograph was taken, ca. 1865–1866. When examined under magnification, the ghostly figures of three Union soldiers walking along Twelfth Street can be seen near the bottom center of the image. This view, from the current city hall, is now obscured by a three-story building that stands where the building with the ladders leaning against it stood. *Carte de visite* attributed to Louis de Planque. *Lawrence T. Jones III collection.*

The city market in Brownsville served as a place for vendors of all sorts of merchandise. In the early 1860s one unidentified photographer operated an "Ambrotype Gallery" from the top floor. The building still stands and today serves as city hall for the city of Brownsville. *Carte de visite* attributed to Louis de Planque, ca. 1865. *Robin Stanford collection.*

The Immaculate Concepción Cathedral in Brownsville, ca. 1870. *Carte de visite* by R. H. Wallis. *Lawrence T. Jones III collection.*

Never tiring of the subject, Louis de Planque photographed this water carrier on Elizabeth Street in Brownsville. Inscribed in period hand verso: "On the Rio Grande, Mexican Water Works." *Carte de visite* by Louis de Planque, ca. 1865. *William L. Schaeffer collection.*

Chapter One

SECESSION AND CIVIL WAR

T he national crisis triggered by the election of Abraham Lincoln and the secession of South Carolina had an immediate and dramatic impact on Texas. Within the small villages and towns on the Rio Grande frontier, as throughout the Lone Star State and the rest of the South, secession was debated with considerable vigor and conviction. At Rio Grande City on December 6, 1860, a number of Starr County citizens gathered to debate the crucial question. Led by John L. Haynes, a well-educated Virginia-born Unionist, several rose to profess allegiance to the Union. Arguing for

secession, but not in favor of a Southern confederation, others spoke of reviving the Lone Star Republic. At the conclusion of the meeting a majority agreed to accept whatever action the state of Texas might take. Upriver at the small river village of Carrizo in Zapata County, Judge Ysidro Vela also called a meeting of the county faithful. Gathering at the small two-story county courthouse on the village plaza a few days after Christmas, with a rare snow blanketing the arid South Texas landscape and a cold north wind sweeping down the valley of the Rio Grande, Judge Vela and the political and ranching elite of the county vigorously pressed for secession. Local customs collector and secession zealot Fenis Mussett spoke of "the felonious aggression of the Abolitionists of the North upon Southern institutions" and warned against submission to "Black Republican rule."[1]

At a large meeting in the courthouse in Brownsville two days after Christmas, Cameron County citizens selected Samuel A. Belden, a prominent merchant, to preside over the assembly. Those in attendance, including Jeremiah Galvan

and William Neale, who were selected as vice presidents, unanimously endorsed a call for a state convention.[2] Three secessionists, New York-born James Walworth, a Brownsville rancher and business partner of Mifflin Kenedy and Richard King; Connecticut-born customs collector Frank W. Latham; and South Carolina-born John S. "Rip" Ford, were chosen to represent the county.

Prominent citizens and public officials in communities such as Laredo also pledged themselves to secession. In early January 1861 voters in Webb and Nueces counties selected Philip Noland Luckett, a Virginia-born physician from Corpus Christi, and Henry A. Maltby, thirty-one-year-old, six-foot-tall, Ohio-born secessionist and former mayor of Corpus Christi as well as editor of the *Ranchero,* to the state secession convention scheduled to convene in Austin on January 28. Virginia-born Edward R. Hord, a Rio Grande City attorney and former member of the Texas House of Representatives and Senate, along with Ohio-born Noah Cox, a prosperous merchant from Roma, were chosen to represent Starr County. Irish-born Edward Daugherty, a rancher from Rudyville, represented Hidalgo County.[3] Although the population along the Rio Grande was overwhelmingly Hispanic, not a single *Tejano* was chosen to the 177-member state convention.

Before a packed and jubilant gallery in Austin on February 1, 1861, the secession convention voted 166 to 8 to present a secession ordinance to the people of Texas, a decision that made the Lone Star State one of only two states in the South to submit the crucial question directly to the people. Three weeks later, Texans voted 46,129 to 14,796 for disunion. On the Rio Grande frontier, the secession ordinance proved to be even more popular than in other areas of the state, including slave-holding and agricultural East Texas. In the counties along the river from Laredo to the Gulf, Webb, Zapata, Starr, Hidalgo, and Cameron, the ordinance was approved by a vote of 1,124 to 41. In Webb and Zapata counties not a single vote was registered against secession, while down in Starr County only two votes were cast in opposition. On the day of the referendum in Cameron County, where the vote was 600 to 37 in favor of secession, trickery, deceit, and the outright intimidation of Unionist voters were said to have been common. Armed men policed the polls and were said to have given suspected Unionist voters a "friendly warning" by slapping "their hands on their revolvers."[4] In Webb and Zapata counties, and to a lesser degree in Starr, Hidalgo, and Cameron, many of those who voted were the landholding elite, well-to-do merchants, or those who were economically and politically subservient to a *patron* system little short of feudalism. Few realized the severity of the crisis and the fact that the country seemed to be

Col. John L. Haynes and his wife, Angelica I. Haynes. Colonel Haynes, a native of Virginia, came to Texas during the Mexican War and afterward lived in towns on both sides of the border. During the Civil War he was an officer in the First Texas Cavalry and commanded the Second Texas Cavalry, the only Union cavalry command organized in Confederate Texas. *Carte de visite* by Austin A. Turner of the New Orleans Photographic Company, ca. 1865. *Lawrence T. Jones III collection.*

approaching the brink of destruction. In Austin Gov. Sam Houston refused to take the oath of allegiance to the new Confederate government. On March 16 the office of governor was declared vacant, and Edward Clark, the lieutenant governor, took the oath. With little hesitation, on March 5 the convention declared Texas independent and voted to join the Confederate States of America.

At the headquarters of the Department of Texas, Gen. David Emanuel Twiggs, seventy-one years old and in ill health, was known to be sympathetic to the South, yet proud and protective of his command. A potentially bloody confrontation developed on February 16, 1861, when Col. Benjamin McCulloch and 250 zealous Texans waving the Lone Star flag swarmed into San Antonio's Main Plaza and occupied the rooftops and buildings housing Federal supplies and men. After ten days of tense negotiations, Twiggs was coerced into surrendering all Federal property in the state. Although he was said to have wept like a child, Twiggs allegedly uttered that, "If an old woman with a broomstick should come with full authority from the state of Texas to demand the public property, I would give it to her."[5] Col. Robert E. Lee, who had been in charge of the Department of Texas a year earlier, arrived in San Antonio only hours after the humiliating capitulation. Pulling his ambulance up in front of the Read House, Lee was surrounded by a crowd of curious men on whose coats he observed a crude red insignia. Told they were state troops and that Twiggs had surrendered, Lee's eyes clouded with tears. "Has it come to this," he was heard to mutter. The Virginian later told a friend that if he had been in control of

The Federal First and Second Texas Cavalry regiments were comprised mainly of Texas Unionists, many of them German Texans, as well as Mexicans living on both sides of the border. This unidentified cavalryman wears the Federal four-button sack coat commonly worn in the field. He is equipped with a revolver and Sharps carbine. His cartridge belt is full and he wears a shoulder belt with a sling that secured his carbine when he was mounted. Tintype by unidentified artist, ca. 1864–1865. *Print courtesy Museum of South Texas History.*

achusetts-born and loyal Unionist Maj. Caleb Chase Sibley received orders from department headquarters directing him to turn over the post to authorities of the state. On March 12, following rather somber ceremonies at the desolate outpost, the Stars and Stripes was lowered and the post was turned over to Charles Callahan, commissioner for the state. With twenty-five days of rations, the troops took up the 230-mile march for Fort Brown.[7] Sibley was hoping to find transportation to the North and, if necessary, even cross into Mexico where he could move down the coast to Tampico to find transportation. While on the way, the Fort McIntosh command, hearing that transportation would be available from Indianola, changed directions and marched for the Texas coast. Downriver at Ringgold Barracks, troops departed on the steamboat *Mustang*. At Fort Duncan at Eagle Pass, Capt. Oliver Lathrop Shepherd and his men evacuated the post at the same time.[8]

In the meantime, a potentially bloody confrontation developed at Fort Brown when the post commander, Capt. Bennett Hoskin Hill, in consultation with Capt. George Stoneman, who had arrived at the post with two companies of the Second Cavalry, refused to surrender the fort to commissioners for the state. Captain Hill even sent Stoneman's cavalry to Brazos Santiago to spike the

the Federal forces in Texas at the time, he would never have surrendered.[6] Had Lee indeed been in command, the Civil War would likely have started in San Antonio instead of Fort Sumter eight weeks later.

At isolated military posts scattered across the vast and arid Southwest and throughout the Lone Star State, the secession winter continued to rage into the angry and defiant spring of 1861. Increasingly heated debate came to characterize a discourse that had once been civil. Consequently, confusion and uncertainty became the order of the day. At sunbaked Fort McIntosh at Laredo, Mass-

guns and destroy the large quantity of ordinance at the seaside depot. By the time Stoneman reached the coast, however, 1st Lt. James Thompson of the Second Artillery had already surrendered the depot. Back at Fort Brown, Hill remained combative and defiant, threatening to arrest the commissioners and destroy Fort Brown.[9]

Forty-four-year-old Col. John S. "Rip" Ford, commanding what the Texans were calling the Confederate Department of the Rio Grande, arrived at Brazos Santiago on February 23 with a force that would eventually number some 1,500 rebellious Texans. Ford reported that Captain Hill was "determined . . . to fight and not to yield." In addition, Captain Stoneman had defiantly proclaimed that "with his two companies of cavalry he would march all over Texas." There was fear the Federals would attack the Texans and inaugurate an unthinkable civil war, which Ford feared, "we may not see the end of."[10] When New York-born Lt. Col. Electus Backus arrived from leave to assume command of the post, tensions were calmed somewhat, and arrangements were made for the state troops to assume control.

On March 20, 1861, after the Stars and Stripes had been saluted and then lowered, six companies of Texans marched into Fort Brown while the Fed-erals departed by steamer for the mouth of the river and Point Isabel, there to find transportation north on the *Daniel Webster*. Up the Texas coast on wind-swept Matagorda Island at the ramshackle village of Saluria on April 24, 1861, Major Sibley and several loyal frontier garrisons from across the vast expanses of the Lone Star State surrendered. "The future was full of uncertainty,

Juan N. Cortina, ca. 1862–1865, by unidentified artist. Probably photographed in Matamoros, this is one of two different views of Cortina that were made at the same sitting. Albumen print (4.5 by 6.5 inches). *Robert G. McCubbin collection.*

dark, and lowering," Colonel Ford concluded.[11]

The fighting that began the Civil War on the Rio Grande was rooted in the Cortina War that swept the Lower Rio Grande Valley in 1859–1860. In September 1859 a charismatic *ranchero*, Juan Nepomuceno Cortina, tired of the land dispossession and second-rate status that he felt had come to characterize the lives of many

Brig. Gen. Hamilton P. Bee was photographed in the summer of 1863 near his headquarters at Fort Brown. Fluent in Spanish, General Bee was in charge of protecting the southern Texas coast, but no less important was his work involving the exporting of cotton and the importing of munitions and other supplies for the Confederacy. One of two wartime photographs of General Bee extant, it is inscribed to a "Miss Clara Boulter" and signed by the general verso. *Carte de visite* attributed to A. G. Wedge. *Martin L. Callahan collection.*

Mexican Texans in the Lower Valley, led some seventy-five angry *Tejano* and *Mexicano* pistol-wielding raiders into the dusty and rutted streets of Brownsville. Shouting "Death to the Americans" and "Viva Mexico," Cortina and his men took possession of the town, killing five prominent citizens and the city jailer. Retreating to his mother's ranch upriver from Brownsville, Cortina issued a fiery and dramatic *pronunciamiento* asserting the rights of Mexican Texans and demanding equality. He eventually recruited a small army of five hundred men from both sides of the border and twice defeated the Brownsville militia and the Texas Rangers. At Rio Grande City on December 27, 1860, however, a combined force of Rangers and United States regulars smashed Cortina, killing sixty of his men and driving what remained of his small army across the river into Mexico.[12] With a burning resentment of the diminished status of the Mexican inhabitants that engulfed the Lower Valley in the years following the war with Mexico, Cortina and a few of his men remained active on the border for several months. In early April 1861, despite being under indictment in Cameron County, Cortina crossed to the Texas side of the Rio Grande to visit his ranch at San José, fourteen miles upriver from Brownsville, bragging that he would return again in a few weeks with a force of Mexicans and Indians.[13] Cortina's appeal to the underprivileged along the twisting and turbulent waters of the Rio Grande even stretched as far upriver as Zapata County.

Zapata County had been administered since its creation in 1856 by a political clique of merchants and large landowners headed by Henry Redmond, a cunning Englishman who had arrived on the border in 1839, shortly after Texas independence. Redmond acquired land on the river, married into an influential local family, and survived the bloody Federalists–Centralists wars that swept the area from 1839 to 1842. By 1861 he had developed a lucrative trading business from his store near San Bartolo or what was called Redmond's Ranch, just upriver from Carrizo, the county seat. Redmond was instrumental in establishing the county that was named after his revolutionary friend from across the river in Guerrero, the mulatto hero of the Republic of the Rio Grande, Col. Antonio Zapata. Redmond became postmaster at Carrizo, justice of the peace and the first county judge, as well as collector of customs at San Bartolo.[14] The political machine that ran the county included John D. Mussett, an articulate Arkansas lawyer and the acting deputy collector of customs at Carrizo, County Sheriff Pedro Díaz, County Clerk Trinidad Zampaño, Tax Assessor-Collector Fernando Uribe, and District Clerk Agustín Díaz. Another player in county politics was Blas Uribe, a wealthy merchant and rancher who controlled the votes at the small rock and adobe village of San Ignacio, upriver from Carrizo. The degree to which the *patron* system controlled the county was indicated by a vote of 212 to 0 in favor of secession. With the overwhelming vote on secession, however, came problems. Judge Isidro Vela had made it known throughout the county that anyone who failed to vote in favor of secession would be fined fifty cents, a considerable amount of money to many of the poor along the river.[15] When several individuals failed to show up at the polls, Vela ordered them arrested.

On April 12, the day before the surrender of Fort Sumter, forty armed *Tejanos* and *Mexicanos* under the leadership of a thirty-nine-year-old *ranchero* named Antonio Ochoa seized control of Precinct Three in the southern part of the county and threatened to kill all the "Gringos" in the county and hang Sheriff Díaz.[16] Ochoa and his followers, directed by or certainly under the influence of Cortina, were said to be "marching about the county in armed bodies threatening the lives of Tom, Dick, and John Doe."[17] Ochoa was even preparing to seize the county seat of Carrizo. The men "were not only attempting to keep the county officers from taking the [Confederate] oath of office," but were "also threatening to forcibly take all public money."[18] Ochoa and his men were met by Judge Vela, owner of Rancho Clareño, who persuaded the men to return to their homes. Although the dissidents backed down, they issued a *pronunciamiento* against the Confederacy, which they pre-

Lt. Col. E. F. Gray, Third Texas Infantry, and acting assistant adjutant general to Brig. Gen. H. P. Bee at Fort Brown. Signed and dated verso, May 8, 1863. *Carte de visite* attributed to A. G. Wedge. *Martin L. Callahan collection.*

sented to Judge Vela. From his fortified ranch near San Bartolo, Redmond was in a state of panic. The insurrectionists demanded, Redmond reported, that their *pronunciamiento* be "forwarded to the U.S.," which Ochoa thought was "a few miles on the other side of Bexar." It is "hard to say how far their ignorance will lead them," Redmond continued.[19]

Amazingly, the insurrection in Zapata County was said to have been inspired by Texas Unionists. Ochoa and his men, it was reported, were in favor of "Old Abe, the rail splitter" and were angrily

Maj. Charles Russell, chief quartermaster on the staff of Brig. Gen. H. P. Bee at Fort Brown. Signed and dated verso, May 16, 1863. *Carte de visite* attributed to A. G. Wedge. *Martin L. Callahan collection.*

demanding to communicate with Federal authorities. With ethnic, social, and economic undercurrents, the threatened violence was, in reality, a reaction to Zapata County boss rule. Although Ochoa owned a small ranch near Clareño, most of his followers were poor *vaqueros* and *labradores*, many from Guerrero, across the river from Carrizo.[20] Some may have ridden with Cortina in 1859 and 1860.

To ensure peace in the county, Capt. Matthew Nolan, commanding a hastily organized Confederate company of twenty-two men, rode downriver from Laredo. After a fifty-five-mile ride, Nolan bivouacked near Redmond's Ranch on the afternoon of April 14, 1861.[21] The captain was determined to crush any resistance to state authority on

the Rio Grande. Judge Vela quickly swore out warrants for the arrest of Ochoa and eighty of his men. Captain Nolan, Judge Vela, and Sheriff Díaz, whom the insurgents were still threatening to hang, immediately took up the line of march for Rancho Clareño, where Ochoa was said to have his headquarters. Reaching the small village before daylight on April 15, Nolan carefully deployed his men around the ranch, and Sheriff Díaz ordered the so-called Unionists, many of whom were still asleep, to surrender. Most were in the process of doing so when one insurgent, according to Nolan, fired at his men, although one of the Confederate volunteers later confessed that not a single shot was fired in defense. Regardless, Nolan ordered an all-out attack. Outnumbered, caught off-guard,

1st Lt. Edward R. Tarver, aide de camp to Brig. Gen. H. P. Bee at Fort Brown. Signed and dated verso, June 1, 1863. *Carte de visite* attributed to A. G. Wedge. *Martin L. Callahan collection.*

and surrounded, Ochoa's men never had a chance. Many were gunned down where they stood, while others were killed as they fled toward the river. Although Nolan later bragged that "nine Black Republicans" were killed in the battle, several of those who died were said to have been noncombatants and may have been unarmed. Ochoa, the leader of the movement, was across the river in Guerrero at the time, but two of his lieutenants, Nepomuceno and Santiago Vela, were killed in the attack.[22] Looking into the incident twelve years later, a committee sent by the Mexican government to investigate border problems concluded that "inoffensive inhabitants were assassinated."[23]

In the days following the massacre at Rancho Clareño, unsubstantiated rumors spread along the Rio Grande that Cortina had formed an alliance with Federal authorities in the North as well as Unionists in Texas. Furnished with arms and horses paid for by the Unionists and hoping to reassert himself on the north bank, Cortina again began recruiting men.[24] Along with Teodoro Zamora, a leading lieutenant and the former county judge of Hidalgo County, as well as Antonio Ochoa, Cortina was preparing to march on Carrizo to avenge the victims of the Clareño massacre. Fearing for his life, Judge Vela took his family and fled to the safety of Redmond's Ranch. Although Vela received assurances from Mexican authorities across the river in Guerrero that they would do everything possible to apprehend Cortina and Ochoa, he did not feel they were sincere. Cortina was so popular that even elements of the Mexican army were said to be in sympathy with the wily revolutionary.[25] When Col. John Ford, who commanded the isolated Confederate units on the vast Rio Grande frontier, received a plea for help from Redmond, he sent Capt. Santos Benavides, a seasoned Indian fighter who had recruited a Confederate company at Laredo, downriver to assist the Zapata County officials.

On May 19, 1861, Cortina and fifty men reached the vicinity of Guerrero, where Ochoa

Capt. George Washington Chilton, Third Texas Cavalry, and ordnance officer on the staff of Brig. Gen. H. P. Bee at Fort Brown. Signed and dated June 1, 1863. Chilton, who owned five slaves, was a delegate to the Texas secession convention. He was passionate in his pro-slavery beliefs and before the war was a member of the Knights of the Golden Circle. Like several of the Confederate officers who were photographed at Fort Brown, including General Bee, the long-haired Chilton wears a French military waist belt and belt plate. *Carte de visite* attributed to A. G. Wedge. *Lawrence T. Jones III collection.*

greeted them. Cortina did not know, however, that the unsympathetic *alcalde* of Guerrero, Juan G. Garza, was keeping Benavides informed on his movements. Garza went as far as to dispatch twenty-five men under José María Hinojosa to the main ford on the Rio Grande, just below Guerrero, to impede Cortina's crossing. Finding another crossing, Cortina splashed across the Rio

"Cotton Buyers, Mata-moros" is the old pencil inscription on the back of this photograph. It was men such as those seen here who made the business of cotton smuggling profitable on both sides of the border. *Carte de visite* by unidentified artist, ca. 1863. *Lawrence T. Jones III collection.*

Grande into Texas. The next day his advance guard ran into three of Benavides's pickets below Carrizo, and a brief skirmish ensued. Reinforced by twenty men from Guerrero and a few men from Zapata County, especially the relatives of those previously killed at Rancho Clareño, Cortina's force was said to be growing hourly.[26] In less than a day Cortina had Benavides's small band of Confederates surrounded at Redmond's Ranch. Cortina also sent two of his men under a flag of truce to the ranch in an attempt to persuade Benavides to leave and let Redmond, Vela, Mussett, and their friends defend themselves. Influential citizens from Guerrero crossed the river to tell Benavides that Cortina's intention was only to seek revenge on Redmond and those responsible for the bloodshed at Rancho Clareño. Cortina was determined, they said, "to have Redmond's head before sundown."[27] But Benavides, who had been Webb County judge at the same time Redmond had been Zapata

Unidentified Confederate first lieutenant at Fort Brown, summer 1863. This photograph was in the same album as the other photographs of Brig. Gen. H. P. Bee's staff officers. The lieutenant, who posed with a French army saber, most likely served on Bee's staff. *Carte de visite* attributed to A. G. Wedge. *Lawrence T. Jones III collection.*

County judge, refused to forsake his friend.

As he had done when he seized Brownsville in 1859, Cortina cut all communications from Redmond's Ranch. One of Benavides's couriers was captured on the road from Roma to Carrizo and another rider, Ángel Jiménez, was seized on the road leading upriver to Laredo. A second rider, however, was able to get past Cortina's pickets and reach Laredo safely.[28] Within hours, thirty-six men under Refugio and Basilio Benavides, Santos Benavides's older brother and uncle, along with Lt. Charles Callahan, were on their way to Carrizo, riding through the night to reach the besieged Confederates.

On the morning of May 22, 1861, after riding sixty-five miles in thirteen hours, the Laredo reinforcements ran into a party of Cortina's men near San Bartolo and a brief fight ensued. Hearing the sounds of gunfire, Benavides and his men rushed to join the fray. Cortina, too, heard the sounds of battle and pushed his men forward. In a running fight that began at 1 P.M. and lasted forty minutes, Benavides completely routed Cortina's raiders. A number of the *Cortinistas* appear to have been preoccupied with sacking the small two-story Zapata County Courthouse and were caught by surprise. Several of Cortina's men were killed in the initial charge while others died as Benavides and his men pursued the partisans to the riverbank. Six or seven *Cortinistas* were said to have drowned while attempting to swim the Rio Grande to Mexico. Cortina, however, and ten of his men, "gained the opposite side of the river in safety, and in ascending its banks, faced about, took an apparent disdainful view of his recent antagonist and master, uncovered, and with characteristic dignity, waved his hat, bidding them in the blandest tone . . . a courteous temporary adieu, informing them that he would give them another call in a few days."[29] Benavides had eleven prisoners, some of whom were badly wounded, either hanged or shot.[30]

After the battle of Carrizo, Captain Benavides set up camp at Rancho Clareño while leaving his brother, Cristobal, in command at Carrizo.[31] From the Mexican bank of the river, a number of Cortina's men continued to snipe at the Confederates. Noah Cox at Roma and H. Clay Davis at Rio Grande City were so fearful that Cortina would cross the river to "rob and murder" and "burn the towns on the Rio Grande" that they hastened to organize local militias.[32] Rumors persisted that Cortina was in camp near Mier with a force of from fifty to two hundred men, boasting that he held a commission from both Benito Juárez and Abraham Lincoln. There were even rumors that Cortina had met José María Jesús Carbajal and the two warriors had agreed to combine their forces.[33] Only one thing was for certain: the Rio Grande frontier had not heard the last of the indefatigable and elusive Juan Nepomuceno Cortina.

Prior to his defeat of Cortina at Carrizo, state authorities appear to have had considerable doubt as to the loyalty of Santos Benavides. When Colonel Ford informed Gov. Edward Clark of Benavides's rout of Cortina at Carrizo, the gover-

Mifflin Kenedy, ca. 1864–1865. A Quaker from Pennsylvania, Kenedy was married to Petra Vela de Vidal. Active in the Cortina War and a business partner of Richard King, he made a fortune in steamboating and in the cotton trade during the Civil War. *Carte de visite* by Louis de Planque. *Brownsville Historical Association.*

nor wrote to praise the Laredo captain: "Whenever our enemies have appeared on our soil, you and your brave men have been present and driven them back with great honor to ourselves and the gratification of our state."[34] Clark even sent an elegantly engraved pistol to Benavides, along with a letter: "I am happy to believe in your hands it will always be used in the defense of your country and prove an instrument of terror and destruction to her enemies."[35] To Colonel Ford and Governor

Clark, Benavides's continued loyalty was critical to Confederate successes along the river and in South Texas.

At Brownsville on the evening of April 18, 1861, news arrived of the opening of hostilities at Fort Sumter. At the time, the entire state was ill prepared for war. Colonel Ford immediately called a council of war, where it was decided to abandon Brazos Island. The island had no reliable water supply, and the fortifications were vulnerable to attack from the sea. Instead, Ford set out to reinforce Fort Brown, and many of the Texas volunteers were put to work fortifying the post. Cameron County Judge Israel B. Bigelow assisted by hiring a number of local laborers to assist with the work, and local merchant Jeremiah Galvan brought several barrels of "pure, good whiskey," as incentive for the workers.[36] In particular, the dense vegetation that had grown up around the post had to be cleared.

After a thorough examination of the fort by various Confederate officers several months later, however, it was concluded that the post was "untenable" and could not be secured.[37] Constructed by the United States Army in 1846 at the beginning of the Mexican War, the earthen fortification had been built for defense against an attack from Matamoros and not the Texas side of the Rio Grande. A large lagoon on the edge of the post afforded protection to anyone attacking the post from the Texas side of the river. Fort Brown, nevertheless, would play a crucial role in the history of the area in the four years of war that lay ahead.

Almost from the beginning, Ford found himself embroiled in the tumultuous and revolutionary politics south of the Rio Grande. The elected governor of Tamaulipas, Jesús de la Serna, a partisan of Benito Juárez and a liberal of the *Rojo* faction, had attacked Matamoros but had been driven across the river by the *Crinolinos,* or conservatives, led by Gen. Guadalupe García, commanding the Line of the Rio Bravo. In Brownsville Ford not only gave protection to Governor de la Serna but allowed the *Rojos* to regroup, rearm, and recruit on the Texas side of the river prior to invading Mexico. Joined by liberal *Juarista* forces from Ciudad Victoria under the command of José María Jesus Carbajal, the Liberals were soon laying siege

to Matamoros. For two months bloody street fighting engulfed the city amid the flames of burning buildings, including the American consulate.[38] Matamoros would remain in the hands of the *Crinolinos* until Gov. Santiago Vidaurri arrived with forces from Nuevo León in January 1862, at which time the new governor of Tamaulipas, Ignacio Comonfort, was able to restore order.

As early as October 1861 Ford had assured military authorities in Matamoros that it was the intention of the Confederate government "to live at peace with her sister republic of Mexico." Ford promised he would do all in his power to "disperse all bands of armed men who may assemble illegally" in Texas for "any hostile descent upon Mexican territory."[39] Under fire for his handling of affairs on the Rio Grande, however, Ford was recalled to San Antonio, where he would serve as the state superintendent of conscripts.

With Ford's departure, Confederate authorities continued to concentrate on a defensive war. In late October 1861 Gen. Paul Octave Hébert, the former governor of Louisiana, who assumed command of the District of Texas, wrote Secretary of War Judah P. Benjamin that Texas was "totally unprepared, confused, and defenseless" and was lacking in "guns, arms, ammunition and a proper military organization." As Ford had observed, the long Texas coastline was "defenseless" and General Hébert admitted his "inability to remedy the evil."[40]

Events were moving fast. Five months earlier, on April 19, 1861, President Abraham Lincoln proclaimed a blockade of all Confederate ports. In the years that followed, the blockade cut the South's seaborne trade to less than a third of what it had been in 1860. Lacking an industrial base, the South needed to import large quantities of war materials, and few places in the South had less industry than Texas. The desire for these materials and Europe's need for Southern cotton, along with profits to be made by carrying such items through the blockade, created a bonanza for blockade-runners. During the war, as many as 500,000 bales of cotton were exported, and 600,000 rifles and a million pairs of shoes were brought into the Confederacy. Although the Union navy initially struggled to blockade the South's 189 harbors and inlets, it did manage to tighten the blockade as the war progressed. In 1861 at least nine out of ten blockade-runners were able to evade the Union navy, yet by 1865 only one in two was successful. Along the South Texas Coast, Brazos Santiago, despite the protests of the American consul in Matamoros who said the port was the "rendezvous for the Texas Navy," remained open to Confederate shipping until the last two years of the war.[41]

No sooner were Union warships off the lower Texas coast than Colonel Ford scurried across the river to meet with the numerous and prosperous merchants in Matamoros. Seeing the possibility of expanding commerce, all were anxious to assist with the exportation of cotton from the Confederate states and facilitate the flow of arms and other vital necessities of war into South Texas. Ford also gained the cooperation of the British and German consuls, who promised to assist. By the summer of 1861 the first big train of cotton, some three thousand bales, arrived on the border from North Texas for shipment to Europe. "An immense trade opened up in a short while," Colonel Ford wrote. "Matamoros was soon crammed with strangers and filled with goods."[42]

John Warren Hunter, who as a fifteen-year-old teamster helped haul cotton to the border in the early months of the war, recalled seeing "a never-ending stream of cotton pouring into Brownsville." Across the river in Matamoros Hunter saw "ox trains, mule trains, and trains of Mexican carts, all laden with cotton coming from almost every town in Texas."[43] To the young teamster Brownsville was "the greatest shipping point in the South," and Matamoros had become "a great commercial center [with] cotton and other commodities . . . pouring into her warehouses." Matamoros was, Leonard Pierce Jr., the American consul, wrote, "the great thoroughfare to the Southern States."[44]

In Matamoros, a Texas Unionist wrote, "cotton was exchanged for English, French, Prussian and perhaps Harpers Ferry Rifles; here the convict gray clothing of England and France found a ready market in exchange for the cotton of Messrs. King & Kennedy [sic] & Co. and here the Jew and Gentile, Gog and Magog, found their first oasis from

Capt. Richard King, Santa Gertrudis Ranch, Texas, 1867. *Carte de visite* attributed to Louis de Planque. *King Ranch Archives.*

the cotton fields of Texas, on their way to Mecca (Liverpool)."[45]

Although most of the cotton firms operating on the border were owned and operated by either English or Germans, the largest and most influential business operating in the area was the Mexican firm of Milmo and Company. The company was headed by Patricio Milmo, the influential son-in-law of the powerful governor of Nuevo León and Coahuila, Santiago Vidaurri, who ran a progressive and popular yet politically autonomous government. The most important private merchant involved in the trade was José San Román, a quiet, politically influential, self-made bachelor, a native of Bilbao, Spain—and the wealthiest man in South Texas.

To avoid the Union blockade, Ford held an emergency meeting in Brownsville with San Román, Charles Stillman, Francisco Yturria, Mifflin Kenedy, and Richard King. Ford urged King and Kenedy, whose steamboats had dominated commerce on the Rio Grande since the Mexican War, to place their boats under the Mexican registry. Although a few officers in the Confederate

Somers Kinney and his young bride in Matamoros, ca. 1864–1865. *Carte de visite* by Louis de Planque. *Brownsville Historical Association.*

army complained that the boats would no longer be under their control, Ford saw no alternative, since under the Mexican flag the steamers would be able to freely "navigate the waters of the Gulf of Mexico and the Rio Grande."[46] At the same time King and Kenedy also began investing heavily in blockade-runners.

Early in the war, when Great Britain and France hesitated to recognize the infant Confederacy, Jefferson Davis and his cabinet urged that cotton be withheld from the world market in hopes of forcing European recognition and possible intervention. Realizing that Mexico offered opportunities for exchanging Texas cotton for badly needed supplies for the war, Confederate authorities exempted shipment into Mexico.[47] Despite the booming economy on the border, the flow of cotton across the Rio Grande combined with the chaotic and revolutionary atmosphere existing in Mexico at the time often produced a confusing state of affairs. As a frontier state and the only Southern state with a foreign border, the blockade presented unique economic opportunities for Texas and those living along the river. Most Texas planters preferred the long and arduous overland wagon trip to the Rio Grande to the dangers of running the Union blockade. Moreover, the cotton trade became a lucrative business as the price of cotton increased from 16 cents per pound in August 1862 to 80 cents in November 1863.

Cotton producers and traders crowded the border. By December 1863, although turbulent Mexican politics frequently interrupted the flow of cotton, more than 150,000 bales had been carried across the river to Matamoros. By the end of the war, 320,000 bales had been sent across the border. At the same time, towns on the Mexican side of the Rio Grande, especially Matamoros, furnished not only Texas but much of Arkansas, Louisiana, and Mississippi with most of their manufactured goods and practically all their munitions of war. Matamoros was to the Confederacy what New York was to the Union.[48] Consequently, the war brought unprecedented prosperity to the border. To many citizens of South

Texas and the Lower Rio Grande Valley, the years from 1861 to 1865 would be remembered not as the Civil War but as the "Cotton Times."

In addition to the Matamoros and Monterrey merchant elite, a number of South Texas businessmen such as Richard King; Mifflin Kenedy; William Marsh Rice, benefactor of Rice University; and Charles Stillman, the founder of Brownsville, along with a host of other speculators, made fortunes from the cotton trade during the war. Yet the vast majority of those involved in the cotton trade, especially the teamsters on the long "cotton road" to the border, were Mexicans who managed only a bare existence.[49]

Teamsters used two main routes to transport cotton across the border. Much of the cotton from Central and East Texas came through Alleyton, the railroad terminus on the lower Colorado River, west of Houston.[50] From here wagons and ox carts carried the cotton across the coastal prairie to the King Ranch, which became a major staging and refitting hub on the Cotton Road, prior to the final 124-mile stretch across the burning and shifting sands of the Wild Horse Desert to Brownsville. Trouble developed on the route in March 1863, when Confederates killed several Mexican herders in the vicinity of the King Ranch. Fearing a repetition of the violent racial intolerance that had characterized the infamous Cart War of 1857, General Bee issued orders for the apprehension of individuals responsible for the murders. Under guard, the perpetrators were to be taken to Corpus Christi for trial.[51] Although the killings stopped, there is no evidence of anyone being arrested or tried.

A second route from Central Texas took cotton to San Antonio and then to the King Ranch. From San Antonio, cotton was also taken across the semi-arid, rough brush country to Eagle Pass, Laredo, or Rio Grande City, where the precious commodity was hauled down the south bank of the river to Matamoros. By early 1863 Confederate authorities were forced to devote precious human resources to policing the cotton trade when teamsters, fearing conscription, began developing alternate routes around San Antonio and King Ranch.[52] Another problem came at Laredo in March 1864, when Colonel Benavides began seizing cotton to pay his men, thus evoking the wrath

of the Confederate Cotton Bureau, which was struggling to bring some semblance of order to the profitable trade.[53] Cotton from as far away as Arkansas and northern Louisiana generally used the San Antonio route. On her way to Mexico during the war, Eliza Moore McHatton-Ripley remembered seeing in San Antonio "hundreds of huge Chihuahua wagons . . . parked with military precision outside" the city "waiting their turn to enter the grand plaza, deliver their packages of goods and load with cotton."[54]

At Brownsville, the cotton was placed in small, shallow-draft paddle steamers operated by King and Kenedy and taken sixty-five miles down the twisting, tortuous, and shallow confines of the river to Bagdad. At the mouth of the river, many of the steamers, operating as lighters, hauled the cotton to the seagoing vessels anchored in the choppy waters of the gulf two to four miles offshore. Later in the war, the majority of the cotton was crossed by ferry to Matamoros and taken in wagons to the mouth of the river at Bagdad, where by 1863 as many as 150 vessels from many nations, including the United States, could be seen on any given day waiting to take on cotton and discharge their cargoes.[55]

At the mouth of the river, Bagdad evolved from a small fishing village to a bustling, vibrant port of fifteen thousand citizens. Yet the *Matamoros Daily Ranchero* referred to the post as a "sand hole on the gulf." A correspondent for the *New York Herald* found the town to be "a dirty, filthy place" where the "streets are covered with slime and mud puddles." The place was sickly, the reporter continued, wondering how "anyone can live there at all."[56] The seaside community consisted of "dirty looking buildings" where "blockade runners, desperadoes, the vile of both sexes, adventurers, the Mexican and the rebel" gathered, and where "numberless groggeries and houses of worse fame [where] vice in its lowest form held high carnival."[57] In early 1863 Lt. Col. Arthur James Lyon Fremantle of the British Coldstream Guards, while on a three-month tour of the Confederacy, wrote that Bagdad consisted of little more than "a few miserable wooden shanties." Yet for "an immense distance," Fremantle continued, "endless bales of cotton are to be seen."[58]

By 1864 as many as ten stagecoaches a day

were making the thirty-five-mile run between Matamoros and Bagdad. Despite frequent flooding, Bagdad offered "first class hotels, boarding houses, stores well fitted with goods . . . and restaurants without number," as well as brothels, saloons, gambling houses, and a small church. Pierre Fourrier Parisot, the French-born Oblate priest assigned to Brownsville, proclaimed Bagdad "a veritable Babel, a Babylon, a whirlpool of business, pleasure, and sin."[59] Bagdad was, Ernst Pitner, an Austrian lieutenant in the Imperial service of Maximilian, recorded, inhabited by "a medley of people from all over the world, but particularly Americans, Spaniards, Italians, French, Germans, Greek, and . . . least of all, Mexicans." In the town, everything was constructed of wood, "everything provisional, everything practical, everything contrived for profit, nothing for solidity; no consideration whatever for health, cleanliness." All the houses were "transportable and built on piles," the young lieutenant continued. "Whenever there is a north wind all the streets are transformed into canals, like Venice, and nowhere are so many rats to be found."[60] A common laborer could earn from $5 to $6 a day, while anyone who owned a skiff or a lighter could make as much as $20 to $40. The *Brownsville Ranchero* described Bagdad as a place where "fandangos were held every night and women as beautiful as houris exhibit their charms, without the least reserve."[61]

On both sides of the border, in an era of compromised business morals, corruption engulfed the cotton trade and reached the highest levels of government and the military. When the English blockade-runner *Rob Roy* reached Bagdad in 1863, William Watson found the Mexican customs officials scurrying to extract as much as possible from various duties and charges. "Everyone competed to grab what he could and many schemes there were to make money out of the crisis," Watson wrote.[62] Off the coast, ships from all over the world waited to take on the cotton. One border resident remembered seeing as many as one hundred vessels ranging from thirty-ton schooners to two thousand-ton steamships anchored off Bagdad, waiting to take on cotton and unload cargo.[63] Ironically, much of the cotton that flowed out of

Texas across the Rio Grande ended up in the flourishing textile mills of New England, where it was made into blankets and uniforms that helped to warm the back of many a Union soldier.

At the mouth of the river in the sand dunes opposite Bagdad, another shantytown, Clarksville, also thrived on the cotton trade. Here too, traders, blockade-runners, gamblers, adventurers, and the riffraff from all over Texas and northeastern Mexico congregated. Many of the small wooden houses in Clarksville, similar to those in Bagdad, were built on stilts. A correspondent for the *New York Herald* said the dwellings were "few, low and roughly built, and the inmates about as 'polished' as their buildings."[64] Daily stagecoaches connected the small community with Brownsville, and a ferry crossed travelers to Bagdad in a matter of minutes.

From the small communities above Rio Grande City, some of the cotton was taken south to Monterrey, and from there the white fiber was hauled hundreds of miles through deserts and mountains to the forty textile mills operating in the Mexican interior in such cities as Quéteraro, Durango, and Guadalajara. From three to four thousand bales each year went to mills in Coahuila and Nuevo León alone. As the cotton trade expanded, the military in Texas used the opportunity to import vast amounts of tin, lead, copper, iron, nitrate of potash, quicksilver, sulphur, saltpeter, powder, and percussion caps, as well as blankets, shoes, and coffee.[65]

From the beginning of the Union blockade, the Confederate State Department realized the free and uninhibited flow of commerce across the Rio Grande was critical to the ultimate success of the Confederacy. By the early summer of 1861, a gifted and talented diplomat, Cuban-born José Agustín Quintero, who was fluent in English and Spanish, was sent by Secretary of State Benjamin as a secret agent to see Gov. Santiago Vidaurri. As the powerful *caudillo* of Nuevo León and Coahuila, Vidaurri had controlled much of the frontier since 1855 and extended considerable influence over politics and commerce in Tamaulipas. Having edited newspapers in New York and San Antonio, Quintero studied law and served as an assistant clerk of the Texas legislature.[66] Well educated and widely traveled, he was the ideal man for the job. Quintero first met Vidaurri in Austin in 1859, and the two had corresponded frequently. After stopping in Austin and Galveston, where he obtained letters of introduction, Quintero sailed for Brazos Santiago and made his way inland to Brownsville.

Crossing the river to Matamoros, the forty-two-year-old Quintero traveled on to Monterrey by stage, arriving on June 17. Although his mission was to be secret and confidential, Union officials such as M. M. Kimmey, the United States consul in Monterrey, and Leonard Pierce Jr. at Matamoros, learned of Quintero's activities by reading the Matamoros and Monterrey newspapers. Able to obtain an interview with Governor Vidaurri, Quintero informed Richmond that he had been "entirely successful in my mission." Vidaurri felt threatened by Benito Juárez's efforts to centralize authority, Quintero reported. Moreover, he "feels great friendship for the South" and was "determined to preserve the peace of the Rio Grande frontier."[67] Able to meet with Vidaurri on two other occasions, Quintero was particularly pleased to learn that Vidaurri was not prepared to permit a Union invasion of Texas from the south bank of the river, something both Austin and Richmond had feared since the beginning of the war. As the friendship between the two men warmed, Quintero excitedly told Richmond that Vidaurri had for several years contemplated the establishment of a Republic of the Sierra Madre with himself as the head. With the birth of the Southern Confederacy, the wily *caudillo*, independent and confident, was even considering the annexation of not only Nuevo León and Coahuila but "several other of the adjoining and interior states of Mexico to the Confederate States."[68] In a "private conversation" in late July, Vidaurri, always the schemer and fearful of the Mexican Liberals under Juárez, told Quintero that he would negotiate annexation with the Confederacy if "one thousand Texians and some flying artillery" could be sent to his defense.[69] Determined to stay in power, Vidau-

Left to right: Pat Daugherty, B. F. Neale, and W. H. Maltby were photographed together in a primitive setting in Matamoros. Note the tobacco spit-stained wooden floor on which they stand. Their casual pose and disheveled appearance might indicate that they had been visiting a local saloon prior to having their photograph made. Maltby's brother Henry was publisher of the *Daily Ranchero*. *Carte de visite* by unidentified artist, ca. 1864–1865. *Brownsville Historical Association.*

rri was convinced that it was only a matter of time before the Mexican frontier became "Americanized." If Nuevo León and Coahuila could be annexed, the governor was sure that the balance of

Left to right: Capt. Fred Noble, Captain Dalzell, and pilot Charles Best. These steamboat captains and their pilot were photographed in either Matamoros or Brownsville after they navigated up the Rio Grande and delivered their cargo. *Carte de visite* by unidentified artist, ca. 1863–1864. *Brownsville Historical Association.*

the frontier states in Mexico would soon follow.

By early July 1861 Quintero was back on the Rio Grande, and by August 17 he had arrived in Richmond to report Vidaurri's revolutionary scheme to annex the northeastern states of Mexico to Secretary of State Robert Toombs and President Jefferson Davis. Although long a proponent of Manifest Destiny, Davis was less than excited about the scheme, concluding that it would be "imprudent and impolitic in the interest of both parties to take any steps at present . . . in reference to the future political relations of the Confederate States and the Northern Provinces of Mexico."[70]

By early September Quintero was told he was being appointed confidential agent of the Confederacy to northeastern Mexico. He would reside at Monterrey with the assignment of continuing to cultivate friendly relations with the border states. Leaving Richmond, Quintero was delayed in New Orleans by rumors that Vidaurri had been defeated by the Mexican Federal troops and that he had fled into Texas. By late October, however, Quintero was back in Monterrey. Although Juárez had proclaimed neutrality in the American Civil War and had given orders to close the border, Vidaurri, who was striving to remain independent of the central government and dependent on lucrative customs receipts, assured Quintero that the Rio Grande frontier would remain open.[71] Quintero also told Richmond that the Oliver Brothers of Monterrey were ready and able to supply the Confederacy with a wide array of goods, including everything from lead and saltpeter to shoes and blankets. Virtually anything could be purchased in Monterrey except small arms. Moreover, Patricio Milmo and Company was eager to exchange flour for cotton.[72]

Before any meaningful agreement could be reached between Vidaurri and the Confederacy, the Mexican central government, always leery of Vidaurri's power and independence and hearing of the possible secession of the Mexican states east of the Sierra Madre, sent a six thousand-man force into Nuevo León, decisively defeating Vidaurri and pursuing him to the Rio Grande.[73]

On the Rio Grande frontier, violence continued to spill across the river, threatening diplomatic relations and causing confusion. In April 1862 a large party of Mexican refugee *Rojos* infuriated Governor Vidaurri by crossing the river into Coahuila, sacking the village of Guerrero and burning part of Piedras Negras, opposite Eagle Pass.[74] Raids into Texas by insurrectionists operating out of Mexico, Union officials realized, could easily paralyze Confederate operations on the bor-

Headed south to Mexico from San Antonio, this wagon train is typical of those used to haul cotton from Texas to Mexico. Stereograph by Henry A. Doerr, San Antonio, ca. 1870. *Lawrence T. Jones III collection.*

der and tie down large numbers of Confederate troops vital to Confederate fortunes elsewhere. Beginning in 1862, Union agents called *enganchados* commenced the recruitment of *Tejanos* and *Mexicanos*.[75] One raider who came under Union influence was thirty-two-year-old Octaviano Zapata, who owned a small ranch near Clareño in Zapata County. A close ally of Cortina, Zapata had escaped the Clareño massacre in April 1861 and, along with his wife and three children, had taken refuge with relatives in Guerrero. Burning with a desire to strike back at enemies in Texas, Zapata was able to recruit between sixty and eighty men in and around Guerrero. Loosely tied to the Union army, potential recruits were offered as much as one hundred pesos in gold and a promise of 50 acres of land in Texas for recruits who were single and 150 acres for those who were married. Such enticements were appealing to many of the poor *Tejanos* and *Mexicanos* who lived along the river.

In early December 1862 Zapata's raiders crossed the river near Roma some eighteen miles above Ringgold Barracks and attacked a Confederate supply train. Three weeks later, on December 26, another train of three wagons en route from Fort Brown to Ringgold Barracks, escorted by five soldiers, was attacked by Zapata's raiders at Rancho Soledad near Las Cuevas, fifteen miles below Ringgold Barracks.[76] The Confederates were caught completely by surprise and made no attempt to resist, except for one soldier who opened fire on the raiders with his revolver, killing two of Zapata's men. The *Zapatistas* killed all the teamsters except one man, who was able to escape to Ringgold Barracks. All the wagons were taken to the riverbank and plundered.[77] In retaliation for the wagon raid, a company of Confederates from Ringgold Barracks rode to Rancho Soledad, where "strong circumstantial evidence" indicated many of the *Tejano* families living in the vicinity had been involved in the raid. As a result, the soldiers burned sixteen *jacales* in the village and rode triumphantly back to Ringgold Barracks.

On the same day as the Rancho Soledad raid, another party of two hundred Mexicans under Zapata crossed into Zapata County, rode to the ranch of sixty-two-year-old Isidro Vela at Rancho Clareño, seized the judge, and hanged him from a tree. Before leaving, the raiders "posted a placard on the body warning that they would kill any person who dared to take the body down for burial."[78] Hearing of the hanging, Gen. Hamilton P. Bee, newly appointed commander of Confederate forces on the Rio Grande, complained bitterly to Gov. Albino López of Tamaulipas that Zapata's raiders had crossed into Zapata County carrying a "Yankee flag" that had "no right on the soil of Texas."[79] Bee demanded that Zapata, who he claimed was attached to the First Texas Cavalry, be apprehended and sent to Brownsville for trial.

One of Zapata's zealous recruits, Guillermo Vino, was successful in stealing several herds of cattle from the Texas bank as well as thirty-two horses from a Confederate company of Capt. Refugio Benavides near Roma.[80] Demanding that the *alcalde* of Mier assist in capturing the raiders, Captain Benavides crossed into Mexico with fifty-four of his Laredo Confederates. Benavides was able to track the *Zapatistas* southeast to Mesquital Lealeño near Camargo, where they were found encamped in a large corral. Eighteen of the *Zapatistas* were killed, fourteen wounded, and several taken captive in the ensuing fight. Zapata, however, was able to escape into the chaparral with some of his men. Fifty-eight horses and fifty-four saddles were seized as well as documents implicating the *enganchados* in the raid on Rancho Clareño. The captives taken in the fray were reported to have "escaped."[81] In reality, they were probably executed, as had been the case following Cortina's defeat at Carrizo in May 1861. After torching several small *jacales*, including that of Jesús Vidal, the Confederates returned to Texas.

Sometime in early 1863 Zapata went to New Orleans at the invitation of Union officials and received a shipment of arms. In March he returned to Bagdad with the arms on the steamer *Honduras*. Fearful of continued raids into Texas, General Bee demanded that Governor López confiscate the arms and arrest Zapata. Although López assured Bee that he would do everything possible to comply, within weeks Zapata was in camp near Guerrero saying Union authorities had given him the rank of colonel. Moreover, in addition to arms, Zapata had been promised money, uniforms, and other rewards to help end the "Confederate War."[82] "*Que Viva la Unión*" became Zapata's battle cry as additional raids on Texas were in the offing. Mexican authorities

finally arrested Zapata, and he was briefly imprisoned in Matamoros. The "outlaw Zapata is again at liberty," Bee protested, "notwithstanding the many crimes and outrages he has committed against the peace and safety on both sides of the river."[83] Moreover, Bee asserted, there was little doubt that Zapata was continuing to conspire with the American consul in Matamoros, Leonard Pierce Jr., to recruit men with the intended purpose of raiding into Texas.

At Mier, Zapata was said to have been responsible for the assassination of Col. Jesús García Ramírez, an officer in the Mexican National Guard and a close friend of Maj. Santos Benavides.[84] In late August 1863 Zapata ambushed and routed Mexican troops on the road between Guerrero and Mier. From Carrizo, Major Benavides rode down river to Rancho Clareño, crossed the Rio Grande into Mexico, found the location of the attack, and followed the trail of Zapata and his men down the Rio Grande in the direction of Mier. Scouts located Zapata's camp in a mesquite thicket early on the morning of September 2. Zapata and all of his officers were killed in the furious attack that followed. Cpl. Natividad Herrera of Benavides's command was said to have killed Zapata with the butt of his rifle while Zapata blazed away at the corporal with his pistol. Mónico Salinas, who claimed the rank of captain in the Union army, as well as Manuel Villarreal and Guillermo Vino, who were said to be lieutenants, were also killed.[85] "Should E. J. Davis ever invade the Rio Grande with his regiment of refugees and outlaws, he will miss his friend Zapata who had the power to do us great injury," Bee wrote.[86]

Another incident several months later seriously threatened diplomatic relations between the Confederacy and the Mexican republic and jeopardized the flow of commerce across the Rio Grande. The nasty incident centered around a band of zealous Confederates and two Texas Unionists, Edmund J. Davis and William W. Montgomery. Davis, a prominent attorney with considerable oratorical abilities, had been a city councilman and deputy collector of customs at Laredo in the years after the Mexican War.[87] Later, as district attorney and district judge of the Twelfth Judicial District in South Texas, he presided at Corpus

Although this photograph was taken ten years after the war, the ferry crossing at Eagle Pass appeared much the same as it did when Confederates used it to export cotton to Mexico. On the south bank of the Rio Grande in the background is the Mexican town of Piedras Negras. Stereograph by Alexis V. Latourette, ca. 1875. *Lawrence T. Jones III collection.*

Christi, Brownsville, and Laredo.[88] Tall, gaunt, and cold-eyed, with a rather commanding persona, Davis expended considerable energy hoping to forestall secession in South Texas. Montgomery, an established Caldwell County horse and sheep rancher and close friend of Andrew Jackson Hamilton, was another leading Texas Unionist who also fled to Mexico.[89] Davis and Montgomery had arrived at Bagdad on March 10, 1863, with permission to raise one or more Union regiments from among the Texans fleeing the state. The two men had spent the first part of March recruiting and assembling Unionists for embarkation on the *Honduras* to New Orleans. A number of those who crossed the river to enlist were Confederate deserters.[90] When bad weather delayed the vessel, Union recruits and a camp of Confederates were left only a few hundred yards apart on opposite sides of the narrow and twisting waters of the Rio Grande. So volatile and perilous was the situation, with both sides shouting insults across the river, that General Bee went to the mouth of the river and issued orders that none of the Confederates were to cross into Mexico or communicate with the refugees.[91]

Far from the capital in Richmond, Virginia, Bee was left very much on his own to conduct foreign relations with Mexican officials. The incident that would challenge Bee's diplomatic skills and ignite international tensions came not from the Confederate pickets at the mouth of the river, but from Maj. George Chilton in Brownsville. Chilton called six companies into formation and asked for 150 volunteers, "for an unexplained, possibly dangerous, night mission."[92] When everyone stepped forward to volunteer, Chilton called on his six captains to choose thirty men each. The men were then told to gather a day's rations and be ready to ride at sundown. Once the men were on the road to Clarksville, Chilton told the volunteers that the purpose of the expedition was to cross the Rio Grande, surprise the Unionist camp, and capture the Florida-born Davis and other leaders of the First Texas Cavalry. R. H. Williams, a British citizen in Duff's Partisan Rangers, recalled that when the men heard the news they went "wild with excitement, and raised such a cheer as to set the chichalakas [*sic*] and turkey-cocks in the chaparral hard by crowing and gobbling vehemently."[93]

In the early morning darkness, the Confederates

Bagdad, Mexico, with a harbor filled with ships. Photographic images of Bagdad during this period are almost non-existent, although it is known that some photography was done there. This engraving was most likely taken from a photograph. *Carte de visite* copy of engraving by unidentified artist, ca. 1863–1864. *Brownsville Historical Association.*

reached the Rio Grande at Clarksville, opposite Bagdad, to find both ferries tied up on the Texas side of the river. Hastily crossing, the Confederates captured the Mexican guardhouse and thirty Mexican soldiers. Leaving five men to guard the captives, Chilton and his men proceeded two miles upriver to the Union camp. In the night, the three hundred *renegados* were caught completely by surprise. Twenty Confederates hurriedly entered the large tent where Davis and his family were sleeping. Despite the desperate pleas of his wife, Anne Elizabeth Britton, Davis was seized and hustled away without bloodshed. Shortly thereafter Montgomery arrived to warn Davis, and he too was abducted. Unlike Davis, Montgomery was said to have "fought like a wild cat and wounded two of the men badly with his bowie-knife before he was overpowered."[94] Davis later claimed, however, that Montgomery surrendered only because Chilton promised him he would "be treated as a prisoner of war and a gentleman."[95] Davis, Montgomery, and four United States Marines were taken to the ferry and by sunup were on Texas soil.

On Sunday, March 15, eight or ten miles down the road to Brownsville, Chilton called a halt. After the men had dismounted, he "moved quietly amongst the boys, evidently taking their opinions on some matter of importance."[96] Within ten minutes, a squad of men led by Sgt. H. B. Adams took Montgomery two hundred yards into a thicket near the road and hanged him from a small mesquite tree. Montgomery would "not commit treason again in this world," Bee wrote.[97] Davis too would have been hanged, Bee supposed, "had it not been for the intercession of his wife" during the capture.[98] Bee, nevertheless, was forced to order an investigation. The raid, Bee reported, "was done without my consent or knowledge and in positive violation of any orders." However, he continued, "it will be a consolation that the indignity cast upon us by the authorities of the United States has been avenged by the gallant sons of Texas."[99]

Four days after the hanging someone cut Montgomery's body down and scratched out a shallow grave under a tree. Arthur Fremantle, the British military observer, came across the site of the hanging in early April. "He had been slightly buried," Fremantle wrote, "but his head and arms were above the ground, his arms tied together, the rope still around his neck, but part of it still dangling from quite a small mosquite [*sic*] tree. Dogs or wolves had probably scraped the earth from the body, and there was no flesh on the bones. I obtained this my first experience of lynch law within three hours of landing in America."[100]

Although most of Chilton's men wanted Davis hanged also, Bee was able to locate the Unionist attorney and three other captives and send a detail to escort them to Brownsville. By March 18 all four of the surviving Unionists had been returned to Mexico, where they were greeted in Matamoros as conquering heroes. A large crowd of more than a thousand gathered to hear several passionate speeches. A Mexican band treated the former captives, along with Governor López and the American consul, Leonard Pierce Jr., with a serenade of American airs including "Yankee Doodle," "Hail Columbia," the "Star Spangled Banner," and "Hail to the Chief."[101] "It is our vow," several of the Unionists in the crowd declared in anger, that "the knife shall do its work on the murderers of Montgomery. We swear it."[102] Taunts and threats echoed across the Rio Grande from the Mexican bank for days, and the Texans returned the insults with rifle fire. Pierce feared that he would be kidnapped and suffer the same fate as Montgomery.[103]

From the beginning of the war, Texas refugees, repressed and intimidated for their views, had poured across the border into Mexico, where Pierce gave them refuge in Matamoros. Originally from Eastport, Maine, the fiery thirty-four-year-old American consul had spent one year in Chihuahua, where he had learned to speak Spanish, before moving to Texas in 1857.[104] For almost two years Pierce opened the consulate door to hundreds of refugees. Some arrived destitute and hungry, others with little more than the clothes on their backs. Probably the best-known Texas refugee to arrive in Mexico was Alexander J. Hamilton, who arrived in Matamoros on July 29, 1862, with fifteen men after a frightful escape from Austin.[105]

Because of the Confederate occupation of the Rio Grande as far upriver as Eagle Pass, some of the refugees were forced to cross as high up as the confluence of the Devil's River. Many of the recruits were Germans from the Texas Hill Country, some of whom managed to escape the infamous Nueces Massacre, when Confederates ambushed sixty-five German Texans on their way to Mexico on the West Prong of the Nueces River on August 10, 1862. One Texas newspaper dubbed the massacre "The Battle with the Traitors."[106] One refugee who later joined the Union army, William Huster, recalled losing seven of his "brave companions in the massacre" and "travel-

An unidentified soldier stands guard in front of a church in Bagdad, Mexico, ca. 1864–1865. A cryptic note accompanying the photograph states that this was a church where prisoners were kept overnight to be shot the next morning. *Carte de visite* by unidentified artist. *Brownsville, Texas, file, Center for American History, University of Texas at Austin, CT-0573.*

ing the dreary road to the Rio Grande." In Mexico, "perfectly destitute" and "without clothes or money," he managed to make his way to Matamoros to find refuge with Pierce at the American consulate.[107] At one Confederate camp on the Rio Grande a skull belonging to a German refugee killed while trying to cross the river was hung from the top of a commissary hut as a trophy of war.[108]

By March 1864 Pierce was able to persuade a local physician, Dr. F. G. Carrasco, to care for the "destitute refugees."[109] During his tour in Matamoros, Pierce was also forced to borrow $23,000, much of it from Jeremiah Galvan, to assist the refugees.[110] Others who arrived in Matamoros included regular army troops who were either captured or stranded in Texas when the war began. A twenty-year army veteran arrived in Matamoros telling how he had been "hunted like a wild buffalo" in Texas.[111] With the arrival of the Union army in the Lower Rio Grande Valley in late 1863, Gen. Francis J. Herron began taxing the sutlers at Fort Brown to raise funds to assist the refugees, many of whom were housed in homes abandoned by secessionists.[112] When Pierce's successor, Emanuel D. Etchison, a dry goods merchant from Maryland, arrived in Matamoros, he too faced the problem of caring for hundreds of Texas refugees, both those fleeing conscription as well as growing numbers of deserters from the Confederate army. The fugitives, old and young, arrived, "destitute, forlorn, hungry and naked, sick and emaciated." Crossing the river far upriver, many had been forced to beg in Mexico, and once in Matamoros, they stood out by their "nakedness, their pale faces & haggard looks, their sunken and glaring eyes."[113]

Jose Augustine Quintero, the Confederate agent in Monterrey, Mexico, ca. 1875. Oval albumen print, size unknown, by unidentified artist. *Prints and Photographs Collection, Center for American History, University of Texas at Austin, CN04170.*

Shortly after the hanging of Montgomery near Brownsville, another Confederate foray upriver at Laredo also riled Mexican officials in Tamaulipas.[114] Capt. Santos Benavides, in preparation for a march downriver to Carrizo, allowed two of his men to cross the Rio Grande to visit relatives in Nuevo Laredo. On March 10, 1863, on the south bank, the soldiers were told by the town *alcalde* "that if they wished to pass about the town, they must leave their pistols which they had in their belts with him until they were ready to return."[115] In a confrontation that followed, twenty-eight-year-old Pvt. Encarnación García was killed. According to Benavides, García and a friend were in the process of complying with the request when they were shot at by the Nuevo Laredo police. The Mexican version of the incident, perhaps more viable, said the two men had "committed some disturbances," at which time the police attempted to arrest the pair, but the Confederates resisted by drawing their pistols and fighting broke out.

The surviving Confederate escaped the fracas and fled across the river to Laredo, where he immediately reported the incident to Benavides, who crossed the river and went to the *alcalde* to ascertain the facts of the case.[116] While the meeting was under way, news that García had been killed spread among the Confederate *Tejanos* on the north bank. Within minutes, forty of Benavides's men had crossed the ferry to avenge the death of their comrade. Benavides met the men at the riverbank and ordered them not to enter Nuevo Laredo until he had completed his consultation with the *alcalde*.

In blunt language, Benavides demanded that the *alcalde* arrest those responsible for García's death. The *alcalde* replied that he had no forces to make such an arrest. Benavides responded that he would assist in making the arrests, but by the time the *alcalde* agreed, the "assassins had all fled," Benavides reported. For several hours, the Laredo Confederates searched the town and surrounding countryside, but no sign of those involved in the shooting could be found. Obviously intimidated, the *alcalde* agreed that the search could continue, but after three days of frantic searching Benavides was forced to admit that he had no "clue of the direction they had taken."[117]

To Governor López the incident was yet another example of rambunctious and out-of-control Confederates trampling on the civil and military authorities of Tamaulipas. To López the invasions of Mexican soil at

Brig. Gen. James E. Slaughter and staff, ca. 1862–1863. This photograph of General Slaughter (seated, second from right) was taken in Alabama before his transfer to Fort Brown late in 1863. At the rear of this group are four African American slaves dressed in Confederate uniforms. These men served throughout the war as personal servants to the white staff officers. As unlikely as it may seem today, in postwar years many of these men considered themselves Confederate veterans and attended veteran reunions. Salt print (2.5 by 3 inches) by unidentified artist, Mobile, Alabama. *William A. Turner collection.*

Bagdad and Nuevo Laredo were among "the most serious crimes against international law" that were certain to "produce bitter feelings."[118] In an apologetic mood, Bee promised López he would immediately investigate the Nuevo Laredo incident. Once Bee, who had been a close friend of the Benavides family ever since he had been a merchant in Laredo after the Mexican War, read Benavides's official report, he forwarded it to Governor López. "From my long acquaintance with Captain Benavides and high appreciation of him as a man of prudence and discretion," Bee wrote, "I am satisfied that the authorities on both sides of the line may equally confide in him as not likely to do any

act to compromise the relation which should exist."[119] More than a year later, when Juan Cortina arrived in Nuevo Laredo with a small army, he heard complaints of how the Confederates from Laredo were in the habit of crossing the river and "mocking the authorities and doing whatever they wanted."[120] Cortina issued orders requiring that anyone crossing from Laredo must have the proper papers and be disarmed. Although preoccupied with events elsewhere, diplomats in Mexico City, as well as Richmond and Washington, were forced to devote more and more of their attention to the growing uneasiness on the Rio Grande frontier.

Chapter Two

BLUECOATS ON THE RIO GRANDE

The men of the Texas Union Expedition, under the command of Gen. Nathaniel P. Banks, came in twenty-six ships out of the grey, cold dawn from New Orleans. On November 2, 1863, the light-draught *General Banks*, with the Nineteenth Iowa Regiment on board, steamed through the foam and pounding breakers off Brazos Santiago. As the steamer crossed the bar at precisely noon, soldiers on board the other ships in the Union fleet "gave three hearty cheers . . . by the waving of hats and handkerchiefs."[1]

The *General Banks* was followed by the dispatch boat *Drew* and the *Clinton* with part of the Thirteenth and Fifteenth Maine on board. Disembarking from the *Clinton,* the men of the Fifteenth Maine, many of them seasick, were the first on Texas soil. Stumbling through the surf and sand in a stiff sea breeze, they waded ashore and raised their regimental flag and the Stars and Stripes. The Nineteenth Iowa quickly followed. "The flag of the Union floats over Texas today," General Banks proudly told Abraham Lincoln.[2] For two days the men in blue continued to wade ashore, many of them up to their armpits. To secure Brazos Island, the gunboat *T. A. Scott* was dispatched to Boca Chica Strait to prevent any Confederates from crossing to the island. The captain of the gunboat, however, mistook the mouth of the Rio Grande for Boca Chica and began shelling "harmless Mexicans on the Rio Grande," instead of "the damned rebels in Boca Chica," *Harper's Weekly* reported.[3]

The Rio Grande Expedition was composed mostly of young men from the Midwest, soldiers from Illinois, Indiana, Iowa, Missouri, and Wisconsin. But there were also men from New England and the First Engineers and Sixteenth Infantry Corps d'Afrique, as well as the First Texas Cavalry under command of Col. Edmund J. Davis. Most of the men were anxious to get to Brownsville and would remember Brazos Island as a barren and inhospitable place where "sand and sand hills meet the eye in every direction."[4]

Three days after landing on Brazos Island, the advance column, guarded by the guns of the *T. A. Scott* anchored just off shore, crossed the narrow straits of Boca Chica and began marching for the Rio Grande. In all, 6,998 bluecoats came to the Rio Grande. They came to cut the flow of cotton and strangle the state economically. In the highest echelons of the Union command there was even talk of pushing upriver to link up with the Union army operating in far West Texas, thus controlling the entire 889-mile Texas–Mexico border. But there were other reasons for sending an army to Texas. Lincoln had long thought the French imperialists, who had intervened in Mexico in 1861–1862, to be in violation of the basic tenants of the Monroe Doctrine. Unable to assist the Republican forces of Benito Juárez, Lincoln could at least show his displeasure with the Mexican empire by waving the Stars and Stripes at the French. The president was also hoping a Federal army presence in Texas could provide a safe haven for the large numbers of Unionists who were continuing to flee the state in droves.

When they first fled Texas, Edmund J. Davis and John L. Haynes had gone to Washington, where they told Lincoln that a Union army presence in Texas would encourage large numbers of Texas Unionists to join the Federal ranks. Moreover, from a base on the Rio Grande, Mexican Texans, many with deep-rooted and legitimate grudges against authorities in Texas, could be recruited for the Union cause.[5] Although both Davis and Haynes were politically ambitious and opportunistic, few understood the Mexican population of Texas as they did. Having served as judge at Brownsville, Corpus Christi, and Laredo before the war, Davis was well known in South Texas. Haynes had represented Starr County in the state legislature, where he had been criticized and ridiculed for attempting to rationalize the causes of Cortina's 1859 raid on Brownsville. Although Davis had escaped Texas with his family, Haynes had been forced to leave his wife and four children behind. "He has to my knowledge lost everything," Davis wrote.[6] "I left Texas," Haynes confessed, "from a sense of duty to my country, to my conscience and I wish to do

Brig. Gen. Edmund J. Davis, ca. 1864. Whole plate albumen print by A. D. Lytle, Baton Rouge, Louisiana. *Print courtesy Texas State Library and Archives Commission.*

my whole duty in the restoration of the authority of the nation."[7]

When Haynes first arrived in Matamoros, Cortina warmly welcomed him and the two appear to have discussed the practicality of a Union presence on the Rio Grande.[8]

Safely in Washington, Davis and Haynes met with Lincoln, who appeared impressed with their proposal to send an army to the border to, in Lincoln's words, "reinaugurate the National Authority on the Rio Grande first, and probably the Nueces also."[9] While in the capital, Haynes also gave Lincoln's general-in-chief, Henry Wagner Halleck, a lengthy letter outlining what Haynes called the "Rebel Plan." The document, based on what Haynes had heard in Texas, proved to be an accurate description of Jefferson Davis's military strategy for winning southern independence. Davis and Haynes also presented a number of different ideas to the War Department relative to a Union invasion of the state.[10] The two Texans also met with Gen. Samuel Peter Heintzelman, who those in the capital speculated would lead the expedition to Texas because of his knowledge of the state and his leadership during the Cortina War. "There was little doubt," Heintzelman wrote, that if Lincoln would commit 25,000 men, such an army "could sweep Texas in a very short time." A Union army on the Mexican border would also "convince Louis Napoleon . . . not to interfere with us,"

Heintzelman confided to his journal.[11]

Also arriving in Texas with the Rio Grande Expedition was Gen. Andrew Jackson Hamilton. The Alabama-born Hamilton, tall and rawboned, was a strong Unionist, having previously served as the state's attorney general and as United States Congressman for the Western District of Texas. Hamilton was honest, deeply conservative, and dedicated to bringing Texas back into the Union. During the secession winter of 1860–1861, Hamilton had remained in Austin despite threats to his life, but in the summer of 1862 he fled in the night for the border. Hamilton, like Davis and Haynes, eventually made his way to the North, where he became somewhat of a hero, delivering speeches in New York, Boston, and several other cities, riling against slave owners and dis-

Brig. Gen. Andrew Jackson Hamilton, provisional military governor of Texas during Reconstruction. *Carte de visite* by Edward Jacobs and Company, New Orleans, Louisiana, ca. 1864–1865. *Lawrence T. Jones III collection.*

unionists. After meeting with President Lincoln in November 1862 Hamilton received a commission as a brigadier general and was appointed military governor of Texas. It was thus that Brownsville temporarily became the capital for the federally-occupied state of Texas. With hundreds gathered outside, Hamilton delivered a fiery, two-hour speech at Market Hall in March 1864.[12]

Even before the arrival of the Union Rio Grande Expedition, General Bee was concerned that Davis and Haynes, as well as Leonard Pierce Jr., were encouraging Juan Cortina to attack Brownsville. Knowing that Cortina was bitterly opposed to the Confederates, Haynes had indeed been in contact with Cortina and the wily Mexican *caudillo* was certain to have known that a Union invasion of Texas was imminent. In September 1863 one of Bee's sentinels reported that Cortina was crossing the river with three hundred men. The "excitement became so very great" that the "confusion was indescribable," Bee wrote. In

their panic, a number of Confederates rushed to the riverbank and opened fire on several Mexican soldiers as well as citizens from Matamoros who were peacefully bathing in the river. Bee apologized to Manuel Ruiz, military governor of Tamaulipas, for the "unfortunate occurrence" and even offered to pay reparations. Yet Cortina was to blame for the "excited state of feeling," Bee asserted. Moreover, Cortina was "notorious for the many outrages committed against the lives and property of the citizens of Brownsville."[13] Ruiz, however, was in no position to confront Cortina and remained somewhat ambivalent toward the Confederates in Texas.

The fact that Lincoln had decided to send a Union army to Texas had been widely reported in both Northern and Southern newspapers for months. As early as June 1863 Bee had sent a spy to New York City to asertain "the intentions of the Federal Government in regard to Texas."[14] A second spy was told to find employment on a ship making the Bagdad-to-New York City run and gather as much information as possible. By August Bee was convinced the invasion would be under way once the "Sickly Season" had passed.

Yet Bee was poorly prepared to meet an invasion. By August 1863 he had been forced to move a large part of his command out of Fort Brown to avoid the summer illnesses and disease that had plagued the post for years. As much as one-third of the Confederate force in Brownsville was sick.[15] At one time every single officer in Brownsville except for Bee was ill. "The panic amongst the troops renders it impossible to keep them here, for at dress parade on yesterday there were but two officers out of four companies, the rest being sick or on duty," Bee wrote on August 15, 1863.[16] Conscripts assigned to the Rio Grande often deserted as soon as they arrived. Bee had been furnished with twenty-five new wagons and more than two hundred wild mules, but there was no one to break the animals. To complicate matters, no one was willing to accept Confederate currency, and the army had problems finding not only teamsters to hire but also anyone to even harness the mules.[17]

Realizing that the small and isolated Confederate forces in the Rio Grande Valley would be unable to hold the area against a Union invasion, both Bee and Slaughter recommended that Santos Benavides, who had served the Confederate cause "faithfully and zealously," be promoted to brigadier general and placed in command of the forces on the river. Benavides, Bee and Slaughter argued, was the only one on the Rio Grande frontier who was capable of rallying "the population to our assistance." Moreover, due to his "strong personal influence" Benavides could create "a guerrilla force" and turn "a quasi-hostile population into most valuable auxiliaries."[18]

Maj. Gen. Godfrey Weitzel, commander, Twenty-fifth Army Corps and District of the Rio Grande, Brownsville, Texas, February 1, 1866. Weitzel graduated second in his 1855 West Point class and was commissioned in the Engineer Corps. After a successful wartime career he was promoted to major general. Weitzel eventually was assigned to command of the Twenty-fifth Army Corps, which was composed entirely of African American military units that officially were called "U.S. Colored Troops." *Carte de visite* attributed to Louis de Planque or R. H. Wallis. *Lawrence T. Jones III collection.*

raids sweeping out of Kansas and across the Indian Territory, Bee was sure the Texas frontier would be temporarily lost.[19] Regardless, the Union army could never hold the entire Rio Grande frontier. "A comparatively small force of the enemy may come to Brownsville but they will never attempt to hold four hundred miles of this river when the same object can be obtained in a march of 135 miles from Saluria to San Antonio." With his small, sickly army, Bee thought it senseless to remain on the Rio Grande. "My force is too small to make any successful defence and I do not aspire to lead a retreat."[20] But when the invasion did come, Bee was still in Brownsville, and the small Confederate army remained ill prepared and was panic-stricken.

With the news that Union forces were landing on Brazos Island, Bee ordered Col. James Duff to send a party to the coast. At the same time, Capt. Henry T. Davis was sent to Point Isabel with a small scouting expedition of nineteen men. Davis climbed the seventy-two-foot-high lighthouse, where he

With the appearance of United States naval officers at Bagdad, Bee became convinced that the attack would come somewhere on the lightly defended Texas coast, which he knew was vulnerable. Bee began issuing orders to move much of the war materials into the interior and asked Mayor George Dye to help organize the citizens of Brownsville into a militia force to help defend the town. Still the main invasion, Bee thought, would not be against the Rio Grande, but against Indianola and Lavaca Bay with the intention of occupying San Antonio. Combined with Union cavalry

had a clear view of the Laguna Madre and Brazos Santiago Pass. He watched for hours with a spyglass as hundreds of Federals disembarked from several vessels, large and small. Moreover, more vessels continued to arrive in the night. Through the haze with his spyglass, Davis counted six regimental flags and twenty-six vessels, both sail and steam.[21] In addition, there were several artillery batteries. "The enemy are in force. Brazos Island is covered with tents," Bee wrote in a frenzy.[22] In the early morning darkness of November 2, Capt. Richard Taylor and fifteen men of the Thirty-third

Texas Cavalry were sent to Clarksville to report on the Union flotilla and the movement of the Federals. Captain Taylor moved up the coast to near Boca Chica, where he spotted the Union fleet and the next day watched as both Union infantry and cavalry began moving inland.[23]

The impending arrival of the Union army on the Rio Grande triggered other events. One was the mutiny of the unpredictable Capt. Adrián J. Vidal, Mifflin Kenedy's impetuous stepson, who had been given command of a cavalry company at the mouth of the river. Vidal had earlier been praised for his gallantry in the capture of a Union gunboat and its crew, and there was no reason to question his loyalty. The Confederate command in Brownsville did not know, however, that Vidal had fallen under the influence of the calculating and conniving Juan N. Cortina. Cortina, in turn, was in contact with Leonard Pierce and John L. Haynes. Vidal may also have been in touch with the commander of the Union ships blockading the mouth of the Rio Grande.[24]

Only days prior to the arrival of the Union army in South Texas, General Bee dispatched two young privates, D. H. Dashiell and Jerry Literal, to Clarksville to order Vidal and his company back to Brownsville to help protect the military supplies and cotton that remained in the town.[25] On the evening of October 28, just as darkness engulfed Bee's headquarters at Fort Brown, rumors reached the town that Vidal and his entire company had mutinied and were planning to attack Brownsville during the night with the help of Texas Unionists from Matamoros. Not doubting Vidal's loyalty, Bee at first dismissed the report as a malicious rumor. Two hours later, however, Private Literal

Maj. Gen. Giles A. Smith, commander, First Division, Twenty-fifth Army Corps and Post of Brownsville, Texas, February 1, 1866. Before his assignment on the Rio Grande, Smith led his division in Georgia and the Carolinas during Gen. William Tecumseh Sherman's storied "March to the Sea." *Carte de visite* attributed to Louis de Planque or R. H. Wallis. *Lawrence T. Jones III collection.*

raced his horse into Fort Brown directly to Bee's headquarters. Badly frightened and bleeding from the mouth due to a "horrid wound through the jaw," Literal could not talk but motioned for a pencil and paper and proceeded to scribble an incredible story.[26] Dashiell, the son of the Texas adjutant general, and Literal had met Vidal and his company on the road fourteen miles east of Brownsville. The two privates had served with Vidal early in the war, and, like Bee, had no reason to mistrust him. They delivered the orders as they had been directed, and the entire party continued along the road to Brownsville. After about four miles, Vidal dismounted and ordered his men to prepare a meal for the evening and asked the two privates to share a drink. Suddenly, Vidal and several of his men opened fire on the two men, killing Dashiell instantly and badly wounding Literal, who was able to mount his horse and race off into the darkness in a hail of bullets.[27]

With so few men, Bee was fearful Brownsville would be overrun. Lt. Jack Vinton and ten men were sent down the road toward the Gulf to locate Vidal and determine, if possible, the reasons for his actions. Lieutenant Vinton proceeded only a few miles outside of town when he ran into Vidal and his company, which numbered more than one hundred men and was advancing on Brownsville. Although outnumbered, Vinton began skirmishing with Vidal's company but was driven back to within one mile of town.[28] With the "garrison and citizens thrown into a panic," Bee called a council of war. At the same time, he issued orders recalling three companies of Col. James Duff's Thirty-third Texas Cavalry, which had been ordered to Houston only days earlier and who were thought to be encamped on the Palo Alto prairie. Fearing that Vidal was intent on sacking Brownsville, Bee organized and hastily armed a six-month militia company commanded by Frank Cummings. Three hundred "old and young, native and foreign" also responded to the emergency.[29] Pistol in hand, General Slaughter was frequently seen during the night among the hastily armed militia.

Bee was also fearful that he would be attacked by either Cortina, Unionists from across the river, or both. A 24-pounder cannon and an 8-inch siege howitzer were pulled into position to guard the arsenal and the garrison. Bee's more dependable regulars were placed on the outskirts of the town and remained on alert throughout the night. But Vidal's contemplated attack never materialized; he had decided to bypass Brownsville.

Crying "*Muerte a los Americanos,*" the *Vidalistas* passed within a mile of Brownsville about 3 A.M. on October 29. Upriver from Brownsville, the raiders continued along the river road for about nine miles, plundering several ranches as they went, killing at least ten unoffending citizens.[30] When the three companies of the Thirty-third Texas Cavalry arrived in Brownsville at daylight on October 29, Bee sent them in pursuit of Vidal. One of the companies commanded by Capt. Richard Taylor reached a ford above Brownsville only minutes after the *Vidalistas* had crossed the river into Mexico. Captain Taylor reported a large body of Texas Unionists on the opposite bank of the Rio Grande waiting to greet Vidal. Conjecturing that Vidal had been in contact with the Unionists all along and believing it would be unwise to cross the river, Taylor returned to Fort Brown.

Furious at the turn of events on the border, Bee wrote Governor Ruiz claiming that Vidal was acting under the orders of

Brig. Gen. Egbert Benson Brown, ca. 1864. Assigned to Texas during Reconstruction, General Brown signed this photograph at Brownsville on June 10, 1865. *Carte de visite* by Schoo & Crouch, St. Louis, Missouri. *Lawrence T. Jones III collection.*

Leonard Pierce. Bee wanted Vidal captured and returned to Texas for punishment.[31] "I at once gave orders that all the troops on the line should unite in pursuing the insurrectionists, and from this city will immediately set forth two detachments of cavalry to reconnoiter the left bank of the Rio Grande," Governor Ruiz assured Bee.[32] Although Bee would later conclude that Cortina was in alliance with Vidal, he initially wrote department headquarters that Cortina, acting under Ruiz's orders, had captured twenty of the *Vidalistas* and that Vidal himself was in hiding in Matamoros. "A wild and reckless boy," Vidal was "daring" and a "crazy young man," the Brownsville *Fort Brown Flag* proclaimed.[33] In Mexico many of the *Vidalistas* became *Cortinistas*.

With the Union army in possession of Brazos Island and advancing on Brownsville, Bee initially contemplated taking what cotton he could and moving his small force upriver to Rio Grande City and Roma. Pressing every wagon and many of the horses in Brownsville into Confederate service, Bee eventually assembled forty-five wagons and had them loaded with military equipment and cotton. Bee finally concluded that it would be impractical due to the "narrow and tortuous road" to advance through the dense chaparral along the river. He decided instead to move his small force east from Brownsville to slow the Union advance and thus give the slow-moving wagon train time to move north toward the Arroyo Colorado. "I received no assistance from the citizens of Brownsville," Bee wrote.[34] The militia company dissolved on the morning of November 3 and disappeared. A number of Confederates deserted at the same time.

Before departing Brownsville, Bee ordered Fort Brown fired. As many as two hundred bales of cotton that could not be ferried or floated across the river also were burned. Unfortunately, the flames spread from the fort to the town, eventually burning an entire block of buildings along Levee Street in front of the ferry. Frightened townspeople were more intent on stopping the spread of the inferno than in assisting the Confederates' escape. Considerable plundering by townsmen and soldiers alike was also evident. To add to the chaos, eight thousand pounds of powder at Fort Brown exploded, breaking windows and terrorizing the citizens. At the fort, a large quantity of commissary stores and quartermaster goods also were destroyed in the blaze. In the mayhem, more than four hundred Unionists lined the south bank of the river to hiss and curse at the panic-stricken Confederates. "Peril was around me on all sides," Bee wrote.[35] Finally, at midnight on November 3, 1863, General Bee bid a fatigued and drunken adieu to Brownsville and headed north with a ten-man escort through the chaparral for the Arroyo Colorado and the King Ranch, turning back wagon trains loaded with cotton as he went. Many of the heavily loaded wagons accompanying Bee were unable to cross the shifting sands of the Wild Horse Desert, and much of the cotton had to be unloaded and burned.

Brig. Gen. George Washington Getty, ca. 1864–1865. Autographed *carte de visite* attributed to Louis de Planque. *Brownsville Historical Association.*

With looting, violence, and disorder engulfing the city, Judge Israel Bigelow sent an urgent plea to Cortina in Matamoros asking for assistance. Cortina replied that Bigelow's problems were not his and refused to intervene. Cortina did, however, prevent troublemakers from Matamoros from joining the plundering and chaos on the north bank.[36] Instead, a forty-five-year-old bandit chief and former officer in the Mexican army, Gen. José María Cobos, stepped forward. With two hundred hastily recruited men, Cobos was able to cross the river, stop the plunder, and restore some semblance of order.[37] Active earlier with conservative forces in Coahuila and Zacatecas, but expelled from Mexico City, Cobos had come to the frontier hoping to procure arms and ammunition, recruit men, and seize Matamoros.[38] Moreover, Cobos had met with the wily Cortina and the two agreed to cooperate in ousting Governor Ruiz.

The Union army entered Brownsville at ten o'clock on the morning of November 6. The Ninety-fourth Illinois Volunteers, the advance guard of the Union Thirteenth Army Corps, led the way down Elizabeth Street as citizens of the community watched in amazement. Many cheered, including Unionists from Matamoros who rushed across the river for the event. General Banks arrived with his staff two hours later. Next came the First Missouri Light Artillery, followed by the Thirteenth Maine Volunteers. Two black regiments along with the Fifteenth Maine were left to guard Brazos Island while the Twentieth Wisconsin was sent to Point Isabel.[39] Arriving on the South Texas border, the Union army, especially the First U.S. Colored Engineers and the Sixteenth Infantry, along with the Eighty-seventh and Ninety-fifth U.S. Colored Infantry, began constructing fortifications at Point Isabel and on the Rio Grande above Brownsville, on Brazos Island, and at Clarksville. The black troopers not only pulled several large guns into place at Boca Chica but even began "bridging the pass."[40] At Freeport in the bend of the river above Brownsville on February 22, 1864, Fort Montgomery, named in honor of William Montgomery, was formally inaugurated with the firing of artillery and a salute to the Stars and Stripes.[41]

No sooner was the Union army in Brownsville than friendly relations were opened with Cortina. General Banks was particularly grateful that Cortina acquiesced in allowing the Federals to take control of King and Kenedy's steamboats. The change of fortunes on the north bank also sparked turmoil in Matamoros. Before daybreak on November 6, just hours before the Union army entered Brownsville, Cobos crossed the river to Matamoros and seized the city with Cortina's assistance. Cortina not only helped Cobos seize Matamoros, but consented to Cobos becoming governor of Tamaulipas while he became head of the *ayuntamiento,* or city council, and military commander.[42] At the same time, Cobos issued a *pronunciamiento,* saying that he had come to save

Maj. Joseph Jones Reynolds, commander of the Military Subdistrict of the Rio Grande and commander of the Department of Texas. Reynolds was heavily involved in the politics and implementation of Reconstruction policies. *Carte de visite* by J. W. Campbell, army photographer, Twenty-ninth Army Corps, Army of the Cumberland, ca. 1863. *Lawrence T. Jones III collection.*

the citizens of Matamoros from anarchy. Although he spoke of independence and patriotism, Cobos appeared ambiguous, perhaps intentionally, about any allegiance to the French. Despite his public pronouncements, the Spanish-born Cobos soon assailed the liberal constitution of 1857 and began criticizing "the accumulation of outrages" thrust upon the people of Mexico by Benito Juárez, a "tyrannical demagogue."[43]

On November 7, only one day after proclaiming himself governor, Cobos and his second in command, Lt. Gov. Rómulo Vila, ordered Governor Ruiz executed. Learning that Cobos was an Imperialist in disguise, Cortina vetoed the plan and had Cobos and Vila arrested, summoned before a hastily-called court-martial, and, when the two were found guilty of treason, ordered them shot. With a large part of the Matamoros populace looking on, Cobos was taken to the outskirts of town near a lagoon and executed by a platoon of *Cortinistas.*[44] Also a Spaniard by birth, Vila was allowed to "run the gauntlet, and was shot upon his flight."[45] The chaos and excitement ran so high in Matamoros that Leonard Pierce feared that the United States consulate might be attacked. In turn, General Banks ordered a battery of artillery into position on the north bank and trained on the town.[46] "If the American flag is assailed or your person threatened," Banks promised Pierce, troops would be sent across the border.[47]

When Cortina released Ruiz, the governor issued two *pronunciamientos* praising Cortina: "Long live Independence! Long live liberty! Long live the National Guard! Long live Lieut. Col. Juan Nepomuceno Cortina."[48] In response,

Head Quarters Gen. Reynolds, Brownsville Texas

C.H.B Jan. 1867

from Dr. Cowles u.s.a.

Gen. J. J. Reynold's headquarters at Fort Brown, ca. 1867. Albumen print (3.5 by 5 inches) attributed to Louis de Planque. *Lawrence T. Jones III collection.*

Cortina deposed Ruiz as governor and sent a twenty-five-man escort to insure "his retreat from the city."[49] Not trusting Cortina, and fearing that he would be shot, Ruiz fled across the river to Brownsville instead. Within days Cortina called for the return of Jesús de la Serna, who had been governor in 1861. No sooner was Ruiz on the north bank of the river than he rode upriver, recrossed the Rio Grande and proceeded to San Fernando, south of Matamoros, where he began to build an army. By early December Ruiz had six hundred men in arms and was preparing to drive Cortina out of Matamoros. Cortina barricaded the streets of the town with Texas cotton and braced for an attack. He also appealed to Santiago Vidaurri for troops.[50] By December 11 Gen. Napoleon Jackson Tecumseh Dana, who had assumed com-

mand of the Union army in Brownsville, reported that Matamoros was in a "great panic and confusion . . . and an attack hourly expected." But one week later Ruiz was still at San Fernando.[51]

By early January 1864 Ruiz had finally arrived on the outskirts of Matamoros to demand the surrender of the town. Cortina seemed determined to fight, and civilians began pouring across the river to Brownsville, including Cortina's family. Cortina finally agreed to negotiate, however, and sent an emissary to meet with Governor Ruiz's representatives.[52] At a tense parley on the outskirts of Matamoros it was agreed that Governor de la Serna would give up his power as governor and retire; Ruiz would resume the office of governor; and Cortina and Ruiz would combine their armies into a single fighting force. Gen. José Macedonio

Administration building at Fort Brown, ca. 1867. An inscription verso states that this building "contains offices of the Post Hdqrs., Library, Reading Room, etc." *Carte de visite* attributed to R. H. Wallis. *Lawrence T. Jones III collection.*

Capistrán, a Ruiz loyalist, would head the army while Cortina would be second in command. Leaving Ruiz in power in Matamoros, the army would march south to meet the French at Tampico.[53]

De la Serna retired to his ranch, Ruiz assumed his seat as governor, and the soldiers prepared to march for Tampico. But Cortina hesitated. After five days, with many *Cortinistas* refusing to depart from the city, Ruiz sent a messenger to inquire why Cortina was not on the road. Cortina replied that his men had not been paid, but when arrangements were made to give the men two months' pay, Cortina raised the stakes by demanding four hundred horses and more ammunition.[54] During this time a Union officer in Brownsville confided to his journal that the *Cortinistas* were "loitered through the city with an easy nonchalance [while] . . . officers rode through the streets with bravado stamped on every action."[55] Violence loomed on the horizon when on the afternoon of January 12, 1864, Cortina's infantry commander, Col. Octaviano Cárdenas, rode up to the house where Governor Ruiz had his headquarters and allegedly insulted the governor, even shouting "death to Ruiz." Cárdenas was seized by the governor's guards, carried into a back yard, and executed.[56]

Less than three hours later, with Cortina vow-

ing revenge, the two armies opened fire on one another in a fierce artillery duel near the Plaza de Hidalgo. Cortina had six hundred men and six artillery pieces, while Ruiz had eight hundred men and four artillery pieces.[57] The fighting continued through the night and into the early morning of the next day with as many as 250 artillery rounds exchanged. At the American consulate, Pierce was panic stricken: "A battle is now raging in the streets of this city," he wrote. "My person and family are in great danger, as the road between here and the ferry is said to be infested with robbers. I have also about $1,000,000 in specie and a large amount of other valuable property under my charge in the consulate, and from the well-known character of Cortina and his followers, I fear the city will be plundered." Pierce asked the Union army in Brownsville to intervene "at the earliest possible moment" to save his family and carry the specie to Brownsville.[58]

At the same time, Governor Ruiz sent an urgent message to Gen. Francis J. Herron, a tough veteran of the siege of Vicksburg who had replaced General Dana, saying that he could not protect the American consulate. In response Herron put three regiments under arms, sent forty men of the Twentieth Wisconsin Infantry to seize the ferry, and dispatched four companies of the same regiment under Col. Henry Bertram, along with a battery of the First Missouri Artillery, across the river to res-

Enlisted men's barracks at Fort Brown, ca. 1867–1868. *Carte de visite* attributed to R. H. Wallis. *Lawrence T. Jones III collection.*

Guardhouse at Fort Brown, ca. 1865–1866. African American soldiers, probably members of the Ninth U.S. Colored Troops, stand at attention on the veranda. This building should not be confused with the military prison at Fort Brown. *Carte de visite* attributed to Louis de Planque or R. H. Wallis. *Lawrence T. Jones III collection.*

cue Pierce.[59] Herron also sent notes to both Ruiz and Cortina explaining that the Federals were crossing into Mexico only to protect the American consulate and would "take no part in the fight."[60] Colonel Bertram arrived at the American consulate during the fighting to find Pierce with the British consul and representatives from both Ruiz and Cortina, who were demanding to know what American soldiers were doing on Mexican soil.[61]

In the fighting that raged through the night, the *Cortinistas*, fighting from house to house and street to street, steadily gained ground on the Ruiz forces until they had reached the Plaza de Hidalgo. Realizing the tide of battle had shifted, the Ruiz forces under the command of General Capistran, demoralized and low on ammunition, began to fall back and eventually flee. Sensing the tide of battle had changed, Cortina's cavalry "dashed through the streets striking down the fleeing fugitive[s]."[62]

By noon the following day Cortina had successfully routed Ruiz and was in complete control of the city. Hundreds of Ruiz's men and officers escaped by swimming across the Rio Grande to Brownsville. After eighteen hours of continuous carnage and bloodletting, the battle for Matamoros was over. As many as three hundred men were said to have died in the fighting, including all of Ruiz's artillerymen, who fell gallantly at their guns. Among the dead was ex-governor Albino López, a prominent Ruiz partisan.[63] "We have lost everything except our honor," Ruiz dejectedly told Benito Juárez.[64]

Within hours of the cessation of hostilities, Cortina proclaimed himself governor of Tamaulipas and issued two *pronunciamientos* justifying his attack on Ruiz. In fewer than five years, through sheer bravado and cunning determination, he had risen from a little-known and illiterate

Post hospital at Fort Brown, ca. 1867–1868. *Carte de visite* attributed to R. H. Wallis. *Lawrence T. Jones III collection.*

April 1864 Gen. John A. McClernand, commanding the Union troops on the Rio Grande, wrote Cortina asking that he use his influence with Juárez to close "all channels of trade and travel on the Rio Grande against the rebels and their property."[67] General McClernand also asked Cortina to seize all the cotton and property in Mexico belonging to the Confederacy and expel anyone aiding and abetting the rebellion in the United States. When McClernand heard that Cortina had agreed to meet with Confederate cotton speculators, he rushed across the river to meet the newly proclaimed governor in person. Cortina told McClernand that the success of the Union army in Texas "was necessary to the security of Mexico, not only against transmarine nations but against the ambitious arms and aggressive spirit of the so-called Confederate government." McClernand was excited by what he heard in Matamoros. Cortina not only professed friendship but issued a *pronunciamiento* that amounted to "little less than a declaration of war against the rebels."[68] As a reward, Governor Hamilton and Federal officers formally and officially presented ten artillery pieces to Cortina in a ceremony in Matamoros.

Cameron County *ranchero* to the pinnacle of power in Tamaulipas. Power had its price, however, and a few months later two Frenchmen in Matamoros attempted to assassinate Cortina. The two were immediately arrested and executed.[65]

With Cortina in power in Tamaulipas, Union authorities in Brownsville opened friendly relations with the unpredictable *caudillo*. General Herron even seized Manuel G. Rejón, Santiago Vidaurri's secretary of state for Coahuila and Nuevo León, and extradited him to Matamoros, where he was executed by firing squad.[66] By early

A note accompanying this photograph states the following: "Paymasters Headquarters, Late U.S. Military Telegraph Headquarters, District of the Rio Grande, Brownsville, 1868." Uniformed military personnel fill the front yard of the building, perhaps awaiting their pay. *Carte de visite* attributed to R. H. Wallis. *Center for American History, University of Texas at Austin, CT-0572.*

Officer's quarters at Fort Brown, ca. 1866. Stereograph by Louis de Planque. *Robin Stanford collection.*

General McClernand also presented Cortina with an elegantly engraved sword. Hearing of the events in Matamoros, Gen. John B. Magruder claimed that the Federals were in violation of the "laws of nations by openly furnishing the Mexican troops with arms with which to carry on [the] war against the French."[69] Magruder was particularly miffed that A. J. Hamilton and Cortina had "walked arm in arm through the streets of Matamoros" during the ceremony.

Despite the optimism in Brownsville, Col. Santos Benavides, in a strange turn of events since the fighting at Carrizo in the early months of the war, was able to complete an agreement with Cortina to protect the Confederate cotton crossing the border at Laredo. Hearing of the news, General Magruder wrote Cortina congratulating the governor on his willingness to "cooperate with Confederate authorities."[70] In addition to Laredo, cotton continued to flow into Mexico at Eagle Pass. In fact, the Union occupation of the Lower Rio Grande Valley did little to stop the flow of cotton across the border; Confederate authorities simply diverted the flow of cotton to Laredo and Eagle Pass. "The occupation of Brownsville has no effect in stopping the trade," M. M. Kimmey, the United States vice consul in Monterrey, told Secretary of State William H. Seward. Kimmey also watched

from Monterrey as Confederate traders continued to send "enormous quantities of goods to Texas through Eagle Pass and Laredo."[71]

The situation at Ringgold Barracks and Rio Grande City was similar to Brownsville. Hearing that the Union army was on the coast and marching on Brownsville, Colonel Benavides called his men together and informed them of what had happened, stating that if any of his men did not want to continue fighting he would issue them a discharge. "The answer was," General Bee would write, "'*Viva la Confederacion! Viva Major Benavides!*' Not a man left him." Benavides was also successful in crossing the cotton at Rio Grande City safely into Mexico. Benavides told Bee that he was prepared to launch "a guerrilla war to the last." Learning that Benavides had remained loyal, Bee issued orders diverting as much cotton as possible to Laredo. To Bee, Benavides was "a gallant, influential leader."[72]

Realizing how critical Benavides was to the Confederacy, General Magruder authorized the money from five hundred bales of cotton that had been sold in Monterrey be used to pay Benavides's men, who had not been paid for six months. As a consequence, families of the men were said to be in a "destitute and starving condition."[73] Another one thousand bales was to be set aside "to his

Officer's quarters at Fort Brown, ca. 1866. Stereograph by Louis de Planque. *Lawrence T. Jones III collection.*

credit for the support of his army and himself," Magruder wrote.[74] Benavides was to use "such inducements as would probably bring to his standard the whole of the border population."[75] Moreover, if Benavides could raise a brigade, General Magruder promised to make him a brigadier general. Except for the small Confederate garrison at Fort Duncan, by late 1863 Colonel Benavides was all that remained of the Confederate army on the Rio Grande. Bluntly put, Benavides was the only hope the Confederacy had for maintaining the cotton trade on the river.

Only weeks after the arrival of the Union army in Brownsville, Col. Edmund J. Davis and more than fifteen hundred men, many of them from the First Texas Cavalry, were already in the field. The Texas cavalry, reinforced by infantry on the captured steamer *Mustang*, seized Ringgold Barracks at Rio Grande City as a small Confederate force of Col. Santos Benavides fled across the river to Reynosa. From Rio Grande City an advance guard of two hundred Federals under Col. John L. Haynes pushed upriver to Roma.[76] Following the occupation of Brownsville, Union forces immediately began rebuilding Fort Brown and constructing fortifications upriver to protect the town from attack from the west.

Less than three weeks after the Union army

occupied Brownsville, a young man crossed the river on the ferry and appeared at the enrolling office identifying himself as Adrián J. Vidal, late of the Confederate army. He was prepared, he said, to raise a company for the Federals, and on November 26 he was mustered into the service of the United States and commissioned a captain. Throughout November and December hundreds of *Tejanos* and *Mexicanos*, many influenced by Vidal and Cortina, joined the Union army. Vidal's company, which was attached to the Second Texas Cavalry, was known simply as "Vidal's Independent Partisan Rangers." General Dana reported that "Vidal's command has been mustered in, armed and equipped to the number of eighty-nine men for one year." In Federal blue, the *Vidalistas* continued their rough and rowdy ways. In early December 1863 a brawl broke out in the company in which a private was mortally wounded. As a result, General Dana promised "to make an example of the murderer."[77]

Although Banks cautioned Haynes about recruiting on Mexican soil, he had no objection "to imparting information that recruits for this service will be received at the U.S. posts on the Rio Grande."[78] As enticement, recruits were offered a bounty of $100, $75 of which would be received at the conclusion of the war. Although hundreds of

Tejanos and *Mexicanos* were lured by the bounty, the amount was less than the $300 given to volunteers elsewhere. In addition, recruits received a blue jacket, pants, shirts, underwear, a raincoat, boots, shoes, and $13 a month.[79] At Mier, one young recruit named Luis Ramirez heard that the Confederates were recruiting soldiers at Fort Brown. Young and bold, Ramirez saddled his horse and rode downriver to Brownsville, only to find that the Federals were in possession of the town; he enlisted in the Union army instead.[80] Another young *Tejano* rode a mule all the way from Carrizo to Brownsville to enlist in the Union army.[81] Some of the first recruits were men who had fought with Cortina at one time or another. "When the Union was in danger, who flocked to its protection? Who enrolled under its banner. Our Mexican patriots responded first," a Brownsville newspaper later wrote.[82] Ironically, the Federal government recruited men the army had fought against during the Cortina War four years earlier.

In his recruiting efforts, Colonel Haynes was assisted by Lt. Antonio Abad Días. Haynes had known the forty-five-year-old lieutenant before the war and realized Días could be an invaluable asset because of his influence along the river. Días was second only to Cortina in his hatred of many of the Anglo-American land barons and politicians of the Lower Valley. Many of the officers in the Second Texas were men such as Días, whom Colonel Haynes had known before the war, a few having previously served in the Confederate army. They

2d Lt. Robert Fletcher, Battery G, First U.S. Artillery, Brownsville, Texas. Lieutenant Fletcher was a West Point graduate who served at Fort Brown during Reconstruction. After completing his military service he pursued a career in education and eventually became director of the Thayer School of Civil Engineering at Dartmouth College in New Hampshire. Inscribed and signed verso. *Carte de visite* by J. S. Mayer, New York, New York, ca. 1868. *Lawrence T. Jones III collection.*

included Jorge Treviño from Reynosa, Clemente Zapata from Zapata County, Cesario Falcón from Nueces County, and Mónico de Abrego and José María Martinez from Cameron County. Colonel Davis, who had been a close friend of Col. Santos Benavides before the war, even tried to lure Benavides and his two brothers, Cristóbal and Refugio, into the Union ranks. It was widely rumored at the time and after the war that Davis had been authorized to appoint Benavides a brigadier general if he would break with the Confederacy. Realizing what a *coup d'état* it would be if Benavides could be lured into the Union army, Colonel Davis purportedly rode upriver to Nuevo Laredo, opposite Laredo, where he requested a meeting with his antebellum friend and political ally. Benavides agreed to talk but was so unpopular in Nuevo Laredo that he declined, asking instead that the meeting be held on the north bank of the river in Laredo. There is no evidence the two men met. Davis perhaps remembered his near death at the hands of the Confederate ruffians near Boca del Rio earlier in the war.[83]

From their base at Brownsville, Union reconnaissances struck hundreds of miles into the interior. Not long after arriving, a Union patrol destroyed the salt works at El Sal del Rey. By December they had crossed the shifting sands of the Wild Horse Desert north of the Arroyo Colorado. From a forward camp at Las Ánimas, Capt. James Speed led seventy cavalry, about one-half of whom were *Tejanos* and *Mexicanos*, in a raid on the King Ranch. Since the beginning of the war, the ranch had served as a major way station on the Cotton Road, a place where weary and fatigued teamsters found water, food, and bunks, and thus it became a Federal target. Two days before Christmas 1863, Captain Speed and his raiders struck the ranch; killed Francisco Alvarado, one of King's vaqueros; drove off horses and mules; plundered the ranch house; and smashed the Kings' furniture before retreating to Las Ánimas.[84]

In the areas south of the Nueces River, the Union army unleashed a vicious guerrilla war. Two of the most active *Tejano* guerrillas were Cecilio Valerio and his son Juan. Loosely attached to the Union army, the senior Valerio was reported by Colonel Ford to be "an active officer; well acquainted with the country; brave and vigilant." The Valerios and other *Tejanos* and *Mexicanos* were active in raiding the ranches in the Nueces Strip and delivering large herds of cattle to the Union army on the border. In fact, the orchestrated and wide-scale cattle raids that plagued the region for two decades after the war had their origins in the Civil War. To feed their army at Brownsville, Federal authorities sent men into the vast expanses of the Nueces Strip to procure beef, for which it was said they paid five dollars per head for every animal driven to Brownsville.[85]

Cecilio Valerio, who legend holds was not only in contact with Union authorities in Brownsville but the Union navy off Padre Island, was said to have been paid in gold by the Federals. At the head of 126 guerrillas, Valerio was attacked by Confederates under Capt. Mat Nolan at a watering hole called Los Patricios in what is today Jim Wells County early on the morning of March 13, 1864.[86] Valerio had posted his men in a dense mesquital when

Capt. Julius H. Higley, 109th U.S. Colored Troops. While the enlisted men and many of the non-commissioned officers of the U.S. Colored Troops were African American, the officers of these regiments were white. Captain Higley arrived at Indianola, Texas, in June 1865 and saw occupation duty there and at various points along the lower Rio Grande until March 1866. *Carte de visite* by J. H. Young, Baltimore, Maryland, ca. 1865. *Lawrence T. Jones III collection.*

the Confederate force struck. Well armed with Burnside carbines, revolvers, and sabers, Valerio, according to Nolan, "fought us most gallantly and could only be repulsed after a desperate fight and at the cost of much blood and property." In the brief but vicious fight, three Confederates were killed while five of the guerrillas lay dead. Nolan and his men found several ghastly pools of blood near the mesquital, indicating that some of the guerrillas were seriously wounded. Valerio left behind 31 horses, 107 blankets, 6 Colt revolvers, 5 Burnside carbines, and 25 sabers.[87]

The most far-reaching of the Federal cavalry expeditions out of the Lower Valley came in March 1864 in a raid on Laredo. With cotton continuing to flow across the Rio Grande at Laredo and Eagle Pass, Union authorities hoped to seize the five thousand bales of cotton spies said were stacked in San Agustin Plaza in Laredo and guarded by fewer than one hundred of Colonel Benavides's men. The expedition of two hundred men, about half of them from the Second Texas, was led by Maj. Alfred E. Holt, a close friend of Col. Edmund J. Davis. From the time the expedition left the Lower Valley, it was slowed by one of the worst droughts in recent memory, which dried up trail grass and left the earth parched. Horses and mules were forced to survive on half-rations of oats and many perished on the two hundred-mile trek.

The Federals hoped to avoid Benavides's pickets, which were known to be at Carrizo, by taking a little-used trail through the chaparral. On March 19, 1864, however, a Laredo vaquero and close relative of Santos Benavides spotted the approaching Federals and raced his horse up the Mexican bank of the river to sound the warning in Laredo. Learning that the town was about to be attacked, Benavides was said to have given specific orders to his brother, Cristobal: "There are five thousand bales of cotton in the plaza. It belongs to the Confederacy. If the day goes against us, fire it. Be sure to do the work properly so that not a bale of it shall fall into the hands of the Yankees. Then you will set my new house on fire, so that nothing of mine shall pass to the enemy. Let their victory be a barren one."[88] Approaching Laredo, the Union cavalry dismounted, formed in groups of forty, and attacked. Three times the Federals advanced and three times they were repulsed by Benavides's outnumbered Confederates.[89] The Bluecoats were "repulsed by the vigorous fire of my gallant men," Benavides, who was ill at the time, reported. After three hours of fighting, the Federals drew off into the chaparral and began the lengthy retreat downriver. On the long and dusty retreat to Ringgold Barracks and Brownsville, several soldiers from the Second Texas deserted into Mexico.[90]

Although the Union army never advanced as far upriver as Laredo again, Union authorities in Brownsville were able to create considerable excitement at Eagle Pass. A Unionist named T. P. McManus was sent to Piedras Negras opposite Eagle Pass to recruit men for the First Texas Cavalry and to "operate against the Rebel trains on the San Antonio–Eagle Pass route."[91] In the process, McManus was to gather as much information as possible on military operations and events in the interior of Texas, a task he accepted with determination and dedication. "To prevent me from sending you an express," McManus

Capt. Anson Withey, Tenth U.S. Colored Troops. The unit was transferred from Virginia to Texas in June 1865, and they served at various locations along the lower Rio Grande until March 1866. *Carte de visite* by S. T. Craig or W. T. Waggoner, Galveston Photograph Company, Galveston, Texas, ca. 1865. *Lawrence T. Jones III collection.*

wrote General Dana, "every mesquite in the state would have to be garrisoned with rebel bayonets."[92] Much of the information McManus was able to relay to Brownsville came from "reliable gentlemen" in San Antonio, Austin, and Houston. From his guerrilla base in Mexico, McManus recruited several hundred Unionists and sent them to Brownsville using the Mexican bank of the Rio Grande. McManus also hoped to either link up with Gen. James Carleton, who he hoped would advance from Fort Bliss at El Paso or Col. John L. Haynes, who he thought might be on the Nueces with units of the Second Texas. With the California column occupying far West Texas and New Mexico but preoccupied with campaigns against the Navajos and Mescalero Apaches, General Carleton had been able to send only small patrols into the vast expanses of the trans–Pecos, some of them as far east as Fort Lancaster.

McManus had sent a courier to General Carleton, but the rider had been overtaken on the Rio Grande forty-five miles above Eagle Pass near San Felipe Springs, where he was badly wounded by four Mexicans McManus asserted had been hired by the "Christ killing Jew[ish] cotton speculators."[93]

In early 1864 McManus began raiding across the river into Texas. On April 3 the Union guerrillas robbed the San Antonio–Eagle Pass stage not far from the border, stole the horses, and fled back into Mexico. On several other occasions McManus was able to attack wagon trains along the route and seize horses and mules. Many of the citizens living along the San Antonio–Eagle Pass route west of San Antonio were said to be in sympathy with the Union guerrillas and bitterly hostile to the Confederacy.[94] Union officials at

Brownsville were even hopeful that the Union guerrillas could penetrate the state as far as Fort Inge at Uvalde and prevent the "killing of Union men on their way out."[95] During the first week of April 1864 Capt. J. B. Weyman, commanding the small Confederate garrison at Fort Duncan, reported chasing various bands of Union guerrillas into Mexico. Weyman complained that Francisco García, *comandante* at Piedras Negras, had promised to apprehend the raiders but would "not deliver the thieves up." Weyman was convinced that McManus held a "Yankee commission to burn, murder, and destroy . . . the people and ranches of Western Texas."[96] On June 17, 1864, forty Union guerrillas brazenly crossed the river five miles above Eagle Pass and raised the Stars and Stripes on the north bank of the Rio Grande. Fearing an attack on Eagle Pass, the new post commander, Capt. James A. Ware, put his thirty-four-man garrison on alert and called out a local militia company. Guards were placed at the post hospital, customhouse, quartermaster's storehouse, and several businesses. Fifteen men were sent to patrol the area to determine McManus's whereabouts. Shortly after noon, just as the Confederates and townsmen had finished barricading the streets of the town with cotton bales, McManus's guerrillas struck. Spurring their horses past the barricades, they captured Captain Ware and several of his men, although a small force of Confederates made a stand at the post hospital. After releasing their prisoners and carrying off what firearms they had seized, McManus and his men retreated back into Mexico.[97] Champion of the Union guerrillas operating on the upper Rio Grande, McManus was able to create so many problems at and near Eagle Pass that Gen. John B. Magruder was forced to temporarily change the route of the cotton being sent into Mexico to the San Antonio–Laredo Road where Colonel Benavides held sway.

From the time the Second Texas had been organized, numerous problems made the regiment less than effective. Union officers constantly protested the lack of discipline in the regiment. In December 1863 Haynes complained that the regi-

Sgt. W. E. Wheeler, Company A, Tenth U.S. Colored Troops. *Carte de visite* attributed to Louis de Planque or R. H. Wallis, ca. 1865. *Brownsville Historical Association.*

ment had not received the 350 boots and shoes they had been promised, so the regiment was having to drill barefooted. Haynes also pleaded for four hundred army hats for the regiment, saying he was "anxious to have a burning of [the] broad brim hats which give an unsightly appearance to the men."[98] Another serious problem facing the regiment was the rampant racism and prejudice in Brownsville and in the Union army. Lt. Benjamin F. McIntyre of the Nineteenth Iowa Infantry said the men in the regiment were "dishonest, cowardly, and treacherous and only bide their time to make good their escape."[99]

Arguing that the authority under which the regiment had been recruited was illegal, the Federal paymaster in Brownsville refused to pay the men in the regiment, including the bounty money Haynes had promised the men. Haynes repeatedly asked that his regiment be treated equally, but such pleadings generally fell on deaf ears.[100] Another serious problem was the fact than the *Tejano* officers in the regiment did not speak English, and few of the white officers, except for Haynes and Davis, knew Spanish. Capt. Adrián J. Vidal, for example, claiming that he did "not understand the English language," attempted to resign.[101] Frustrated with his inability to keep company books, Vidal wanted to return to his family in Brownsville. Although Haynes agreed and an honorable discharge was issued, the orders arrived in Brownsville too late. Impatient with army bureaucracy, Vidal fled into Mexico along with most of his men.[102] What started out in late

1863 as a few men deserting to their homes in Mexico, had increased to such proportions by early 1864 that the regiment was on the verge of dissolving. Those leaving the regiment included not only enlisted men but officers such as Capt. Mónico de Abrego.

To halt the large numbers of desertions, it was decided that drastic measures would be necessary. The victim became a twenty-five-year-old Brownsville farmer named Pedro García, who had enlisted in Company E of the Second Texas. On May 26, 1864, García, along with another man, deserted while on picket duty at Rancho Punta del Monte, a Union camp in northern Cameron County.[103] When García and his companion were found missing, Corp. John Tuscan and two privates went in pursuit. Fifteen miles west of Punta del Monte, the pursuers caught sight of García and the second man, and they were able to approach within thirty yards before García and his accomplice spurred their horses into the chaparral. Pursued, the two deserters escaped on foot in the dense underbrush, where the two men separated

A company of the Ninth U.S. Colored Troops stands at attention in front of their tents at Fort Brown. A sergeant at the immediate left of the front line of men appears to be engaged in a heated discussion with the soldier next to him. Muskets are stacked nearby and a drummer stands in the background behind and to the left of the sergeant. *Carte de visite* attributed to Louis de Planque or R. H. Wallis, ca. 1865–1866. *Lawrence T. Jones III collection.*

and García became lost.[104] García was later apprehended by a Union patrol operating out of Charles Stillman's Santa Rosa ranch southwest of Punta del Monte. Back in camp, García told Capt. A. B. Slaughter that he had been out hunting turkey. García, who finally admitted that he had deserted, seemed very sorry and begged to be forgiven, even telling Slaughter that the captain could "cut his throat or hang him if he ever did it again."[105]

Taken to Brownsville, García was charged with desertion, leaving his post, and of "conduct to the prejudice of good order and military discipline." At a hastily organized court-martial in Brownsville on June 6, 1864, García was found guilty on two of three counts and sentenced to be executed "by musketry at such time and place as the commanding general may direct."[106] In his defense and in broken English, García said only that he had left his post in hopes of visiting his wife in Brownsville and that he was ignorant of any order that prohibited him from doing so. García later told Pierre Fourrier Parisot, the Oblate priest in Brownsville, that he was "very anxious about his family and asked permission to come down and provide for his children," but that his "request was refused."[107] Because of "the great number of desertions from the Texas Cavalry Volunteers and the large amount of government property thereby lost," it was decided that an example had to be made of García.[108]

In stifling heat, at six o'clock in the afternoon of June 23, a large part of the Union army in Brownsville, including several regimental bands, was ordered out to watch the execution. Numerous townspeople, including women and children, also gathered on Washington Plaza near the head

Col. George H. Hanks, Ninety-ninth U.S. Colored Troops and Twenty-ninth Battalion, U.S. Colored Troops. After leaving military service Hanks became the Adams Express agent in Brownsville. The inscribed notes on the album page detail a harrowing journey across the Gulf of Mexico to Texas. The notes were written by an unidentified soldier who also made the journey: "We crossed the Gulf of Mexico together on a propeller and a very frail craft. Our ingine (sic) broke down and we drifted about 12 hours. While we was laying too (sic), he went swimming and came very near being killed by a shark." *Carte de visite* by M. H. Kimball, New York, New York, ca. 1865. *Lawrence T. Jones III collection.*

of Elizabeth Street. The army formed a large open square, after which a squad of soldiers approached followed by a band playing the somber notes of the "Death March." Behind came four men with a coffin and a cart carrying the victim. Nearby walked Father Parisot. After slowly passing around the entire square, the cart was halted beside an open grave and the coffin was placed nearby. García, who gave the impression of being

In October 1865 the U.S. Army quartermaster at Fort Brown erected a tent on the roof of a Brownsville bookshop, which faced Levee Street. Photographed from the rear in this view, the vantage point provided the Federals with an observation post from which they could monitor activities across the river in Matamoros. *Carte de visite* attributed to Louis de Planque. *Lawrence T. Jones III collection.*

Pvt. William Thomas, Company H, Ninth U.S. Colored Troops. Private Thomas was wounded in action on August 16, 1864, at Deep Bottom, Virginia. He later served with the Federal occuption troops at Fort Brown from July 1865 to October 1866. *Carte de visite* by unidentified artist, ca. 1865–1866. *Lawrence T. Jones III collection.*

"stout, rugged and in the enjoyment of health," stepped from the cart and approached the grave as Parisot administered the last rites.[109] He received, Parisot reported, the sacraments "with perfect resignation and with lively sentiments of faith and contrition."[110] He then pulled off his shoes and knelt before the coffin. A blindfold was placed over his eyes, but García defiantly pushed it aside and faced the firing squad. "Each one who gazed upon the spectacle," Lieutenant McIntyre wrote, "felt cold blood curdling in his veins and would prefer never again to witness an alike exhibition." The word "fire" could be heard as a dozen rifles cracked simultaneously. As the rifle balls pierced his body, García lurched backward and fell upon the bare earth. A surgeon came forward to examine the body and announced that García was still alive. Two soldiers, acting as supernumeraries, approached to within a few steps of the prone private and shot into his head. The sounds of the "Death March" struck up again as the army passed slowly by the grave to view the "gory corpse of the ghastly dead."[111] Not only did the news of García's heart-rending execution cause considerable consternation in the Lower Valley, but it was said to have even provoked a serious discussion in a Confederate camp near Rio Grande City. The Civil War on the Rio Grande had entered a new and even more tumultuous phase.

Chapter Three

CONFEDERATE CAVALRY
OF THE WEST

The Union occupation of the Lower Rio Grande Valley never seriously curtailed the stream of cotton flowing into Mexico nor the flow of war materials into Texas. With Laredo and Eagle Pass open to the rush of Confederate cotton, the length of the new cotton road was extended by as much as three hundred miles, however, and the cost escalated by 50 percent. The recapture of the Lower Valley thus became a major Confederate objective.

When Gen. John B. Magruder replaced Gen. Paul Octave Hébert in command of the District of Texas, a renewed effort was undertaken to defend the state and reoccupy the Lower Rio Grande Valley. The man given the job of driving the Federals from the Rio Grande was none other than Col. John S. Ford, who knew as much about the geography and people of the region as anyone. On December 22, 1863, General Magruder wrote the black-bearded, white-haired Ford suggesting that he recruit and assume command of a cavalry force sufficient to reoccupy the Rio Grande frontier. Relieved of his conscription duty, Ford set up headquarters at San Antonio and began to immediately recruit. "These were the days when strong passions ruled," he wrote at the time.[1] At Magruder's suggestion, Ford was to give the impression that he intended to occupy Indianola and the central Texas coast, but upon leaving San Antonio to march for the Mexican border instead. "You will not let a soul know of your intended movements," Magruder wrote. "By making a sudden and rapid movement, you may be able to create a panic among the enemy."[2]

With Texas Confederate manpower already seriously depleted, Ford found recruiting difficult. Arriving in San Antonio in December 1863, he found several applications from men asking for authority to raise companies. Many from the Austin and San Antonio area and the small German communities on the edge of the frontier had managed to avoid conscription, some in hiding while others fled across the vast deserts of the Texas trans–Pecos to El Paso. Most crossed the Rio Grande to make their way to New Orleans and enlist in the Union army. In fact, Ford was so desperate for men that he persuaded General Magruder to authorize pardons so Ford could appeal to men who had deserted from the Confederate army, many of whom were in Mexico. "It is highly important that the expedition be organized and placed in the field immediately," Ford proclaimed. "Shall it be said that a mongrel force of Abolitionists, negroes, plundering Mexicans, and perfidious renegades have been allowed to murder and rob us with impunity?" Ford asked, in appealing to the raw emotions of Texans. "Shall the pages of history record the disgraceful fact, that

Col. John S. "Rip" Ford, ca. 1865. This photograph shows Ford wearing the uniform of a Confederate colonel. *Carte de visite* by Louis de Planque. *Lawrence T. Jones III collection.*

but individuals who had been exempt from the draft, as well as old men and teenagers. Many of the young men were between the ages of fifteen and seventeen and were from Travis, Williamson, Gonzales, Karnes, Guadalupe, and Caldwell counties. Ford was fortunate, nevertheless, to have several good officers.[4] Fortunately, most of the recruits who enlisted arrived with their horses. Nevertheless, there were few supplies in San Antonio to be purchased at any price, and Ford had a particularly difficult time securing funds to properly equip as well as forage and subsistence his cavalry. Able to exchange Confederate cotton for blankets, saddles, and forage, Ford was able to put part of his army in the field by early 1864. As soon as recruits arrived in San Antonio they were sent forward to advance camps on the Nueces River. By the second week in February Ford himself rode out of San Antonio for the Nueces. So sure was the fighting colonel of the ultimate success of his mission that he sent his wife, Addie, and daughter, Lulu, to Eagle Pass and then along the south bank of the Rio Grande to Matamoros. Arriving in Matamoros, Addie "received polite attention from Cortina," who offered "her anything she might require." Cortina "attended to having her mail sent off," Ford wrote, "and did everything a gentleman could."[5] Ford had no doubt that Cortina's courtesies were in exchange for the kindness he had shown Cortina's mother during the Cortina War four years earlier.

Encouraged by Gov. Pendleton Murrah, Ford was determined to drive the Federals out of the Lower Rio Grande Valley or die fighting. There was little doubt that the "repulsion of the Yankees

Texians have tamely and basely submitted to these outrages, and suffered the brand of dishonor to be inflicted upon an unresisting people?"[3]

In the end, Ford's Cavalry of the West came to consist of not only veterans who agreed to reenlist

from the Rio Grande would be almost equal to that following the recapture of Galveston."[6] Ford, nevertheless, worried that a Federal force, perhaps part of the California column, would push across the vast expanses of the trans–Pecos to occupy Eagle Pass and perhaps even San Antonio and then link up with the Federals in the Lower Valley. Communications with Confederate sympathizers living in El Paso del Norte, opposite Fort Bliss, were largely dependent on Henry Skillman, a skilled and rambunctious frontiersman who knew more about the upper Rio Grande and the trans–Pecos than anyone in Texas. But Skillman and several of his men were ambushed and killed by a Union patrol out of Fort Bliss in the early morning darkness of April 15, 1864, while camped at Spencer's Ranch near modern-day Presidio.[7] Even before Skillman's death, Ford recommended that James Magoffin, the well-known El Paso trader and Confederate sympathizer, be sent to a "proper point in Mexico to ascertain the doings of Yankees and by establishing a line of couriers to convey intelligence."[8] To avoid what had happened to Skillman, all the couriers would travel on the Mexican side of the Rio Grande and deliver their dispatches at Eagle Pass. From Fort Duncan, Capt. George Giddings was under orders to keep a detachment on the San Antonio–El Paso Road.[9]

Another major obstacle facing Ford's Cavalry of the West was a severe four-year drought that plagued South Texas, particularly the Lower Rio Grande Valley.[10] "You cannot imagine how desolate, barren, and desert-like this country is; not a spear of grass, not a green shrub, with nothing but moving clouds of sand to be seen on these once green prairies," Maj. L. M. Rodgers wrote Ford on February 7, 1864. "Around water holes . . . could be seen hundreds of domestic animals, dead, their flesh seemingly dried upon their bones," Ford wrote, and it took great effort, "to move cavalry across the region between the Nueces and the Rio

Grande."[11] Even the Nueces River was dry for miles.

The situation in South Texas was so bad that Ford attempted, without success, to acquire several camels, part of a herd that had once been stationed at Camp Verde during the 1850s. To assure that his men would have enough to eat once they reached the Rio Grande, Ford even issued orders

Santos Benavides and his wife, Augustina Villareal de Benavides, ca. 1864–1865. Although previously published, this is the only known wartime photograph of this courageous cavalry commander. Benavides was the highest-ranking Mexican Texan in the Confederate army; he even raised his own regiment late in the war. *Carte de visite* by unidentified artist. *Courtesy of Hector Farias.*

Pvt. J. F. Robinson, Company A, Thirty-third Texas Cavalry, ca. 1862. The Thirty-third Texas Cavalry served primarily on the lower Rio Grande and several companies fought at Palmito Ranch. Sixth plate ambrotype by unidentified artist. *Lawrence T. Jones III collection.*

should move in the direction of the upper Rio Grande, "hang upon his rear and harass him day and night—beating up the pickets, capturing his trains, stampeding his animals and allow him no rest."[14]

Striking the Nueces River and following what remained of the meandering stream downriver to San Fernando, an isolated Confederate outpost west of Corpus Christi, Ford was able to link up with Maj. Mat Nolan. Ford had known Nolan ever since the young man had joined Ford's company of Rangers as a bugler in 1850.[15] Nolan informed Ford of his vicious and bloody fight with Cecilio Valerio in the brush country. In camp at San Fernando, Ford sent out scouts who reported that there were no Federals north of the drifting sands of the Wild Horse Desert. He did learn from Colonel Benavides at Laredo that some five hundred Federals with two cannon were at Ringgold Barracks.[16] Moving on to the King Ranch on Santa Gertrudis Creek, Ford received news from Colonel Benavides of the Union attack on Laredo.

Leaving Major Nolan to help guard the Brownsville–Corpus Christi Road south of the King Ranch, Ford struck out for Los Ojuelos, one of the few reliable springs in the Nueces Strip, some forty miles east of Laredo, where he hoped to link up with Colonel Benavides and Colonel Giddings, who would leave a small force to guard Fort Duncan. Pushing through the drought-ridden landscape, Ford continued past Los Ojuelos to Laredo, where he arrived on April 17, 1864. At Benavides's home on St. Augustine Plaza, Ford was surprised to find Santiago Vidaurri.

While at Laredo, Ford and Benavides received information that Federal authorities had gone to Monterrey to discuss with Juárez the idea of using the south bank of the river to advance on Laredo and Eagle Pass by way of Camargo and Mier. Both Ford and Benavides felt that such a movement against the upper Rio Grande from Mexico "would be tantamount to a declaration of war by the Juárez government" on the Confederate States

prohibiting the crossing of cattle, swine, or domestic animals into Mexico. He even contemplated subsisting his army on jerky.[12] South of San Antonio, Ford was surprised to see large amounts of cotton that had been secreted in the brush country. On the lower Nueces he was angered to see evidence of the trade that had developed with the Federal army in Brownsville. "Men who furnish the Yankees are aiding and abetting the enemies of our country," he wrote, "and are committing treason."[13]

Learning that a Union force had left Brownsville for either Corpus Christi, Laredo, or Eagle Pass, Ford issued orders to Captain Nolan, who was already in camp on the Nueces River, to make contact with Colonel Benavides at Laredo. If necessary the two could combine their forces in the vicinity of old Fort Ewell and, if the Federals

of America. If such a plan ever reached fruition, Ford was willing to place his small army "side by side with the French" if necessary.[17] "Would I not be justifiable in crossing the Rio Grande to meet the enemy?" Ford asked General Magruder. Unknown to the Confederates was the fact that Juárez had refused the Federal request, saying that "Mexico was too small and weak a nation to wage war against either the United States or the Confederate States."[18]

There were also problems in Ford's rear at Eagle Pass. With conscription and a virtual reign of terror west of San Antonio by Confederate authorities against Unionists and draft dodgers, many of the German Texans who had hoped to sit out the war by joining local militias fled for the border. Many of those who left Texas departed with an unbinding hatred for Confederate authorities. By the spring of 1864 small bands of *renegados*, as the Confederates called them, were continuing to arrive in Piedras Negras, opposite Eagle Pass, almost daily. "Renegades from all portions of the State are continually arriving on Mexican territory in this vicinity, animated with the strongest personal hatred to ourselves and cause," Capt. J. B. Weyman, who had replaced Giddings in command at Fort Duncan, wrote in early April 1864.[19]

Taking part of Colonel Benavides's command with him, including the *Tejano* company of Capt. Refugio Benavides, Ford proceeded east from Laredo to Los Ojuelos. One day's march beyond the springs, where the road turned abruptly to the southeast, he went into camp near Rancho Las Ánimas. Continuing south, the column reached the Rio Grande above Roma. Lt. Eugenio Garza ran into a party of some thirty Mexi-

can raiders, who had left their horses on the south bank of the river and waded across. In a brief firefight, Garza reported killing the leader of the band.[20] Advancing downriver, Garza and his advance party of *Tejanos* were able to pass themselves off as Federals and were able to determine that a small Union scouting party was only a few miles downriver. Garza did not hesitate at Ringgold Barracks but continued downriver to within sight of the village of Las Cuevas. Hearing the sound of cannon upriver at Rio Grande City, Lieutenant Garza raced his men upriver to learn that a noisy fiesta was under way across the river at Camargo.

Ford, with the remainder of his command, reached Ringgold Barracks on May 2. Here he set up his headquarters and began to consolidate his Cavalry of the West for the final push against Brownsville. Yet Ford remained apprehensive that he would be attacked from the south bank of the river. On good terms with José María García Villarreal, *alcalde* of Camargo, who provided badly needed supplies for the Confederates, Ford realized that he would need to open friendly relations with those in power on the south bank. Ford even discussed an agreement with Villarreal by which property, especially animals stolen from one side of the river, would be returned to the proper owners on the other bank.[21] In Camargo, Ford also met with José María Silva, secretary of state of Tamaulipas, who said Governor Cortina would even consider selling thirty pieces of artillery and a large amount of rifles and revolvers that had been purchased in the United States for the *Juarista* army. Ford also discussed with Silva an "arrangement to

1st Lt. Enrique B. D'Hamel, Company G, Thirty-third Texas Cavalry. D'Hamel, a native of Cuba, served at Fort Brown as assistant post adjutant and assistant provost marshall of the Rio Grande District. This photograph of Lieutenant D'Hamel was taken while he was on furlough visiting his family in Cuba. *Carte de visite* by S. A. Cohner, Havana, Cuba, ca. October 1864. *Lawrence T. Jones III collection.*

detach the Mexicans from the Yankee service." Learning that large numbers of *Tejanos* and *Mexicanos* were deserting from the Second Texas Union Cavalry and crossing the river with their weapons, Ford sent agents to Matamoros to purchase the arms. "Gen'l Herron's and Col. Davis's horse[s] are now in our camp," Ford bragged.[22] Moreover, Vidal, who was under arrest in Brownsville, was willing to desert with all his men.

In preparation for the attack on Brownsville, Capt. Refugio Benavides was given the task of impressing as many horses as possible.[23] At the same time, Col. John Swisher was sent to purchase arms from Matamoros. Not only did Swisher purchase arms, but he was able to provide Ford with drawings of the Union fortifications at Fort Brown and at Freeport

Capt. Cristobal Benavides, Company H, Thirty-third Texas Cavalry and Benavides Regiment, Texas Cavalry, ca. 1863–1864. *Martin L. Callahan collection.*

above the city. From what intelligence he could gather, Ford estimated the size of the Federal force in and around Brownsville at from five thousand to seven thousand.[24] From spies, Ford was even able to ascertain the exact number of Federal artillery pieces in Brownsville and the size of each gun. Units from Benavides's regiment were able to scout as far north as the Nueces and to within twenty miles of the coast. Ford also sent a small force of *Tejanos* downriver along the river road to recruit as many Mexican Texans as possible. At the same time he extended an invitation to many of the farmers and small ranchers who lived on the north bank and who had sought refuge in Mexico "to return to this bank and peaceably pursue their vocations."[25] Although greatly outnumbered, Ford was not deterred in his dogged determination to drive the Union army out of the Lower Rio Grande Valley.

Once in the Lower Valley, Ford was able to

open negotiations with his old nemesis, Juan N. Cortina, who had taken power in Matamoros. "The present feeling in Tamaulipas is now more favorable to us than at any preceding period," Ford told General Slaughter. Moreover, an agreement to purchase arms and even rifled cannon had been tentatively agreed to on "most favorable terms."[26] Ford was also informed that Capt. Adrián J. Vidal had indeed deserted from the Union army in Brownsville and had crossed the river with sixty of his men. Had not there been a sudden rise in the Rio Grande, Ford was told, Vidal could have taken as many as four hundred men and ten wagons with him. More importantly, Ford was heartened to learn that Gen. Francis J. Herron had begun the process of transferring most of the Federals in the valley to Louisiana, leaving only a skeleton force to defend Fort Brown and Brownsville.[27] Still, the situation on the Mexican bank of the river remained unsettled. Widespread rumors of a French expedition to secure Bagdad, Matamoros, and the Rio Grande frontier were becoming more pervasive. Should the *Imperialistas* indeed occupy Matamoros, Ford was told that Cortina and his army, along with all their arms and equipment, were preparing to cross into Texas.[28]

In late June Ford sent a reconnaissance in force to feel out the Federals and ascertain if they were indeed evacuating Brownsville. He first sent Lt. Dan Showalter and Capt. Refugio Benavides to the Como Se Llama Ranch on the Arroyo Colorado north of Brownsville. With Colonel Giddings, Ford pushed along the river road to John and Salomé McAllen's San Tomás de la Blanca Ranch before he turned north to Charles Stillman's Rancho Santa Rosa and joined Showalter and Benavides at the Como Se Llama on June 23, 1864. The combined forces, about four hundred men in all, subsisting entirely on jerky, then moved toward the Rio Grande.

They reached the river at the Carricitos Ranch, just below the village of Las Rucias, little more than a stone's throw from where the Mexican War had begun in 1846. Learning that a sizeable Federal force was on picket at Las Rucias, Ford, by using "an obscure trail through the chaparral," advanced on the Federals with 250 men and was able to "get within a few hundred yards of the enemy without being discovered."[29] At eleven o'clock in the morning of June 25, the Confederates attacked.

The Federals stationed at Las Rucias were men from Companies A and C of the First Texas Cavalry

Maj. Matthew "Mat" Nolan, Second Texas Cavalry. When Nolan had his photograph taken in Brownsville he wore a Confederate officer's frock coat with yellow collar and sleeve cuffs, the color designated for cavalrymen. Active on the Rio Grande early in the war, Nolan was murdered in Corpus Christi on December 22, 1864. *Carte de visite* by Louis de Planque, ca. 1864. *Brownsville Historical Association.*

was killed instantly. Captain Benavides had his horse shot from under him while Sgt. Samuel Cockerel and Pvt. Eugenio Sanchez were killed.[31]

Outnumbered and outgunned, the Union Texans fell back to the dense vegetation along a lagoon while others fled into the tall cane and dense underbrush along the Rio Grande. Ford sent Capt. Refugio Benavides in a flanking movement to a spot "behind a fence to the bank of the laguna [to] turn the right flank of the enemy and command the ground in [the] rear of the houses."[32] Captain Benavides evidently misunderstood the order and moved to the extreme right and attempted to turn the enemy's left flank instead. With his men on horseback, the Laredo captain twice charged the Federals, but each time he was stopped by the sickle-

commanded by Capt. Philip G. Temple. Greatly outnumbered by the attacking Confederates, the Union Texans hastily took up defensive positions in a large brick building and in several small *jacales* as well as from behind a large pile of rubble and several mesquite fences.[30] The fighting opened with the charge of Capt. James Dunn and Capt. Cristobal Benavides and their men. Dunn, a Mexican War veteran, spurred his horse to a gallop, charged headlong into the Federal defenses, and

shaped lagoon or *resaca*. Benavides then ordered his men to dismount as they joined the remainder of Ford's command in a final assault on the Federals. Twelve of the Union Texans were able to escape by throwing their rifles into the river and swimming to safety in Mexico. In the fighting, which lasted for thirty minutes, Ford estimated that twenty of the enemy were killed, ten or twelve wounded, and thirty-six taken prisoner.[33] Several of the wounded Federals were said to have drowned while attempting to cross the lagoon and the river. The wounded who were able to reach the south bank of the river, among them Captain Temple, were taken in wagons downriver to Matamoros and then to the hospital at Fort Brown.

Two wagons and teams, twenty-eight horses, a number of saddles, as well as a considerable amount of commissary and quartermaster stores, fell into the hands of the Confederates. Ford learned from a letter addressed to Captain Temple that the majority of the First Texas Union Cavalry had been ordered to New Orleans and that among the Texas Union recruits there was considerable "insubordination produced by the order to leave Texas." In particular, the execution of Pvt. Pedro García of the Second Texas had caused "considerable demoralization among the renegades."[34]

Three Confederates were killed and four wounded at Las Rucias. Ford singled out Captains Refugio and Cristobal Benavides for their gallantry in the battle.[35] Unable to carry the captured Union supplies, Ford contemplated burning the saddles and other equipment, but it was raining so heavily that he would have had to do so inside the small *jacales* of the local Mexican Texans. Calculating that the support of the *Tejano* population of the Lower Valley was more important, the supplies were left as they had been found.

Those captured at Las Rucias were said to have been treated in a most "inhuman manner" and were marched to Hempstead to be confined in the stockade at Camp Groce, where eleven of the men died of disease and exhaustion. One man was able to escape and made his way back to the Federal camp on Brazos Santiago. Months later, a few of the Las Rucias prisoners were exchanged.[36]

From Las Rucias the Confederates advanced downriver through drought-breaking rain. Ten miles from Brownsville, the Confederates were fired on, and a brief skirmish erupted before the Union Texans fell back. Continuing to skirmish as they slowly advanced, the Cavalry of the West was able to drive the Federal pickets into the fortifications at Freeport. The Federals, who were still evacuating the town, were in no position to engage Ford in an open fight, and the Confederates were in no position to assault the Brownsville fortifications with the Union artillery still in place. Colonel

Ford thought of establishing a forward camp on the Arroyo Colorado but did not have the necessary supplies to sustain his men for any length of time. After five days the Confederates broke camp and retreated upriver to their base at Ringgold Barracks.

At Ringgold Barracks Ford continued to consolidate and recruit as more and more of the Union forces in Brownsville departed for New Orleans. On July 30 a Confederate reconnaissance approached Brownsville to find the outer defenses deserted. Somewhat surprised, they rode into the town to find the Federals gone. Two days earlier the last of the Federal forces had evacuated Fort Brown and departed for the coast. Confederate sympathizers from Matamoros led by E. W. Cave had crossed the Rio Grande to restore order. In contrast to the chaotic Confederate evacuation of the town in November 1863, there had been little lawlessness.

Within hours of the Confederate occupation of Brownsville couriers brought word that General Herron and the rear guard of the Federal force were in camp about eighteen miles east of the town on the road to Brazos Island. Ill and unable to mount his horse, Ford sent Col. Dan Showalter and several companies to attack the bluecoats. Spotting the Federals on the prairie east of town, Showalter sent Capt. Refugio Benavides out as a reconnaissance-in-force. Benavides charged into the Union camp, drove the Federals back in disarray, and captured several supply wagons. "We expected Colonel Showalter every moment," Benavides told Ford, but all "at once we saw a heavy column of the enemy moving upon us. I then looked for Colonel Showalter, and saw his command going the other way, about a mile and a half off. The *carajos* came, and took all our wagons away from us." When Showalter was "not under the influence of liquor," he was "as chivalrous a man as ever drew a sword," Ford wrote.[37]

Within days of the Confederate reoccupation of Brownsville, sympathizers began to cross from Matamoros and resume their livelihoods. Within weeks the lucrative arms and cotton trade had resumed. Col. John Salmon "Rip" Ford had won a signal victory.

Chapter Four

LONG ROAD
TO PALMITO RANCH

The fighting in the Lower Rio Grande Valley did not end with the Federal evacuation of Brownsville. For the remainder of the war skirmishing continued along the river and on the treeless, windswept coastal plain between Brownsville and Brazos Santiago, where the Federals maintained a garrison and continued to construct fortifications. The coastal plain offered little more than "burning sands and unhealthy shrubs, broad prairies and uninteresting hills . . . sand crabs, fleas, flies and mosquitoes . . . for miles and miles in every direction," the *New York Herald* reported.[1] Confederates were fearful of assaulting the entrenched Union forces because of the narrow and unpredictable waters of Boca Chica Pass and the large Federal guns on the island.[2] Isolated and demoralized, the Union garrison of 1,590 men and officers chose not to attack Brownsville.

On August 9, 1864, the commanding officer at Brazos Santiago, Col. Henry M. Day of the Ninety-first Illinois Infantry, sent seventy-five men of the Eighty-first Corps d'Afrique Engineers on the steamer *Hale* across the bay to Point Isabel to secure a supply of lumber. Finding a small Confederate patrol in possession of the seaside village, a skirmish erupted in which two Confederates were killed. Fearing a counterattack and the loss of the *Hale,* the Federals retreated to the safety of the big guns on Brazos Island. Not wanting several small boats at Point Isabel to fall into the hands of the Confederates, Colonel Day next sent a detachment of the Ninety-first Illinois and the Nineteenth Iowa across the bay to destroy the boats. Although they were fired on by a small number of Confederates, the small Union force was able to land and destroy the boats.[3] The Confederates fared better in other

skirmishing down the coast. Capt. Refugio Benavides "ran a Yankee force of more than double his number into the works on Brazos Island, and remained in close proximity to the works for a considerable length of time," Ford reported. In the fighting, nine men under Lt. Eugenio Garza were reported to have driven one hundred Federals "from a good position." But Ford remained cautious; certain Union tents on the mainland near Boca Chica were unoccupied and deliberately placed, he concluded, "to invite us to attempt to capture them and place ourselves under the guns of the enemy."[4] Moreover, by November 1864 the garrison at Brazos Santiago had grown to more than two thousand men with the arrival of the Sixty-second U.S. Colored Infantry.[5]

One month later Colonel Day received information that the Confederates had corralled a herd of cattle in a bend of the river at White's Ranch, sixteen miles from Brazos Santiago, which they intended to sell to the Imperial troops occupying Bagdad. On September 6, 1864, Colonel Day sent a squadron of the First Texas Cavalry under Maj. E. J. Noyes along with a battery of the First Missouri Artillery and a 12-pounder howitzer to seize the cattle. No sooner were the Federals across Boca Chica than they ran into Ford's pickets. Although the pickets were easily driven back as far as Palmito Ranch, the Confederates made a stubborn and determined stand and a brisk skirmish ensued. But when the Union artillery opened on the Confederates, the gray-clad Texans retreated upriver. When Colonel Day and a detachment of the Ninety-first Illinois Infantry arrived on the scene, most of the cattle were gathered and driven back to the island to feed the Federal army.[6]

The tumultuous and chaotic situation in Mexico also required considerable attention by both the Union and Confederate armies. At this crucial time in Mexican history, events on the Rio Grande were dramatically impacted by events in the interior of the country, particularly the flight of Pres. Benito Juárez and his liberal Republican government from Mexico City. After a siege of almost two months, the French army under Gen. Elie Frédéric Forey captured Puebla on May 16, 1863, and less than a month later the *Imperialistas* triumphantly marched into the capital.[7] By December 1863 Gen. Tomás Mejía had driven Juárez and his ragtag army from San Luis Potosí, and it appeared as if both Tampico and Matamoros would fall to the forces of the Empire. Nothing, it seemed, could stop the French. In Monterrey, Santiago Vidaurri, the "Lion of the North," began to sway in the wind. To assure his allegiance, Juárez named him military *comandante* of Tamaulipas. But Vidaurri was still vacillating by the time Juárez arrived in Saltillo in January 1864. Vidaurri was fearful Juárez would demand the customs receipts from Piedras Negras, opposite Eagle Pass, where Texas cotton diverted from the Lower Rio Grande Valley continued to flow into Mexico, producing revenues of $40,000 to $50,000 a month.[8]

As Juárez entered Saltillo with his small army, Cortina sent his brother, Col. José María Cortina, to see the president. José María carried a badly needed $20,000 for the ever-dwindling Mexican army of little more than thirteen hundred men, along with a letter from Cortina pledging his loyalty to the Liberal government.[9] Throughout February 1864 Cortina continued to correspond with Juárez, always assuring the president of his loyalty and promising to send more money while at the same time maintaining contact with Vidaurri. Late in February, however, alarming news reached Matamoros from Monterrey.

Although the fiercely independent Vidaurri warned Juárez to stay away, the president entered Monterrey on February 12, 1864, with his small army. Vidaurri was nowhere to be seen, having barricaded himself in the Ciudadela, a fortress within the city. When the president finally did make contact, a heated exchange ensued in which the *caudillo*'s son drew a pistol and threatened Juárez.[10] As the beleaguered little president fled through the streets in his carriage, Vidaurri declared himself in open revolt and pronounced against the government. Reaching Saltillo, Juárez struck back by issuing a decree separating Coahuila from Nuevo León and declaring Vidaurri in open rebellion.

In the meantime General Slaughter learned through José Quintero, the Confederate agent in Monterrey, that Vidaurri had large quantities of munitions that he was willing to sell at "reasonable rates." Santos Benavides had been directed to "write or send someone to Monterrey" to make arrangements for purchasing the badly needed war materials and to keep the entire mission secret and not to "breathe a word of it to any one."[11]

With a Liberal army advancing on Monterrey, Vidaurri fled for the border with a small army and body guard. With "eighteen pieces of light artillery, a large quantity of ammunition, a number of Sharp's carbines, and 15 million percussion caps," he hoped to deliver the badly needed war materials to Colonel Benavides at Laredo.[12] Halfway between the Nuevo León capital and the border, on a barren plain near the foothills of the Sierra Madre in the desert at Villa Aldama, Vidaurri's army was overtaken and crushed by sixteen hundred Liberals. As many of the defeated *norteños* swore allegiance to Juárez, Vidaurri and a small "party of faithful friends," along with the state archives and treasury, raced on to the Rio Grande and safety in Laredo with his longtime friend and loyal Confederate, Col. Santos Benavides.[13] Before being overtaken, most of the war materials were hidden in the homes of political allies of the governor. Colonel Benavides immediately dispatched a relative, Nicolás Sanchez, to Villa Aldama with letters from Vidaurri to the parties who had helped hide the armaments. The *Juaristas*, however, had found the war materials, and when Sanchez attempted to procure the supplies he was arrested and almost executed.

By early April Juárez had set up his government in Monterrey but was forced to flee when the army of the Empire, supported by French money and prestige, marched on the city in August. Fleeing the advancing French and riding in an old carriage with a small escort, Juárez disappeared into the arid desert wastes of northern Mexico, later to appear at El Paso del Norte, a community on the Rio Grande that would change its name in 1888 to honor the gallant president. At this point the cause of the Mexican Liberals appeared to be on the verge of collapse. With the governors of Chihuahua and Sonora wavering as Vidaurri had done, the Liberal cause seemed all but dead. When Ferdinand Maximilian Joseph and Marie Charlotte Amélie Léopoldine arrived from Austria to assume the throne in Mexico, a new era dawned on the Rio Grande.

On August 22, 1864, the French landed four hundred Marines at the mouth of the Rio Grande and seized Bagdad.[14] Confederates in Brownsville were fearful that the Empire would curtail, if not halt, the flow of supplies to the Confederate army in Texas. As a result, Ford immediately dispatched two officers as emissaries to Bagdad. "Will you

Capt. James M. Butler, Thirty-fourth Indiana Infantry. Captain Butler resigned on May 20, 1865, one week after his regiment was defeated at the battle of Palmito Ranch. *Carte de visite* by Theodore Lilienthal, New Orleans, Louisiana, ca. 1864. *Lawrence T. Jones III collection.*

respect persons and property covered by the flag of the Confederate States of America?" Ford inquired.[15] A. Veron, commanding the French expeditionary forces, responded by sending an emissary of his own to Brownsville. "If the exigencies of war should take me to Matamoros you may rest assured that I shall see that all persons and property covered by the flag of your nation are duly respected," Veron told Ford.[16]

But there was always the unpredictable Cortina. Colonel Ford knew when he led his gray-clad cavalry into Brownsville that relations with Cortina would be difficult. Although bitter enemies during the Cortina War, circumstances now compelled the two to open communications and exchange diplomatic greetings. Ford never trusted Cortina, while the wily Mexican revolutionary would always associate Ford with the forces of oppression in Texas he had rebelled against five years earlier. Although many of the Americans living in Matamoros were hostile toward Cortina, he was said to have "treated them kindly and honorably."[17]

From contacts in Matamoros, Ford remained concerned that Colonel Day, commanding the small Federal garrison on Brazos Island, was promising to make the *caudillo* a brigadier general in the United States Army, providing Cortina could capture Brownsville.[18] Cortina held "an old and deep-seated grudge against Brownsville," Ford complained. He "hates Americans, particularly Texans."[19] If Cortina could only "force his way through our lines, plunder our people and get within the Yankee lines, it would be a finale he would delight in," the Confederate colonel concluded.[20]

Ford sensed a change for the worse when Cortina stopped the passage of forage from the Mexican side of the river and insisted that the ferries operating between Brownsville and Matamoros be tied up on the Mexican side of the river at night. Then in late August 1864 Cortina's men began sniping at Confederate forces from across the river. "I shall cordially act in concert with you in speedily arranging a plan to check these outrages," Ford told Cortina in a terse note. Yet a week later Cortina's men, this time with artillery and small arms, opened fire on Confederates camped at Palmito Ranch, killing several of Ford's men. To Ford, the attack was "unprovoked and unwarranted."[21] Just as Ford was preparing to reinforce his men at Palmito Ranch, he learned that Cortina had moved six hundred men and an artillery battery to the riverbank above Matamoros. At the same time, six cannon were pulled into position overlooking Brownsville. Through the dense early morning fog on the following day, the Confederates stared out across the narrow waters of the Rio Grande and watched as the Mexicans pulled two more cannon into position.

Colonel Ford was so sure that Cortina and the Federals were preparing to attack that on September 6, in a heavy rainstorm, he sent his wife and children through the streets of Brownsville to safety at the Catholic convent. "We anticipated Cortina and the Federals would be on us early the next day," he wrote. "Troops under your command are patrolling the banks of the Rio Grande," Ford curtly told Cortina in a panic, "your artillery is bearing upon the City of Brownsville, you stopped communications with this bank. I would respectfully inquire, if by these acts you intend to indicate that war exists between your government and that of the Confederate States?" Failing to receive a conclusive answer, Ford appealed to the French at Bagdad for assistance. "Our position of perfect neutrality towards the United States as well as towards the Confederacy prevents us from doing the service you request," Commander Veron replied.[22]

If Cortina was intending to attack Brownsville, as Ford surmised, the Confederates on the river had no alternative but to strike first by attacking Matamoros. In so doing, Ford had no doubt that he might well provoke an international incident that would result in President Lincoln sending a large army to the Rio Grande to cut the flow of badly needed supplies into Texas.

Events were changing rapidly. On September 2, with the Imperial forces under Gen. Tomás Mejía occupying the village of Burrita, downriver from Matamoros, and other forces advancing from San Fernando and Monterrey, Cortina appeared doomed. Although the crafty *caudillo* had some fifteen hundred men and twenty guns and could put up a bloody fight, his eventual demise appeared inevitable. At a hastily called and contentious meeting with his officers and political supporters, Cortina determined the only way he could save his army and artillery was to cross his entire army to the north bank and ally himself, at least temporarily, with the Federals on the Texas coast. Col. Servando Canales, rather than surrender or sign on with the French, fled across the river to Brownsville, where Ford granted asylum providing Canales disarm and disband his regiment.[23] Although Cortina concluded that with the help of the Union forces he could capture Brownsville, his main objective was to avoid a humiliating surrender. Communicating with the Federals on Brazos Island through Leonard Pierce Jr., the United States consul in Matamoros, Cortina devised a plan by which he would proceed downriver, feign an attack against the French advancing from Burrita, ford the river, and join the Federals, who by design would advance from Brazos Island. The two armies would then drive the Confederates out of Brownsville. With Cortina's plan in place Pierce dispatched a messenger to Brazos Island asking that the Federals push back the Confederates camped on the river below Brownsville, thus allowing Cortina to cross. Once in the United States, Pierce suggested the *Cortinistas* could serve "as beef hunters or muster in as rangers." Exactly "how this matter will end no one can tell," the consul admitted.[24]

On the evening of September 8 Colonel Day, who met with Cortina, dispatched a detachment of the First Texas Cavalry under Maj. Edward J. Noyes to the Rio Grande to provide safe passage for Cortina's men. Pushing upriver from White's Ranch to a few miles above Palmito Ranch, Major

Noyes found that Col. Miguel Echazarete was already across the river with more than three hundred of Cortina's *Exploradores del Bravo* and three 6-pounder brass cannon. No sooner had Noyes begun negotiating with Colonel Echazarete to disarm the Mexicans than Col. George Giddings's Confederates arrived on the scene. Outnumbered, Noyes quickly rearmed the *Cortinistas,* who were reported to have fought bravely in the fighting that ensued.[25] The Mexican artillery was particularly effective in repulsing the Confederate advance with heavy losses. But when Capt. Refugio Benavides and Capt. W. H. D. Carrington arrived with reinforcements, Colonel Giddings ordered a second attack on the Federal center. When this also failed, a third attack finally succeeded in forcing the First Texas and the *Cortinistas,* who were short of ammunition, downriver two miles.

In the hasty Union retreat, Major Noyes was said to have "discarded his clothing and private papers."[26] In the confusion, a few of the *Cortinistas* fled back across the river. Fearing that Colonel Giddings would be reinforced and that Noyes and Echazarete would be overrun and the Mexican artillery captured, Colonel Day led two hundred men of the Ninety-first Illinois and two pieces of artillery to White's Ranch, where he then ordered Noyes to fall back. When the Confederates followed, Colonel Day reported he "routed them with my artillery." Nevertheless, on the morning of September 12, along with what remained of the *Exploradores del Bravo*, Day retreated to the safety of the Federal guns on Brazos Island. Colonel Ford claimed as many as 550 of the Mexicans and Union soldiers were either killed or wounded in the fighting on the river. Colonel Day wrote that none

Capt. Henry Spencer, Thirty-fourth Indiana Infantry. Spencer participated in the battle of Palmito Ranch. *Carte de visite* by W. W. Washburn, New Orleans, Louisiana, ca. 1864. *Lawrence T. Jones III collection.*

of his men were killed, although one Union soldier and twelve *Cortinistas* had been captured. Day was certain "the killed and wounded of the enemy must have been great."[27] Yet Ford reported a loss of "two or three killed, a few wounded, and three missing."[28]

As soon as the commander of the French forces at Bagdad learned that Colonel Echazarete and the *Exploradores del Bravo* had crossed the river, he dispatched his aide-de-camp to Colonel Day to complain. "I am bound to consider the forces of General Cortina as troops belonging to the United States," Veron wrote. The French commander warned that he had better not encounter Cortina, "on my road, either now or later."[29] When Maj. Gen. John G. Walker, a Missourian in command of the District of Texas, learned that Cortina's men were in Texas and had joined the Federals, he sent orders that if Cortina was captured he was not to "be treated as a prisoner of war, but as a robber and murderer, and executed immediately."[30]

A week after the fighting on the river, Colonel Ford sent a flag of truce with a lieutenant and a private to Brazos Island to inquire if the Mexicans he had captured were indeed in the service of the United States as they claimed.[31] In reply, Colonel Day explained how Cortina's men had been armed and that the *Cortinistas* were indeed "in the service of the United States and fighting under the U.S. flag."[32] On Brazos Island, Colonel Day seized all of the *Cortinistas's* muskets, Enfield rifles, horses, mules and their artillery. Nevertheless, Day reported all 303 *Cortinistas* were pleased with their treatment. Several even enlisted in the United States Army, although most eventually returned to Mexico.[33]

Desperate for artillery of any kind and anxious to purchase Cortina's guns that remained in Matamoros, Confederate authorities in Brownsville, despite the fighting in early September, once again opened friendly relations with Cortina. Gen. Thomas F. Drayton, who had arrived on the river to take temporary command, even signed an agreement with Cortina calling for the resumption of "free and unrestricted intercourse of persons and the passage of merchandise across the Rio Grande."[34]

In late September, Cortina appeared at the ferry and invited Ford to "come over and hold a friendly talk with him." Although a number of Confederates warned Ford that he would be killed if he crossed the river, "we needed artillery and knew Cortina would be glad to sell his," Ford recalled, so the "Mexican and the Texian agreed to do business."[35] A variety of proposals were said to have been presented to Cortina, none of which the unpredictable *caudillo* found acceptable. Yet Ford was in the process of inspecting Cortina's artillery when a rider galloped up to say that the Imperial Guard was entering the city. As a consequence, Ford "left in some haste and made Brownsville in good time." He later concluded that "the whole thing was fixed up by Cortina to let General Mejía find Ford in the hall where the artillery was," and thus embarrass him and damage future relations with the *Imperialistas*.[36]

With the Imperial forces entering the city, Cortina made a decision that would haunt him for the rest of his life. He declared for the Empire and gave up his hold on Matamoros. Many years later he would say that he had no alternative if he was to keep command of his army and his artillery.[37] It was widely thought at the time and later that Mejía arranged to give Cortina a large sum of money to buy his allegiance.[38] On September 26, with flags flying and drums beating, Gen. Tomás Mejía triumphantly entered Matamoros, and Cortina, an enigmatic man of many colors, put on the uniform of the Empire.

Three days later, Confederate authorities in Brownsville rushed across the river to not only congratulate the conquering Imperialists, but to assure General Mejía of their friendly intentions toward Maximilian and the Empire.[39] In Matamoros, Mejía graciously embraced the Confederates, saying he would reciprocate by crossing to Brownsville in a few days, and telling the Confederates that the flag of the Empire meant "peace and progress." The appearance of "General Tomás Mejía upon the Rio Grande was viewed with pleasure by [the] Confederates," Ford would later write. Ford would remember Mejía as someone with "rugged features," who was "honest, sincere, and truthful," and "who had fought his way up from a low position to the top of the ladder."[40] Despite the deep-rooted corruption in the Imperial Mexican army, where everyone regarded "state property as a milch cow," an Austrian officer wrote, Mejía was "one of the best and most honest citizens."[41]

As Mejía occupied Matamoros, skirmishing north of the river continued. On October 14, 1864, a company of Confederate cavalry was spotted approaching Boca Chica Pass by the Union artillerymen on Brazos Island. A few well-placed shots from the large 20-pounder guns were said to have dismounted four of the Confederates and sent the others scurrying.[42] Despite sporadic communication and brutal Texas winter storms called northers, the blue-coated defenders on the island continued to fortify and entrench in the months that followed. Realizing that the tide of war in the east had shifted dramatically against the struggling Confederacy, the small Confederate army in Brownsville grew increasingly demoralized. Plagued by pandemic desertions, Gen. James Slaughter, commanding the Confederate army on the Rio Grande, went as far as to estimate that "fully one-fourth" of his small army was ready to lay down their arms. Slaughter went on to say that he "would not be surprised if they joined the enemy."[43] The Confederates were not only deserting into Mexico but riding out of camp to make their way north to home.

With the war winding down and many of the Confederates growing increasingly weary, Gen. Lew Wallace presented Union commander-in-chief, Gen. Ulysses S. Grant, with the idea of negotiating an end of the bloodshed on the Rio Grande and possibly the entire 600,000-square-mile Confederate trans–Mississippi. Astute in Mexican affairs, Wallace saw an opportunity to possibly end the war and aid Juárez and his shrinking Liberal army at the same time. Unless the Union intervened, Wallace told Lincoln and Grant, the United States ran the risk of allowing the dispirited Confederates in Texas to cross into Mexico, where in the political chaos of the times they could easily join the French or create an independent empire of their own and carry on the war indefinitely.[44] "The adoption of the Juárez flag on the bank of the Rio Grande as the basis of a compromise would stagger the Rebellion next to the giving in of the State of Georgia," Wallace confidently proclaimed.[45] The army veteran and future author of *Ben Hur* proposed to parley with General Slaughter on the old Mexican War battlefield of Palo Alto near Brownsville. "If I win him to my views," Wallace told Grant, "all the bad luck will be to Maximilian." On January 22, 1865, Grant issued orders sending Wallace "to Western Texas [to] inspect the conditions of military affairs in that vicinity and on the Rio Grande."[46]

If his peace endeavors failed, Wallace asked that he be assigned to a new command in the Lone Star State. With a division of infantry and a brigade of cavalry from a base at San Patricio on the Nueces River, upriver from Corpus Christi, Wallace could easily isolate the Rio Grande frontier from the rest of the state. By stationing small Union garrisons at Fort Brown, Ringgold Barracks, and Fort McIntosh, he could cut the flow of cotton into Mexico and stymie the importation of foodstuffs and war materials into Texas.[47]

Arriving in New Orleans after a perilous steamboat voyage down the Mississippi River, Wallace met by chance Charles Worthington, a Texan and collector of customs at Brazos Santiago. Arriving on Brazos Island, Wallace sent Worthington to Bagdad and then to Matamoros to contact General Slaughter if at all possible. Crossing the river, Worthington found Slaughter readily "disposed to talk freely about the situation and about a settlement of difficulties." Slaughter agreed to meet with Wallace under a truce flag at Point Isabel. All agreed that to disguise the real purpose of the meeting, the public would be led to believe the conference was to discuss "the rendition of criminals." On the day designated for the conference, a cold and bone-chilling norther swept over the coastal plain, making it impossible for Wallace to cross the choppy waters from Brazos Island. He was able, nevertheless, to convey a message to Slaughter offering to meet two days later. On March 11, with General Slaughter and Colonel Ford arriving at Point Isabel, Wallace crossed from Brazos Santiago with his staff, provisions, and a tent for the evening. The two parties cordially talked into the night and until noon the following day. General Slaughter was anxious "to bring about an accommodation upon grounds of humanity and an unwillingness to see his state invaded and ruined and the war decline into guerrilla murders," Wallace said. Slaughter and Ford were both convinced they could carry on the war indefinitely, but they admitted in the end "the North would ultimately conquer the South as a desert."[48] With Richmond and Confederate forces east of the Mississippi growing weaker and weaker, the Confederates on the Rio Grande realized their cause was inevitably doomed.

On the second day they agreed on a list of propositions as a basis for peace. Confederates wishing to remain in the United States, as Lincoln had always insisted, would need to take an oath of allegiance to the Union. If they desired, they would be free to go abroad and take their "property" with them. Contrary to the Emancipation Proclamation and the recently enacted Thirteenth Amendment, Slaughter and Ford wanted a provision that would set forth a system for the gradual emancipation of slaves. The Confederates did agree, however, "that the right of property in slaves shall be referred to the discretion of the Congress of the United States."[49] Before departing Point Isabel, it was also agreed that Colonel Ford would carry the preliminary draft of the peace proposal to Galveston to Gen. John G. Walker, commanding the District of Texas. Both parties realized the implications of what they called "delicate business." In particular, Wallace was fearful that he would be accused in the North of "hobnobbing and sleeping with rebels."[50]

Any hope of achieving peace on the Rio Grande was dashed when General Walker received the draft of the proposal. Unwilling to acknowledge the almost certain defeat of the Confederacy, Walker was furious and stopped little short of

Brownsville to the Gulf of Mexico: May, 1865

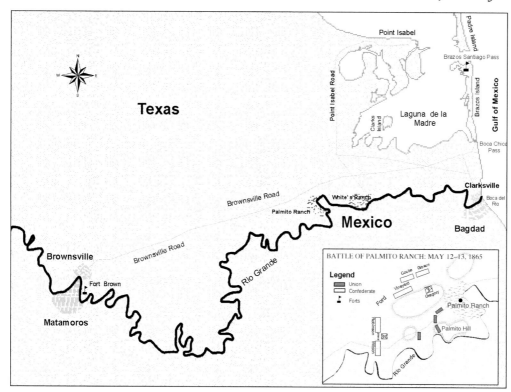

account of Lee's surrender, but of President Lincoln's assassination at Ford's Theatre and the fact that Gen. Joseph E. Johnston had surrendered his army to Gen. William T. Sherman in a North Carolina farmhouse. Three days later Gen. Richard Taylor surrendered what remained of the Confederate army east of the Mississippi River. In Brownsville more soldiers departed for home.[53] Confederate officers scurried to cross as much cotton into Mexico as possible. At Laredo the agent in charge of crossing cotton absconded with what funds were available and fled into Mexico.[54] Elsewhere in Texas, once proud Confederate units degenerated into rowdy mobs that broke into stores and arsenals as entire towns were looted. Even the state treasury was rifled.[55]

Yet on the river, Ford and many of his men were determined to resist to the very end, although they would later claim they did not know the war was over. With a stubborn reluctance to admit defeat, Ford asserted that the "honor and manhood" of his men were at stake.[56] Moreover, he was not about to surrender to invading black troops. Perhaps even more important was the large quantity of King and Kenedy cotton that remained to be sent across the river. If Ford did not resist, the cotton would be confiscated by the invading Yankees and thousands of dollars lost. As one northern newspaper put it, the Confederates "held out until the very last moment for the purpose of sending rebel cotton into Mexico."[57]

At 9:30 P.M. on May 11, 1865, Col. Theodore H. Barrett, the new commander of Union forces on Brazos Santiago, sent Lt. Col. David Branson with 250 men of the Sixty-second U.S. Colored Infantry and fifty men of Company A of the dis-

accusing Slaughter and Ford of treason. Had the propositions outlined in the agreement been submitted in advance, "the interview would not have been accorded," Walker bluntly wrote Wallace. "Your proposition is nothing less than . . . we of the Trans–Mississippi States are to lay down our arms, surrender at discretion, take an oath of allegiance . . . and in return accept such terms of amnesty, pardon, or foreign exile as our conquerors shall graciously afford us," Wallace bluntly concluded. "With the blessings of God," the Confederacy would never "be reduced to the necessity of seeking an obscure corner of the Confederacy to inaugurate negotiations."[51] The bloody war would continue, even in an obscure corner of the Confederacy.

In late April 1865 news reached Brownsville that Gen. Robert E. Lee had surrendered his once grand but now decimated and starving Army of Northern Virginia to General Grant at Appomattox Court House, Virginia. "Everyone here is blue and despondent," Richard King wrote a friend.[52] On May 1, 1865, a passenger on a steamer heading up the Rio Grande tossed a copy of the *New Orleans Times* to Confederates camped at Palmito Ranch. The newspaper gave not only a detailed

mounted Second Texas U.S. Cavalry across Boca Chica Pass on a "foraging expedition."[58] Branson was an able officer who had once been a private in an Illinois regiment. A stern disciplinarian, Branson respected his black troops, and they respected him. After marching through the night the Federals reached the Rio Grande at White's Ranch, where they bivouacked in the underbrush along the river. On arrival, however, they realized they had been spotted by civilians across the river in Mexico. Any hope of surprising the Confederate pickets on the river was lost, so Colonel Branson ordered his men upriver toward Palmito Ranch.

Stationed at Palmito Ranch were 190 men of Capt. George L. Robertson's company of Lt. Col. George H. Giddings's Texas Cavalry Battalion. Skirmishing, the Confederate camp was overrun, three prisoners and some horses captured, and the abandoned supplies burned. The Union reconnaissance then fell back to a small hill near the Rio Grande, where they rested, cooked, and bivouacked for the evening. A few of the Federals who had been wounded and those "unable to make a heavy march," along with the captured cattle and horses, were sent back to Brazos Santiago.[59] Receiving orders from Colonel Ford to maintain contact with the Federals, Captain Robertson renewed the fighting before daylight on May 12.

Pushed back to White's Ranch, Lieutenant Colonel Branson dispatched a courier to Brazos Island for reinforcements. Before daylight the next morning, May 13, 1865, Colonel Barrett arrived with two hundred men of the Thirty-fourth Indiana Volunteer Infantry.[60] Taking command, Barrett cautiously sent the black Sixty-second Infantry and the Sec-

Enlisted men of Company C, Thirty-fourth Indiana Infantry, who were present during the battle of Palmito Ranch. *Carte de visite* by A. Constant, New Orleans, Louisiana, ca. 1865. *Lawrence T. Jones III collection.*

ond Texas along the riverbank, while the Thirty-fourth Indiana advanced on the Union right. In continued skirmishing, the small Union army slowly pushed Robertson's outnumbered Confederates upriver to Palmito Ranch, where in the early morning a fierce skirmish ensued in a thicket along

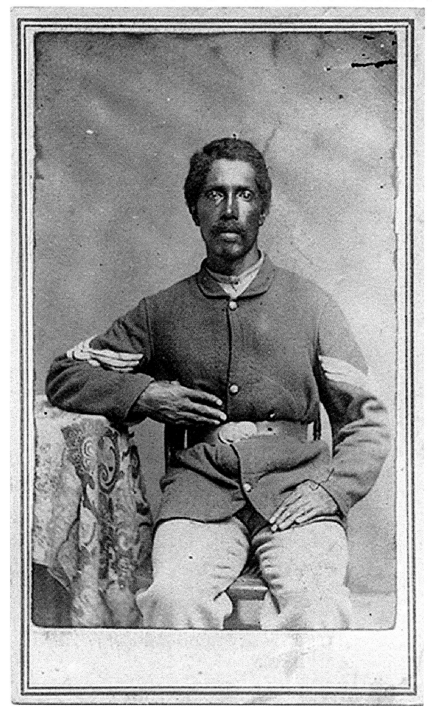

Sgt. Charles Poindexter, Company H, Sixty-second Infantry, U.S. Colored Troops. An ex-slave from Missouri who was freed on condition that he enlist in the Union army, Poindexter participated in the battles of White's Ranch and Palmito Ranch. *Carte de visite* by unidentified artist, ca. 1863–1865. *Private collection.*

huts the Confederates had been using for barracks.[61]

After continuing the pursuit west along the river for several miles, the exhausted Federals fell back to a small hill about one mile west of Palmito Hill. From here a detachment was sent to Brazos Island with the Federal wounded and the prisoners taken in the skirmish as well as those captured the previous day.

At 3 P.M. on May 13 Colonel Ford arrived from Fort Brown with three hundred men of the Second Texas Cavalry, along with men from Col. Santos Benavides's cavalry regiment and additional men from Colonel Giddings's battalion. After pushing through the night, Capt. O. G. Jones's six-gun battery of field artillery also arrived on the scene. "This may be the last fight of the war," Ford later remembered thinking, "and from the number of Union men I see before me, I am going to be whipped." Dressed in civilian clothes and with a spyglass in hand, the fighting colonel made a short inspirational speech. Concealed by a small grove of mesquite on the flat coastal plain, Ford formed his men in line of battle. From a mile away at four in the afternoon, three of Captain Jones's guns under Lts. William Gregory and Jesse Vineyard, assisted by volunteer French cannoneers, opened fire on the Federals. No sooner had the fighting commenced than a steamboat was spotted steadily moving upriver. Unable to see the "flag she bore," and fearful

the river. Fearing he would be overrun, Robertson fell back across the open prairie in the direction of Brownsville. At the ranch, the black troopers shared their rations with the Indiana Volunteers, and both took time to destroy what supplies the Confederates had not carried off or burned the previous day. They also torched several makeshift

the boat might be from the Union navy, one of the Confederate cannon opened fire. Two shots fell harmlessly in the muddy water before the Confederates realized the steamboat belonged to King and Kenedy. The artillerymen then turned their guns on the Federals. One Confederate cannon, commanded by Lt. M. S. Smith, "threw several well-directed shells and round shot into the enemy's lines," Ford recalled, causing considerable confusion. Following the Confederate artillery barrage, Captain Robertson and his men moved against the Union left near the river. At the same time, two companies of Giddings's battalion hit the Federal right while the remainder of Ford's troops charged the center. Ford was hoping the Confederate artillery could gain a position on the Federal flank and open an enfilading fire.[62]

The Confederates opened "a fire upon us with both artillery and small-arms," Colonel Barrett wrote. With a "heavy body of cavalry and a section of a battery, under cover of the thick chaparral on our right," Barrett continued, the Confederates "succeeded in flanking us with the evident intention of gaining our rear."[63] The situation for the Union forces was "extremely critical," he concluded.

Caught by surprise and in danger of being outflanked, the Federals had no alternative but to retreat. "Having no artillery to oppose the enemy's six twelve-pounder field pieces our position became untenable," Barrett continued. "We therefore fell back fighting."[64] In his memoirs, Ford remembered the Union forces having left the field in a "rather confused manner." To cover his retreat, Barrett ordered out forty-six men of the Thirty-fourth Indiana as skirmishers. Although Colonel Barrett had given the order to retreat "double quick," several times the black troops and a few men from the Second Texas were forced to halt to protect the skirmishers of the Thirty-fourth Indiana. The Hoosier riflemen, nevertheless, were surrounded by the pursuing Confederate cavalry and forced to surrender. Others in the Thirty-fourth Indiana panicked and fled the field. Pvt. John R. Smith, standard-bearer of the Thirty-fourth Indiana, who was exhausted and lame, tried to swim the river to Mexico with the regimental flag, but was fired on by Imperialist troops holding the south bank. Swimming back across the river and pressed by the advancing Confederates, Smith hid the flag in some weeds near the river.[65] The national banner that Cpl. George W. Burns was carrying also was hidden near the riverbank, but the Confederates found the flag and took it back to Brownsville as a trophy of war.[66] A few of the Thirty-fourth Indiana infantrymen who successfully crossed to the south bank later re-crossed the Rio Grande and returned safely to Brazos Santiago.

In command of the Sixty-second Colored Infantry, Lieutenant Colonel Branson watched as the Hoosiers "broke ranks and forced their way through my regiment."[67] "For God's sake, men, don't break my ranks," Branson screamed out, hoping his men would not panic. Colonel Barrett rode up and told several soldiers in the Thirty-fourth Indiana that although he was personally opposed to liquor, he would issue them some if they would make a stand at Palmito Hill. Many in the regiment took off their hats and cheered the colonel.[68] Before reaching Palmito Hill, part of the Second Texas was sent out as skirmishers, and they, like the skirmishers of the Thirty-fourth Indiana, were overrun and captured. Barrett blamed Lt. Col. Robert G. Morrison for the men from both the Thirty-fourth Indiana and the Second Texas being captured. Although Barrett gave the order to "retreat in good order," Morrison "stood as one paralyzed, or not knowing what to do."[69] Only by deploying the more disciplined black troopers in a long skirmish line that stretched for more than a mile from the river across the open prairie did the Federals avoid being completely overrun.

Totally exhausted and with blistered feet, many of the stragglers in the Thirty-fourth Indiana fell out beside the road and were unable to continue.[70] Even the horses in the Confederate artillery became so jaded they were unable to continue. For seven miles, to a point about halfway between White's Ranch and Boca Chica Pass, Ford continued to pursue. So desperate and disorganized were the Indiana men that on reaching Boca Chica Pass they rushed into the water, desperate to seize any boat to cross the narrow pass to safety. In their retreat and along the sandy road to Brazos Island, the footsore bluecoats left "many stands of arms, threw others in the Rio Grande, and left clothing scattered on their whole line of retreat," Ford recalled.[71] Although the Sixty-second U.S. Colored Infantry reached the safety of Brazos Island "with colors flying and music playing," the "34th Indiana crossed the same night in total confusion."[72]

Capt. W. C. Durkee of the Sixty-second Infantry said that it was impossible to restore order in the Indiana regiment, and it was difficult in the darkness to get the wounded safely across.[73] The twelve-mile chaotic retreat that had become a panic had lasted four painfully long hours.

"Boys, we have done finely," Ford remembered saying, as he sat on his horse within sight of Brazos Island. "We will let well enough alone and retire."[74] Late in the afternoon, General Slaughter arrived from Fort Brown and assumed command. The general had been delayed by the fear that Cortina, who had realigned himself with the *Juaristas* and who remained in close contact with the Federals, was preparing to attack Brownsville. Only after obtaining assurances from General Mejía that the Imperialists would cross to secure the city if Cortina did attack, did Slaughter head east.[75] Now in command, General Slaughter ordered the pursuit continued. Realizing the Federals were manning the large guns on Brazos Island and reinforcing the south end of the island, Ford responded by only sending out skirmishers. When the Federals also sent out skirmishers, a brisk firefight ensued in which John J. Williams, a private in Company B of the Thirty-fourth Indiana, was killed. Members of the regiment would later present his family with a medallion remembering the Indiana lad as the last soldier killed in the Civil War. Colonel Barrett claimed the "last volley of the war was fired by the 62nd U. S. Colored Infantry about sunset on the 13th of May 1865."[76] When the Confederates fell back, they were briefly shelled by a Union warship anchored off Brazos Santiago, and a seventeen-year-old Confederate blasted away in the direction of the exploding shell with his Enfield rifle, "using a very profane expletive for so small a boy, causing a hearty laugh from half a score of his comrades."[77] The last shot of the Civil War had indeed been fired.

Federal casualties in the fighting at Palmito Ranch and the retreat that followed included 111 men killed, captured, and wounded.[78] Ford reported that he had only five men wounded. Years later, however, one of Ford's officers, Capt. W. H. D. Carrington, recalled burying Confederate dead after the battle. A few days after reaching Brazos Santiago it was learned that Ford's men

had found the regimental flag of the Thirty-fourth Indiana and somehow taken it to Bagdad. First Lt. John Markle was immediately dispatched to retrieve the banner, which he found in possession of the French commander.[79] A few of the Federal prisoners were able to escape on the march back to Fort Brown. Captives from the Second Texas, several of them Unionists from Central Texas, were afraid they would be declared traitors and executed. Although few in number, the prisoners from the Sixty-second Colored Infantry were afraid they would be "either shot or returned to slavery."[80] Capt. Harrison L. Dean, commander of Company E of the Thirty-fourth Indiana and who was on staff duty at Brazos Santiago at the time of the battle, was able to enter Brownsville under a flag of truce and obtained the release of the prisoners. All the captives, except two men General Slaughter ordered held because they were deserters from the Confederate army, were set free. Although Slaughter admitted to Captain Dean the war was over, some of the Confederate officers said they intended to continue fighting and thought they could hold out in Texas for at least five years.[81]

Col. Theodore Barrett would blame Lt. Col. Robert G. Morrison of the Thirty-fourth Indiana for the Union debacle at Palmito Ranch. Barrett charged Morrison with disobedience of orders, neglect of duty, abandoning his colors, and conduct prejudicial to good order and military discipline. In a dramatic and fiery court-martial at Fort Brown that lasted through the stifling heat and humidity of July and August 1865, however, Morrison was acquitted on all counts, despite a powerful argument and compelling testimony by a host of prosecution witnesses. Surprisingly, one of those who testified for the defense was a Brownsville civilian, former Confederate officer John S. Ford.

Early on Saturday morning, May 21, 1865, shortly after the release of the Federal prisoners, three Union officers arrived in Brownsville under a flag of truce and were welcomed into the city "as guests of the Confederates."[82] The Union officers were not only treated with eggnog at Ford's house, but, along with several Confederate officers, crossed the ferry to Matamoros, where they were guests of Gen. Tomás Mejía at a grand review of his Imperial army. As General Mejía stood on a veranda overlooking Plaza de Hidalgo, the Americans stationed themselves on the opposite side of the square. Seeing the Federals and Confederates clustered together in a jovial and talkative mood was said to have caused considerable consternation and "great surprise to the Mexicans."[83]

Yet General Slaughter remained defiant and combative. Hoping to cross as much cotton as possible and learning that General Brown was marching on Brownsville, he fired off a letter warning the Federals that any "forward or aggressive movement" was in violation of a previous agreement and he would resist such an advance with force. Another battle like Palmito Ranch would "produce excitement throughout the State of Texas," Slaughter warned, and "prevent the speedy and peaceable settlement of difficulties." Union forces were not to be deceived "as to the strength of my command," he cautioned.[84] In response, Brown politely but tersely told Slaughter that he was not aware of any prior agreement that prevented him from occupying Brownsville. The only way to end the war on the Rio Grande, Brown wrote, was for the "armed opponents of the government to yield to its demands and surrender."[85]

On May 26, 1865, Gen. Edmund Kirby Smith surrendered the Confederate Trans–Mississippi Department. By this time, much of what remained of the once proud Confederate army on the Rio Grande had melted away. As men and boys in

Pvt. C. R. Battaile. This is one of the few known wartime photographs of a Confederate enlisted man who served with Col. John S. Ford's cavalry command and who fought at Palmito Ranch. Sixth plate ambrotype by unidentified artist, ca. 1862–1863. *Lawrence T. Jones III collection.*

homespun and butternut struck out north for home, some pillaging as they went, others crossed into Mexico to join the French or the *Juaristas.* Angry soldiers who remained on the border, demoralized at the collapse of the Confederacy, hungry and not having been paid in months, threatened to sack Brownsville or even Matamoros. Drunken soldiers were everywhere. Officers quarreled among themselves and then turned on each other. As chaos and mayhem engulfed the once proud Confederate command, General Slaughter used the *Mexico,* a steamboat flying the Imperial flag, to rush as much cotton as possible across the river. At the same time, he sent his artillery battery of six guns, along with considerable ammunition and military equipment, to Matamoros, where it was sold to the Imperialists. Crowds cheered as the guns were dragged through the streets to the courtyard adjacent to the Imperial barracks.[86]

In Brownsville, angry Confederates arrested General Slaughter, accusing him of embezzlement and forcing him to divide $20,000 with them.[87] A militia company comprised of local *Tejanos,* along with Mexican Liberals, helped to restore order and patrol the streets.[88] The presence of a force of *Juaristas* in Brownsville was said to have caused considerable consternation in Matamoros.

On the south bank of the river weeks earlier, embittered Confederates, upon hearing details of

Lincoln's assassination, were said to have publicly rejoiced. Adjacent to the customhouse and not far from General Mejía's headquarters on *Calle de Comercio*, a spurious grave was dug for the martyred president, around which "buffooneries and gross indecencies" were performed that would have "shamed an Apache or Comanche Indian," a Texas Unionist recalled.[89] A grave was also dug for Lincoln in Bagdad, where there was much celebration by drunken Confederates and southern sympathizers.

Union soldiers entered Brownsville at daylight on May 30 to find General Slaughter and his small command gone. Five hundred bales of cotton, which the Confederates had been unable to get across the Rio Grande, along with several hundred cattle and a few horses and mules that belonged to the vanquished Confederate army, were seized.[90] Within two weeks, 1,915 men from the Sixty-second U.S. Colored Troops, the Thirty-fourth Indiana Infantry, and the Second Texas Cavalry (only fifty of whom were mounted) had arrived at Brownsville.[91]

Released from arrest, General Slaughter rode upriver to join Col. Santos Benavides at Rio Grande City. Although Federal authorities in Brownsville ordered his arrest, he confiscated 630 bales of cotton at Ringgold Barracks and sent it across the river to Camargo, where it was sold to Francisco Yturria for $25 a bale.[92] Slaughter defiantly rode south into exile with the money from the sale of the cotton.

From Ringgold Barracks, Colonel Benavides wrote his brother-in-law, Capt. John Z. Leyendecker: "Unfortunately our war is already terminated. I am doing all I can in order to protect the interests of the government and my soldiers. Have brother Refugio keep order and not allow the soldiers to rob . . . I will do the same as the only in command of the line."[93] Finally in July 1865 Benavides, who was on a scouting expedition against Indians, received a polite letter from Union officers in Brownsville asking that he sign and forward his parole papers. There was one last brief respite on the great river before the turning of the tide. Reconstruction had come to the Rio Grande frontier and what had once been a singular corner of the proud and defiant, but now battered and vanquished, Confederate States of America.

Chapter Five

BLOODY SIEGES AND
BORDER RAIDS

With the collapse of the Confederacy on the Rio Grande in May 1865, fear and anarchy initially threatened to engulf the north bank of the river. For many Texans the loss of the war spawned a sense of bitterness and foreboding that would transcend generations. As many as eight to ten thousand former Confederates, convinced their antebellum way of life was lost and fearing they would be imprisoned or even hanged for treason, fled to Mexico. Prominent former

Confederates crossing the Rio Grande included Gens. Edmund Kirby Smith, John B. Magruder, and Joseph O. Shelby; former Texas governor Edward Clark and the last Confederate governor of the state, Pendleton Murrah, who died in Monterrey of tuberculosis; as well as former executives from Louisiana, Kentucky, and Missouri.[1] General Shelby, after leading a large contingent of his Missouri brigade through Texas, paused at Eagle Pass to symbolically bury a Confederate battle flag in the murky waters of the Rio Grande. That event, known as "the grave of the Confederacy incident," became an important part of the legacy of the "lost cause" and would be memorialized in poetry:

A July sun, in torrid clime,
Gleamed on an exile band,
Who, in suits of gray,
Stood in mute array
On the banks of the Rio Grande.[2]

But many of the Confederates who sought refuge south of the border did not fare as well as General Shelby. After obtaining a passport from the *Imperialistas*, Mosby Monroe Parsons, another Confederate general from Missouri, along with several members of his staff and their families, were robbed and brutally murdered by a band of bandits loosely associated with the Liberals at a ranch seven miles from China, Nuevo León, on the road from Camargo to Monterrey.[3]

With orders to seal off the border to Confederate refugees and bandits, by the early summer of 1865 Gen. Frederick Steele and a large part of the Twenty-fifth Army Corps, mostly black troopers, had taken up station on the Rio Grande. General Steele, a New York-born hero of the Vicksburg campaign, whom Ford called a real gentleman, set up army headquarters on Brazos Island in a "few miserably constructed wooden shanties."[4] Here an endless sea of tents, erected on small platforms among barren sand dunes, dotted the horizon. Eventually seven large barracks, designed to house as many as three thousand men, were built in two rows. The long wooden structures were constructed four feet off the ground to avoid flooding. A sizeable hospital also was built at the same time. The largest building on the island was a large commissary, where supplies were stored before being transported into the interior. In late September 1865, however, a strong gale swept across the island, killing five men and injuring eight who were working on the building.[5] At the same time, the army also rebuilt four wharfs on the north end of the island. Nearby, the Brazos Beacon guided ships into the harbor and the straits separating Brazos Santiago and Padre Island. Several residences, all open to the sea, helped make up the forlorn community. Close by stood the Brazos Hotel, a low, whitewashed building with large windows entirely devoid of glass. Although beds cost only a dollar a night, guests and weary travelers, fleeing armies of fleas, frequently bolted from their beds in the middle of the night to sleep on the beach. Since little drinkable water could be found on the island, water had to be hauled nine miles from the Rio Grande.

To speed communication and transportation to Clarksville and Bagdad, the army began construction of a makeshift bridge across the salt flats at Boca Chica. The army also began building a telegraph line south to the Rio Grande and then west along the river to Brownsville. Even before the telegraph could be completed, the small poles set into loose sand began to blow down and the line had to be rebuilt. Bandits also wrecked the telegraph by cutting the wire and frequently dragging long strands of it off into the underbrush. Others chopped down the poles and carried them off for wood or building material. Yet on September 20, 1865, the first message arrived in Brownsville from the island.[6] The outside world of rapid communication had come to the Texas–Mexico border.

The army's most impressive project was the building of a railroad from Brazos Santiago down the island and across Boca Chica inlet to White's Ranch. Most of the rails were removed from railroads in the South and shipped from Mobile, Alabama.[7] Yet the lack of rails and crossties, as well as frequent flooding, delayed the project and by October 1865 only seven miles of what came to be known as the Brazos Santiago and Rio Grande Railroad had been built. Reaching the only significant natural obstacle at Boca Chica inlet, short cypress pilings were driven into the shallow saltwater flats every twelve feet and two revetments were constructed to support a bridge some 162-feet long and three feet high. Continuing toward the southwest across the sandy coastal plain for

eleven miles, the line finally reached the Rio Grande in December 1865, where a small terminal was constructed on the banks of the river for freight to be transferred to steamers bound for Brownsville or points upriver. At White's Ranch travelers could also catch a stage for the four-hour trip upriver to Brownsville. Those heading for Bagdad either crossed the river for a stage ride down the south bank or caught the stage across the marshy flats to Clarksville before crossing by ferry into Mexico.[8] The railroad, the only one in Texas ever built to the track gauge of five feet, was sold in July 1866 to private interests and then reverted back to the military when the line proved to be unprofitable. Washed away in the "Great Storm" of October 1867, the rails were taken up and shipped to Indianola for construction of the San Antonio and Mexican Gulf Railroad.[9]

More men of the Twenty-fifth Army Corps from Virginia under Gen. Godfrey Weitzel came to reinforce General Steel. From newly established army headquarters in a dilapidated and rundown Fort Brown, Weitzel's subordinate, Gen. Egbert Benson Brown, a balding and bearded New Yorker, issued orders, in the words of the bitterly anti-Federal *Matamoros Daily Ranchero*, putting "citizens at work on the public streets, under negro guards, shoveling filth."[10] But Brownsville was "kept very clean . . . the streets are swept and the dirt carried off," the *New York Tribune* reported. On any day, "one may see strong details of negro troops marching down a street by fours, with heads up, each man carrying a rod-broom on his shoulder," the *Tribune* continued.[11]

Initially there was not the dramatic change in Brownsville as evidenced in other areas of the battered and beleaguered Confederacy. To many of the locals Brownsville had simply changed hands yet another time.[12] In response to defiant and bellicose threats by Gov. Pendleton Murrah and other Confederate authorities to resist by arms the occupation of the state, General Brown publicly announced that any person "found in arms resisting the authority of the United States" would be "treated as a common felon."[13] Talk of continued resistance by disbanded Confederate units proved to be little more than idle bluster.

General Steele was directed to move a part of

his army upriver as far as Laredo but was unable to do so immediately because of lack of transportation.[14] Troops were dispatched upriver by steamer to occupy Ringgold Barracks and then sent by land to Fort McIntosh at Laredo. Most of the troops sent to the border were African American, many of them seasoned veterans of the siege of Petersburg and the bloody battle of the crater. They also held the distinction of being the first to triumphantly enter Richmond in April 1865. "The line of the Rio Grande is growing dark with troops," one newspaper commented.[15] Within a year the Fourth U.S. Cavalry, along with the Thirty-eighth, 111th, and 114th U.S. Colored Troops, and one company of the First U.S. Artillery, were stationed at Fort Brown. The Thirty-fourth Indiana, veterans of the debacle at Palmito Ranch, occupied Ringgold Barracks in the early summer of 1865 but were replaced in July by 777 men of the Eighth and Twenty-ninth U.S. Colored Troops under the command of Gen. Richard Henry Jackson.[16] The black troopers were joined in August by two batteries of the First U.S. Artillery. In October the 117th U.S. Colored Troops arrived at Ringgold Barracks to replace the Eighth U.S. Colored Troops, who were sent to Fort Brown to be mustered out.[17] By the summer of 1866 Col. Thomas D. Sedgwick also arrived with 712 men of the 114th U.S. Colored Troops to patrol the border. Besides the more established military posts, Colonel Sedgwick stationed troops at Santa María, Edinburg, and a camp upriver at Redmond's Ranch near Carrizo.[18] By the summer of 1866, Lt. Col. William R. Shafter arrived at Ringgold Barracks with four companies of the Forty-first U.S. Infantry.

The Second Texas Cavalry first occupied Fort McIntosh at Laredo in the early summer of 1865. By late October 1865, however, 365 men and officers of the Sixty-second U.S. Colored Troops under command of Capt. H. R. Parsons had arrived at the isolated post.[19] In December Captain Parsons was relieved by Lt. Col. David Branson, who sent scouts as far upriver as Eagle Pass. By early March 1866, one company of the Fourth Wisconsin Cavalry and a company of the 117th U.S. Colored Troops had also arrived in Laredo.[20] With mostly infantry at the post, the military at

Fort McIntosh proved to be ineffective in curtailing Indian raids that had plagued the Laredo area for decades. So desperate was the army for reliable cavalry and scouts that in May 1869 Maj. Nathaniel Prime issued orders calling for four companies of civilians in Webb County, two in Duval County, and two in Encinal County to assist the military. Many of those who heeded the call to arms were former Confederate veterans such as Santos Benavides.[21]

Many who came to the frontier found the topography and climate of the Lower Rio Grande Valley in striking contrast to what they had experienced in the east. "The more one sees of this country the less he likes it," the *New York Tribune* wrote. "It is a sort of exile to come out here, and the person who stays out for months deserves immortality."[22] Many of the soldiers who would occupy the military posts and camps on the Rio Grande frontier would perish, some dying from fever and disease while others succumbed to scurvy.

In early 1867 the barracks at Brazos Santiago were torn down and the lumber hauled to Fort Brown. By February 1869, 115 laborers, 15 carpenters, and 16 masons were at work constructing new quarters at the post.[23] With its fragrant and gentle winter climate, Fort Brown would remain a favorite duty post for the army in Texas.

From the time the predominantly black American army arrived on the border, racial relations, especially in Brownsville, became tense. Many of the African Americans had enlisted to gain some semblance of social and political equality and they were not easily deterred by the prejudices of those in political power on the Rio Grande. During the latter part of 1865 and much of 1866, as was the case elsewhere in Texas, a number of nasty racial incidents heightened anxieties. Although despised by many of the white citizens they had come to protect, blacks even aspired to participate in the Cameron County judicial system. Seasoned veterans of a war that had eliminated slavery, the African Americans considered themselves equal to those who administered the city, many of whom were former Confederates. In Brownsville, one black soldier, who entered a Brownsville barbershop only to be refused service, drew his revolver and threatened to kill the barber. "G–d d--n you," the soldier swore, "I'll blow the top of your head off."[24] Race-conscious Mayor William Neale accused the black soldiers of "drunkenness, riotous conduct and frequent breaches of the peace." The mayor went on to assert that the black troopers were roaming the streets at night, "shooting" and "indiscriminately thieving."[25] The *Brownsville Daily Ranchero* blasted the conduct of the "nigger troops" and demanded they be transferred upriver to fight Indians.[26] Racial unrest reached a peak in January 1867 when two city policemen encountered a black patrol, ethnic epitaphs were exchanged, and a gun battle erupted. In the week that followed a few of the black troopers were even shot and killed.[27] Not until January 1869 would Brownsville establish a "school for colored children" and even then it was the army that took the initiative.[28]

Absorbing American military concerns on the Rio Grande was the volatile situation in Mexico. With the conclusion of the Civil War, diplomatic pressure to force the French Imperialists out of Mexico intensified. Yet Secretary of State William H. Seward remained adamant that the American army not provoke the Mexican Imperialists. Even before General Brown marched into Brownsville in late May, 1865, relations with the *Imperialistas* were tense and volatile. In a meeting at Bagdad on May 26, Gen. Tomás Mejía, who was leery and suspicious of a large American military presence on the Rio Grande, told Brown that despite the surrender of Confederate forces east of the Mississippi, the "Rebels in Texas were a recognizable power."[29] There was even talk in Mexico, Brown learned, that Texas would be returned to Mexico as a protectorate. Although Mejía "presented a feeling of kindness towards the government of the United States," he could not be trusted, Brown asserted. Although Mejía had received the Confederate arms and artillery in Matamoros and had given permission to General Slaughter to cross his troops into Mexico at any time, he denied both. Brown did secure permission to purchase badly needed beef and horses in Mexico; he did not trust General Mejía. Arriving in Brownsville, Brown tried to calm Mejía's concerns and trepidations relative to the American military presence on the border. "In the conflict we take no part," Brown quoted Secretary of State Seward as proclaiming, "we practice absolute non-intervention and non-interference."[30]

With many of the blue-coated African American soldiers on the border in sympathy with Juárez and the Liberal cause, tensions heightened, nevertheless, between the Federal army and forces of General Mejía, who complained that Brownsville had become a haven for enemies of the Empire and that American soldiers were firing on Imperial troops on the south bank of the river.[31] Black soldiers were reported to have secured temporary leaves-of-absence to join the *Juaristas*. In Brownsville it was said men could receive up to $50 a month to enlist as "bodyguards" to assist unnamed parties having "business" in Mexico.[32] In fact, both the Imperial and Republican armies on the border included large numbers of Americans, many of whom were former Confederates or discharged Federal veterans. Yet while Washington pondered military intervention, authorities were hesitant to interfere directly in the internal affairs of Mexico. Although orders arrived from Washington to "prevent aid or supplies being given from the United States to either belligerent," war materials, overtly and covertly, flowed across the river to support the struggling and beleaguered armies of Benito Juárez. Smuggling, long a way of life on the Rio Grande, became even more rampant and lucrative than before the war. Yet absolute "non-intervention and non-interference" remained official United States policy. "Troops under my command," General Brown repeatedly told Imperialist and Liberal alike, "will not be permitted in any manner to interfere in the present relations of Mexico."[33]

The most contentious dispute that came close to driving the Americans and the Imperialists to actual combat was the dispute over possession of the arms and ammunition that General Slaughter carried to Matamoros in the final days of the war. Although he already knew that Slaughter had sold the artillery and arms to Mejía, Brown wrote Slaughter in early June wanting to know at what point on the Rio Grande the equipment could be transferred to the forces of the United States.[34] When Mejía finally admitted having the guns,

Col. Charles Dupin, commander of the Contra-Guerrillas, Mexican Imperial army. Dupin's savage methods in dealing with Mexican Liberals are reflected in a statement he made when occupying a town or village: "I am Colonel Dupin. Obey or you are dead! All resistance is futile . . . I protect the good but have no mercy for evil men. I kill men, I rape women, I murder children; I exterminate the enemy by fire, by steel and by blood; remember my words!" *Carte de visite* by unidentified artist, ca. 1865. *Enrique E. Guerra collection.*

Brown demanded they be relinquished. Saying he wanted to settle the matter amiably, Mejía responded that he did not have the authority to hand over the guns. At the same time, he called for the Americans to give up the war materials the *Cortinistas* carried into Texas in October 1864. With Mejía continuing to stall, General Sheridan issued orders for General Steele to demand the return of the guns. With the arrival of more and more Federal soldiers on the Rio Grande, the Americans became more forceful in demanding that the guns be given up.[35] By early July, with still no word from Mejía, orders were issued for the troops on the Rio Grande to prepare for "active service." Until the guns are given up "annoy the French authorities as much as you can . . . without provoking actual hostilities," Sheridan told Steele.[36] Finally, in early July 1865, an express arrived from Emperor Maximilian relinquishing the artillery and ordnance.[37] Tensions continued, nevertheless, when the artillery and arms previously taken from the *Cortinistas* were "quietly" turned over to Cortina.[38]

On June 23, 1865, Union cavalry hero Gen. Philip H. Sheridan arrived for a firsthand look at the tense and unpredictable situation on the border. After a fatiguing tour, Sheridan eventually said goodbye to the "dust and dirt" of Brownsville and departed on the stern-wheeler *Cora*. Proceeding down the Rio Grande through the night with a gentle, summer rain falling, he arrived the next morning at Clarksville.[39] The brilliant but ruthless Sheridan then headed up the coast to Galveston, where he checked into a local hotel. Approached by a stranger who wished to know what the general thought of Texas, the five-feet-four-inch Sheridan slapped the dust off his uniform and replied: "If I owned hell and Texas, I would rent Texas out

Capt. William Norris, Contra-Guerrilla Squadron, Mexican Imperial army. Norris was one of several Anglo volunteers in this unit, whose motto was "Catch in the act, shoot on the spot." One of his medals (right) is the French medal for service in Mexico. This is the only known existing photograph of an American volunteer serving with the Contra-Guerrilla Squadron. *Carte de visite* by Louis de Planque, ca. 1865–1866. *Brownsville Historical Association.*

sand-man Imperial army, only three hundred of whom were French and Austrian, remained firmly entrenched. Yet the *Imperialistas* consistently found themselves under attack from the rag-tag Liberals who lurked on the outskirts of the city. "Guerrillas continue to swarm about Matamoros," a correspondent for the *New York Herald* reported in July 1865.[41] Three hundred *Cortinistas* "circle about the city, killing or capturing every living thing which moves." When pursued by Mejía's cavalry, "they flee to the chaparral—low thick, tangled woods [with] whose devious winding paths they are perfectly familiar, and where it is impossible to pursue them."[42] Only with a small fleet of steamers and gunboats, along with supplies from across the river, were the Imperialists able to sustain themselves.

By the early summer of 1865 the Matamoros merchant elite, who had watched their trade decline with the end of the Civil War, cheered as Mejía went on the offensive and successfully reestablished communications upriver to Camargo.[43] For the first time stages reached Monterrey, Bagdad, and Camargo without being robbed.[44] With the *Juaristas* on the defensive, the prospects for the Empire appeared generally good. Each week large crowds gathered on the plaza to hear the festive martial airs of the Imperial band. In August 1865 the social elite from both sides of the river, along with leading officers in both the Federal and Imperial armies, despite their diplomatic differences, gathered for a grand ball in Matamoros. A month later, the *dieciséis de septiembre* celebration also included an elaborate banquet at the recently completed new theater, where elaborate red, white, and green streamers decorated the hall. The gathering was said to be the most splendid ceremony ever held in the city. A week later Generals Steele and Weitzel again crossed the river to join the officers of the

and live in hell!" Sheridan's flippant "hell and Texas" remark rapidly became newspaper copy throughout Texas. In rebuttal, one small newspaper praised the general for sticking up for his place of origin.[40]

On the south bank, General Mejía's three thou-

Imperial army for a festive ball to celebrate General Mejía's birthday.[45]

There was one dinner after another. A young Austrian officer wrote, "I do not believe that in my whole life altogether I have enjoyed so much champagne, Rhine wine, claret and all sorts of delicacies as in the five weeks of my stay here." At one festive gathering there were "3,000 elegantly served places at tables in the open in the great square" where "every man [had a] bottle of claret, masses of English beer and champagne . . . stewed fruit and roasts and pieces of ham, in a word everything imaginable."[46] In contemplation of a visit by Emperor Maximiliano and Empress Carlota, Mejía undertook to build an opera house to entertain the royal couple. With an American architect and a Belgian company in charge of construction, the Teatro del Imperio was completed in 1865.[47] On another occasion, several thousand spectators gathered to watch an Italian acrobat walk across the ferry cable connecting Matamoros with Brownsville. Although motley Liberal bands continued to hover on the outskirts of the city, to many in Matamoros it appeared as if peace had at last been restored.

As the Federal army had done in Brownsville, the Imperial army in Matamoros set out to enforce sanitation regulations and improve living conditions in the city. Municipal Prefect Manuel Reves Arreza issued rules fining citizens who failed to keep the front of their houses clean as well as anyone caught dumping dead animals, broken bottles, or rubbish in the streets.[48]

A serious blow to the Imperial cause came at San Fernando on the coastal plain some eighty-five miles south of Matamoros, as early as April 1, 1865, when Cortina reasserted his loyalty to Juárez and the Mexican republic. Despite such pronouncements, Cortina remained politically and militarily autonomous, frequently refusing to follow orders from his Liberal superiors, although he did combine his forces with those of Gen. Miguel Negrete to attack Matamoros on May 1, 1865. After three days of bloody repulses, Negrete withdrew, leaving Cortina in charge of the resistance.[49]

With the arrival of the Federal army on the frontier, Cortina was allowed to set up a recruiting office in Brownsville. He also began to operate freely from camps in the United States.[50] Like others who opposed the French occupation, Cortina had no trouble procuring arms in Brownsville. Establishing his headquarters at his mother's Rancho del Carmen above Brownsville, Cortina seized the steamboats *Senorita* and the *Bell* and forced them to tie up on the north bank of the river.[51] On his way downriver from Ringgold Barracks, however, Gen. Frederick Steele took possession of the *Senorita* and brought it to Brownsville. Also in July Cortina seized the *Camargo* on its way upriver and forced the steamer to tie up near Rancho del Carmen.[52] The French protested Cortina's actions to Federal authorities but to little avail. In one daring sortie, the crafty Cortina slipped through the Matamoros defenses, killed an Imperialist colonel and several of his men, retrieved military supplies he had previously cached in the city, stole a few horses, and, in typical Cortina style, galloped out of town unscathed.[53]

"Cortina is giving the Imperialista a great deal of trouble," General Steele wrote from Brownsville. "They hold Matamoros and Camargo and he appears to have full sway every where else on the Rio Grande, interrupting their communications both by land and water."[54] In hope of obtaining arms from the Americans and permission to sell captured cotton in Texas, Cortina did everything possible to win the friendship of the American military on the border, even giving them permission to cross the river into Mexico at any time.[55]

The American military did solicit Cortina's assistance in apprehending Confederates fleeing into Mexico. Although without sufficient cavalry, Federal officers even devised a plan to cross the river and join Cortina in catching the fleeing Confederates. Steele was especially interested in capturing Gen. John B. Magruder and Gen. Kirby Smith as well as other prominent Confederates, who were known to be moving south from San Antonio to cross the river at Eagle Pass.[56] When it was learned that Gen. Joseph O. Shelby was already in the Mexican interior with a large quantity of rifles and two pieces of artillery, Steele wrote Mejía demanding that he be arrested, turned over to Federal authorities, and the arms and ammunition returned.[57]

At a festive Fourth of July celebration in Brownsville, Cortina and a number of his richly attired officers appeared as guests of the Federal army. In response, three weeks later, Cortina invited a number of the officers stationed at Fort Brown to a festive fandango at Rancho del Carmen.[58] So friendly were many of the Federals toward Cortina that in late August, when Imperial soldiers fired on a band of *Cortinistas* on the Texas bank of the Rio Grande, General Steele strongly protested to General Mejía.

The Brownsville merchant elite and the Cameron County political establishment, who had borne the brunt of Cortina's bloody 1859 raid, were dismayed to see *Cortinistas* freely walking the streets of the city. Cortina's men, many of whom were under indictment in Cameron County, were easily identified by the six-guns strapped to their hips and the white handkerchiefs they wore. "There is a perfect mystery why this notorious assassin and outlaw has not been picked up by the law loving authority of the United States," Henry A. Maltby, editor of the pro-Imperial *Matamoros Daily Ranchero*, moaned.[59] Despite the Imperial occupation of Matamoros, the vast majority of the underclass in the city remained sympathetic to the Liberals and Cortina.

By the summer of 1865 Cortina and his raiders drove the Imperial garrison out of his hometown of Camargo and harassed them as they retreated toward Monterrey.[60] Combined with other *Juaristas*, the emboldened Cortina also attacked a convoy containing a large quantity of specie on its way from Matamoros to Monterrey. The *Cortinistas* were repulsed and suffered heavy losses; several were captured and executed on the spot.[61]

Surgeon Joel L. Morse and his wife. Surgeon Morse served with the 117th U.S. Colored Troops along the lower Rio Grande. On May 27, 1866, an unknown assailant murdered Morse near Brownsville. *Carte de visite* by unidentified artist, ca. 1863–1864. *Lawrence T. Jones III collection.*

Seven weeks later, an Imperial night patrol out of Matamoros surprised Cortina's pickets some sixteen miles upriver from Matamoros, overran his camp, and captured saddles and weapons and even an elegantly engraved sword Ignacio Comonfort had presented Cortina in Ciudad Victoria.[62]

During much of 1865 Cortina remained active in what degenerated into a vicious, no-holds-barred guerrilla war in Tamaulipas and Nuevo León with the swashbuckling, cigar-chomping, sombrero-crowned Col. Charles Dupin and his battalion of Contra-Guerrillas.[63] Based at Ciudad Victoria, the Contra-Guerrillas were under orders to eradicate the numerous guerrilla bands infesting the primitive roads in the region. Colonel Dupin's cavalry "fought fire with more fire" and achieved the worst reputation of any part of the French army.[64] Called the "hyena of Tamaulipas," Dupin was accused by the Liberals of hanging "invalids and cripples" and sacking entire towns.[65] In the valley of Rio Blanco in the heart of the Sierra Madre, south of Monterrey, Dupin's Contra-Guerrillas executed civilians, pillaged homes, burned crops, destroyed the municipal archives, drove off all the animals in the vicinity, and even "killed all the hogs and chickens," besides "throwing . . . offal into the streets and public squares till the smell was intolerable."[66]

Many of the Contra-Guerillas were recruited from Matamoros and a few were American. Superbly mounted, well paid, and well equipped, they were feared all over northeastern Mexico and in the towns along the Rio Grande. Even individuals thought to be in sympathy with the *Juaristas* were summarily shot by the Contra-Guerrillas. In the unending violence that engulfed the frontier,

On June 23, 1866, the remnants of General Mejía's Imperial forces embarked on the steamboat *Antonia* at Matamoros. They were transported to Bagdad, at the mouth of the Rio Grande, and two days later sailed for Veracruz and home. *Carte de visite* attributed to Louis de Planque. *Lawrence T. Jones III collection.*

Liberal guerrillas were equally brutal. "Every prisoner, upon either side, after going through the form of a trial—a mere mockery—is taken out and shot," one newspaper reported.[67]

One victim of the vicious guerrilla war was the colorful and impulsive Adrián J. Vidal, who, after deserting from the Union army, had joined the *Cortinistas*. In June 1865 Vidal was seized by the *Imperialistas* at Camargo while hiding on the *Alamo*, hastily tried as a guerrilla spy of Cortina, found guilty, and ordered to be shot.[68] Although Vidal's wealthy and influential stepfather, Mifflin Kenedy, used "powerful means," evidently bribes, to save his stepson, on the morning of June 14, 1865, Vidal was executed. "I write with a heavy hand, as my boy has been shot at Camargo," Kenedy vividly recorded. "As bad as he is, I would have saved him if [I] could, but my efforts have failed. . . . He died at 20 years, one month and five days old, and to all appearances less concerned than any one present. He took the bandage from his eyes, and faced the guard, requesting them not to shoot him in the face, which was not complied with. He requested his body be sent to his mother. My brother being at Camargo at the time with the *Alamo*, he has brought him down, and [he] is buried here in Matamoros."[69] The young captain had served both the blue and the gray, deserted from both, joined a third army, and was shot by a fourth. Vidal's short and violent life was perhaps symbolic of the difficult times along the Rio Grande in the years during and after the Civil War. The execution of other captured *Cortinistas* on the outskirts of Matamoros became part of the daily routine of the "heroic city."

Merchants at Reynosa, Camargo, and Mier, towns that frequently changed hands during this turbulent period of Mexican history, also suffered at the hands of the Liberals. With the customs receipts from Matamoros and Bagdad flowing into the Imperial coffers, the only money to feed, clothe, and equip the struggling *Juarista* army in Tamaulipas and Nuevo León came from impressed loans on businesses and prominent citizens in the river communities.

The primary objective of Liberal forces in northeastern Mexico was to drive the Imperial army out of Matamoros. Following his failure to negotiate an end to the Civil War on the Rio Grande, Gen. Lew Wallace had joined with José María Jesús Carbajal to procure arms, munitions, money, and volunteers for an expeditionary force to Mexico.[70] On October 14, 1865, after Gen. Mariano Escobedo learned that Carbajal had been successful in New York in purchasing arms, he began the long anticipated push against Matamoros with his Army of the North. Five days later he issued two *pronunciamientos* from his headquarters at Santa Rosalia. The first was an attempt to rally as many troops to his cause as possible, saying he would lead them in casting off "the yoke of the so-called empire." The second was an attempt to persuade the Imperial Mexican troops in Matamoros to throw down their arms and join the Liberal army.[71] Learning of the impending attack, General Mejía declared both Matamoros and Bagdad in a state of siege.[72] Certain he was to be attacked, Mejía had the chaparral outside the cordon of forts guarding Matamoros cleared of vegetation and several small *jacales* in the vicinity demolished.

In the early morning darkness of October 25, 1865, Escobedo's Liberals, with several companies of African Americans in their ranks, attacked the fortifications guarding the city.[73] At first only small parties of thinly-clad soldiers could be seen approaching the city, but then a much larger party attacked one of the poorly-constructed artillery redoubts along the southeastern defenses of the city. Here a fierce fight ensued and the Liberals successfully stormed the fortifications. Hearing that part of his fortifications had been overrun, Mejía heroically galloped out at the head of five hundred Imperial cavalry and drove the *Juaristas* from the captured works and pursued them into the chaparral.[74] As other attacks continued against the breastworks closer to the river, many of the foreign citizens of the city, especially the European merchant elite and their employees, hastily erected barricades of cotton bales near the Plaza de Hidalgo. Hundreds of frightened citizens crowded the banks of the Rio Grande awaiting passage to Brownsville.

In what became known as the battle of La Laguna, the gunboat *Paisano* steamed to the scene and began shelling the attackers. As the *Juaristas* began to fall back, several companies of Imperial troops pursued them. At the same time, the *Antonia*, a steamboat that had been sold to the French by King and Kenedy and converted into a gunboat, was fired on from the American side of the river while approaching the city from downriver. Nearer the city, the sixty French marines on board watched as large numbers of *Juaristas* struggled to cross the Rio Grande. Realizing the French had been ordered not to fire on individuals on the north bank, several Mexicans, said to be *Cortinistas*, shouted obscenities and even pelted the French marines with rocks. Two individuals on horseback who had fired on the *Antonia* downriver were warmly greeted in a camp of the American army, the French alleged.[75] General Mejía, along with Lt. D. de la Bedolliero, commanding the *Antonia*, and the commander of the French fleet in the Gulf of Mexico, G. Cloue, all wrote General Weitzel protesting the incident as a "flagrant violation of neutrality."[76] The tone of Cloue's letter was so disrespectful, Weitzel angrily responded, that he returned it without an answer. Any communication should be in a "proper tone and couched in proper language." Unlike the *Antonia*, another gunboat, the *Paisano*, had deliberately fired on American troops on the north bank of the river, Weitzel bitterly complained. He excused the incident by saying that he did not have enough men to properly patrol the river and to do so would require "all the cavalry of Europe and American combined." The Liberals by their gallant "fight for freedom," he continued, had "awakened the warmest sympathies in every American breast."[77] With Escobedo's officers and hundreds of *Cortinistas* using Brownsville as a safe haven to rest and take their meals while the siege of Matamoros progressed, Clouse went as far as to proclaim the city "the headquarters of the *Juaristas*."[78]

For sixteen days Matamoros remained under attack. The city is so closely "besieged that no one dares to stir an inch beyond the fortifications," it was reported.[79] Downriver, the Liberals seized the steamboat *Rio Grande* and ran it to the American side of the river at Clarksville, hoping to convert it into a gunboat. On the north bank, however, the Americans seized the steamer.[80] The only means of communicating with Bagdad was by gunboat or steamship or by using the American side of the river. For over a week in late October, as rain showers dampened the bloody scene, skirmishing lingered on the outskirts of the city. The Liberals occasionally lobbed an artillery shell into the city, scaring an already frightened populace. On the morning of November 9, an Imperial patrol rode out to find the Liberal trenches empty and only a few arms and blankets scattered on the bare earth.

The caissons and cannon of General Slaughter's Confederate artillery were photographed on the parade ground at Fort Brown. General Mejía and French authorities in Matamoros returned them at the United States' demand. At the extreme right of this view three U.S. soldiers stand at one end of the line of caissons by the large flagpole at Fort Brown. *Carte de visite* attributed to Louis de Planque, ca. October 1865. *Lawrence T. Jones III collection.*

General Escobedo and his Liberals, like hungry wolves, had retreated into the chaparral to regroup and attack another time. Low on ammunition, Escobedo moved his small army some six miles upriver to Santa Rosalia. The ship loaded with arms and ammunition that Carbajal had promised had not arrived.

In the battle of La Laguna, as many as five hundred of the *Juaristas* were killed or wounded and fifty-eight captured. Imperial losses were placed at less than twelve. As many as one hundred of the wounded *Juaristas* were carried across the river and cared for in makeshift hospital tents the United States Army erected. It was later revealed that during the siege a plot had been undertaken by former Confederate officers in the Imperial army to assassinate General Mejía and turn the city over to the Liberals. One of the conspirators, Capt. W. W. Gholson, who commanded Fort Matanzas, was arrested, tried, found guilty, and executed the same day.[81]

Although defeated, the determination of the Liberals to drive Mejía and his *Imperialistas* out of Matamoros did not slacken. On November 10 the steamer *Antonia*, carrying a detachment of French marines and two field pieces, was attacked and run aground seven miles upriver from Matamoros.[82] *Cortinistas* opened a furious fire on the boat by from both banks of the river, and several of the marines were wounded. A week later, a detachment of Contra-Guerrillas was ambushed and surrounded by a band of *Cortinistas* near the site of the attack on the steamer, and several Imperial cavalry were killed. Skirmishing resumed within a few miles of Matamoros.

A serious setback to Imperial attempts to consolidate power in northeastern Mexico came when General Escobedo seized Monterrey in late December 1865. Although seven hundred Imperial cavalry were able to recapture the city, the Liberals were emboldened by the episode.[83]

A month earlier tensions had erupted anew at

Bagdad. A small band of American filibusters led by a grandiose and illusionary dreamer named William D. St. Clair and encouraged by Francisco de León, who claimed to be the *Juarista* governor of Tamaulipas, seized the steamboat *Rio Grande.* Shortly after midnight on November 5, St. Clair and three other men crossed the river from Clarksville in a small skiff and pulled up beside the *Rio Grande,* which was docked at the Mexican Express Line wharf just upriver from the seaside community. Only one guard was on duty and the boat was easily taken. The steamer was "hard aground" and it took two hours to get her under way while fifty other filibusters anxiously stood on the American bank waiting to pull the boat across the Rio Grande. "She is a fine vessel and I think after she is properly fitted, I shall force Matamoros to surrender," St. Clair boasted. "I have already challenged the *Antonia* to a fight."[84] St. Clair, who claimed the vessel in the name of the Republican government, was hoping to turn the steamer into a gunboat. The incident, he gloated, had "created great excitement in Bagdad as well as Clarksville."[85] Moreover, he was hoping the seizure of the steamer could be publicized in northern newspapers. As it turned out, the steamer, which was seized by the American authorities in Clarksville, belonged to a maritime entrepreneur in New Orleans and not the French Imperialists.

A much more serious challenge to Imperial authority on the Rio Grande came in January 1866, again at Bagdad. The previous November Lew Wallace had persuaded R. Clay Crawford, a blustery and charismatic adventurer, to undertake a filibustering expedition against the French. At the same time Wallace notified army headquarters that Crawford was on his way to the border and that the military would be advised not to be "too vigilant about his activities."[86] On his way to Brownsville from New Orleans, Crawford paused in Galveston, where Gen. Grenville M. Dodge offered assistance in securing arms and raising recruits.[87] Arriving on the Rio Grande, Crawford and another filibuster, Arthur F. Reed, a former lieutenant colonel in the 110th U.S. Colored Troops who had been cashiered in June 1865, opened a recruiting office offering "Fifty Dollars a Month in Gold" and all expenses for anyone who would join in an invasion of Mexico.[88] A few days before Christmas 1865 Crawford, who claimed to be a major general in the Republican army, sent one of his lieutenants, George P. Edgar, to Bagdad to spy on the Imperial troops stationed there. Specifically, Edgar was to report on the size of the *Imperialista* garrison and the number of artillery pieces at Bagdad, as well as the size and nature of the vessels anchored at the port.[89]

From the time the French occupied Bagdad in August 1864, the *Imperialistas* had maintained a small force in the town. A reporter for the *New York Herald* found the soldiers "sauntering about in a uniform that was a disgrace to any nation aspiring to military honors." Poorly armed and bedraggled, the garrison was "devoid of spirit, seemed indolent, and were positively little better than a pack of . . . ragamuffins."[90] Believing Bagdad to be vulnerable, the American filibusters under Crawford and Reed struck the town on the early morning hours of January 5, 1866. The invaders were mostly army deserters, outlaws, filibusters from Galveston, and border riffraff of all descriptions, as well as a few men still in the United States Army stationed at Clarksville.

For several weeks filibusters had secretly gathered at Clarksville. The adventurers quietly congregated at a saloon and store Thomas D. Sears owned in the town.[91] Reed, who claimed to be a lieutenant colonel in the *Juarista* army, also obtained a pass that allowed him access to the camp of the 118th U.S. Colored Troops, who were encamped on the outskirts of Clarksville. Several of the American officers, including Lt. Col. J. D. Davis, who commanded the 118th U.S. Colored Troops, knew the filibusters were planning to raid Bagdad but remained silent. With the promise of money and a share of the plunder, Reed was able to enlist, allegedly unbeknownst to the officers of the regiment, a number of black enlisted men. On December 18, 1865, Reed wrote Crawford from Clarksville that his recruits were prepared to cross the river at any time.[92] Two weeks later, on January 3, 1866, he wrote Crawford again to say that plans had been completed and his recruits were "impatient to strike."[93] Throughout January 4, a number of the filibusters crossed the river and quietly began to congregate at the Globe Hotel. At 4

A.M. in the early morning darkness of January 5, the filibusters, said to be a "promiscuous crowd of adventurers," struck.[94] Imperial soldiers guarding the ferry, part of a force of 180 who were assigned to the town, were caught largely by surprise and easily subdued. At the same time, more than 150 men, many of them in uniform, crossed from the north bank. With a frightened populace awakened by gunfire, the garrison commander and the captain of the port were taken prisoners while in their beds.[95] In the violence and confusion, the Imperial *alcalde* of Bagdad, a man named Alonzo, was dragged out of his headquarters and executed on the street.

As the assault progressed, the Imperial gunboat *Antonia*, anchored at the docks, was attacked. The ship, lined with cotton bales, raked the raiders with an incessant fire, killing two of the filibusters and wounding two others. Wearing the uniform of an American colonel and riding a black horse, Reed led a second charge on the gunboat, which also failed. The raiders, however, were able to pull one of their captured cannon into a wooden frame house and fire through the walls at the thinly protected vessel from only a few paces.[96] Several shots pierced the pilot house, killing an Austrian cadet and a French non-commissioned officer, while other shots ripped into the boat just above the waterline. Although badly battered, the *Antonia* was able to gather enough steam to escape into open water.

With the first rays of dawn streaked across the Gulf, French warships at the mouth of the river began bombarding the town. As the fighting continued, Crawford sent a dispatch to the collector of customs at Clarksville requesting that the ferry be used to evacuate women and children. After two hours of bloody fighting, the Imperial garrison under the command of Colonel Rico surrendered. Crawford seized their arms and placed 175 of the prisoners on the *Prince of Wales* and sent them across the narrow channel.[97] Reaching the dock at Clarksville, the ship was refused permission to land. Not deterred, Crawford then steamed up the Rio Grande and discharged the prisoners on the American side. In the bedlam the American filibusters continued to pillage the town. Stores, warehouses, saloons, business houses, and even

private residences were ransacked as the frightened populace fled in terror. It was reported that "every species of movable property was crossed from Bagdad to Clarksville."[98] In possession of the town, Crawford ordered Bagdad barricaded with cotton bales. As many as fifty lighters loaded with plunder began to cross the Rio Grande. One merchant lost thirty-three chests of tea, fourteen cases of claret, and twenty-four boxes of axes. "Upon taking possession of the town, the work of pillage and plunder was immediately inaugurated," the *New Orleans Daily Crescent* reported. Within a few hours several large warehouses had been emptied. In the fighting, the raiders lost four men killed and eight wounded while the Imperial losses were placed at eight killed and twenty-two wounded. Frank Benter, the collector of customs at Brazos Santiago and Clarksville, later seized both the *Prince of Wales* and the *Rio Grande* and a large quantity of the plundered goods that were crossed to the north bank.[99]

Along with the American filibusters, as many as thirty to forty men of the 118th U.S. Colored Troops were said to have been involved in the plunder, which included 100 boxes of assorted merchandise, 102 boxes of shoes, 37 barrels of flour, 4 barrels of whiskey, and a large amount of dry goods. Goods later seized in Clarksville included 108 muskets, 21 boxes of ammunition, 4 cannon, and several kegs of powder.[100] Although a few of the black troopers were arrested, Maj. Edmund De Buck of the 118th U.S. Colored Troops later admitted that due to the "great confusion" and the intoxicated condition of many of the men, few of those who had been involved in the raid were apprehended.[101] One resident later testified that he lost clothing, money, jewelry, and everything of any value.[102] Another businessman in the seaside community said that before the raid he was worth over $30,000, but after the raid he was "not worth a dollar in the world" and was "fortunate to have escaped with [his] life."[103] The man later found the safe from his business blown open on the American side of the river. Within two days even the doors and windows from the buildings in Bagdad had been removed.

Goods customs officials seized in Clarksville were later taken to Brownsville. Many of the plundered items remained in the hands of the filibusters and for days, it was said, "mules, asses and carts" could be seen on the Brownsville road carrying the stolen items.[104] Hearing that Bagdad was under attack, Lt. Col. Frank J. White, commanding the Second U.S. Colored Troops at Brazos Santiago, hurried down the coast to find citizens crowding the north bank of the Rio Grande, pleading that he intervene to restore order. Crossing the river, White found the town in "great disorder" and many of the houses and businesses already "plundered and gutted."[105]

The raid on Bagdad caught General Escobedo and the Liberals by surprise. Escobedo initially informed Weitzel that his forces had seized Bagdad, but within hours he asserted that Crawford had done so without his orders and he asked the Americans to detain him.[106] In Bagdad, Francisco de León, one of seven individuals claiming to be governor of Tamaulipas, had time to send an urgent plea across the river requesting that Lieutenant Colonel Davis send a company of troops to Bagdad "for the purpose of restoring order and protecting American citizens."[107] Panic stricken, the French consul in Matamoros called a hasty meeting of many of the European inhabitants of the city to ponder the capture of Bagdad or what he termed "matters of grave importance."[108]

Lieutenant Colonel White and 450 of the Second U.S. Colored Troops were ordered to Clarksville on January 16 to relieve the Forty-sixth U.S. Colored Troops. White was under orders not "to occupy Mexican territory unless common humanity required" it, however.[109] In Clarksville, White met Cortina, who had arrived with forty of his men. Cortina admitted that he did not have a sufficient force to hold the town and if the Americans were withdrawn before civil order was restored, he asserted, chaos would once again engulf the community. At Cortina's urging, White immediately crossed the river with three hundred men of his Second U.S. Colored Troops and took possession of the town.[110] Although Cortina hoped to assume command at Bagdad himself, Gen. Mariano Escobedo refused to recognize him and instead placed Col. C. S. Garza in command. Rebuffed, Cortina headed back to Brownsville as the Second U.S. Colored Troops continued to

patrol the largely deserted community.[111] A handful of Americans who had remained in the town and survived the violence crossed to the north bank. As late as January 24 it was said that $40,000 in specie belonging to Dröge, Oetling and Company was seized in Bagdad and taken to Clarksville. The sheriff of Cameron County, George Dye, was able to seize the specie, however, and the robbers were arrested.[112]

Shocked at the audacity of the Bagdad raid and perhaps fearful that Matamoros too would be attacked, more than 150 merchants from the city issued a protest, charging the raiders with violating the neutrality laws of the United States. The petitioners called on the United States to "check the arbitrary interference of its officers in Mexican affairs." The merchants also complained that the United States army was going out of its way to protect "the traitor Cortina and his banditti from the vengeance of the Imperial Government."[113] Embarrassed by the raid, Gen. Horatio Gouverneur Wright, commanding the Department of Texas, with several aides, under orders from General Sheridan, arrived on the Rio Grande from Galveston to investigate the incident. Wright was to do everything possible to maintain neutrality and arrest Crawford and other filibusters implicated in the raid.[114] Not trusting the Americans to objectively inquire into the facts of the case, an Imperial officer recorded that Wright was a "crafty and knavish scoundrel in a general's uniform."[115] Convening a court of inquiry, General Weitzel ordered the 118th U.S. Colored Troops, who were scheduled to be mustered out of the army, held until the inquiry could be completed and anyone found guilty arrested.[116]

Convening at Brazos Santiago behind closed doors on the morning of January 23, 1866, the court heard testimony from several officers in the 118th U.S. Colored Troops as well as citizens from both Bagdad and Clarksville. Every officer that testified denied complicity in the raid. Reed was arrested in Clarksville on January 28 and sent under guard to Brownsville, but Crawford and Sears, along with Francisco de León and several colleagues, fled to New Orleans on the steamer *Crescent* and were not available to testify.[117] After more than a week of testimony, the commission concluded only that the port had been sacked and that American soldiers, paid by leading filibusters, had been involved. The commission was unwilling or unable to implicate any United States officers in the raid.[118] Seeing the findings of the court as a cover-up, one Imperial officer branded the American officers "coarse, mean, devoid of honor and character, completely mercenary and only brave when there is something to steal."[119]

On the night of January 24, Escobedo's small Liberal army under Col. Adolfo de la Garza evacuated Bagdad and crossed to Clarksville on the *Prince of Wales*. Not only was the steamboat immediately impounded by the Americans but so were the *Juaristas*' arms and artillery. Although the Liberals claimed the arms and artillery had been lawfully captured during the raid on Bagdad, the Imperial forces who re-occupied the community demanded they be returned to Mexico.[120] There were even rumors that if the Americans did not comply with Imperial demands, the French were preparing to blockade Brazos Santiago. Although General Sheridan compared Emperor Maximilian to a lowly Caribbean pirate, he ordered the arms delivered to the Imperialists.[121]

Far from the banks of the Rio Grande, diplomatic reverberations from the Bagdad raid continued for months. In Washington Matias Romero, Mexican minister to the United States, received a letter from Col. Enrique A. Mejía protesting Sheridan's decision to turn the arms and artillery over to Tomás Mejía, "chief of the traitors in Matamoros."[122] Acting under Escobedo's orders, Colonel Mejía had gone to Galveston to seen General Wright, but Wright had referred him to Sheridan. Romero wrote Secretary of State William Seward demanding to know why arms and artillery taken by the U.S. forces from a Republican officer who sought refuge in the United States were turned over to an enemy of the Mexican Republic who the United States did not diplomatically recognize.[123] In Washington diplomatic circles it all seemed very confusing. Secretary of War Edwin M. Stanton, along with General Grant and Secretary Seward, did not have an answer for Romero. What had transpired at Bagdad was a "delicate matter" and an embarrassment, Grant admitted, and he and everyone in Washington

were anxious to put the incident behind them. In the final analysis, General Weitzel perhaps put it best: "The whole affair was disgraceful in the extreme from beginning to end."[124]

On the night of January 21, 1866, not long after the Bagdad raid, a band of *Cortinistas* crossed from the Mexican bank of the river and plundered the Sabineto Ranch, fifteen miles below Brownsville, mortally wounding the ranch owner, Cristobal Rosa. Cortina's men also fired on a steamer on the river, mistakenly thinking it was bound for Matamoros rather than Brownsville.[125] As many as thirty *Cortinistas* were later arrested in Brownsville.[126] The continued violence along the river provoked Henry Maltby of the *Ranchero*, who, along with his younger brother, William H. Maltby, and Somers Kinney, to editorialize that "thugs and thieves, ruffians and robbers, pickpockets and pillagers, filibusters and free niggers, burglars and bandits, Mexican outlaws and midnight assassins . . . held complete sway . . . over the greenback side of the lower Rio Grande Valley."[127]

In the five years following the end of the American Civil War, one hundred murders were committed within a five-mile radius of Brownsville on the American side of the river. The district court in Brownsville was so busy convicting criminals that at one time forty-three malefactors, including a "motley crowd [of] Mexicans, Negroes, an Indian and fifteen young Americans," all heavily chained and guarded by sheriff deputies armed with Spencer carbines and a squad of the Eleventh U.S. Cavalry, left Brownsville in six wagons for the long journey to the state penitentiary in Huntsville.[128] In fact, all along the border from Eagle Pass to the Gulf, a general breakdown in law and order led to a number of highway robberies, murders, kidnapping, and general thievery. On the road from San Antonio to Eagle Pass, sixty people were said to have been killed in only a few months following the end of the war. One of the most prominent individuals to fall victim was Ramos Larrache, a wealthy merchant from San Luis Potosi, who along with three other men was killed by *Cortinistas* near Rio Grande City.[129]

A rare glimpse into the history of the Lower Rio Grande Valley in the troubled years after the Civil War can be seen in the photographs of the

A two-story building inside the armory at Fort Brown served as the military prison. Condemned murderer Robert Rodgers dug his eighty-foot escape tunnel beneath these walls before he was captured. *Carte de visite* by R. H. Wallis, ca. 1871. *Lawrence T. Jones III collection.*

This portrait of convicted murderer Robert Rodgers was taken in his Fort Brown prison cell shortly before his execution by hanging on June 11, 1866. *Carte de visite* attributed to Louis de Planque or R. H. Wallis. *Lawrence T. Jones III collection.*

1st Lt. David Bond, Ninth U.S. Colored Troops. Lieutenant Bond was in charge of the military prison at Fort Brown, and it was he who originally collected and brought home all of the photographs related to the executions of Robert Rodgers and the three *Cortinistas*. *Carte de visite* by Samuel Anderson, New Orleans, Louisiana, ca. 1866. *Lawrence T. Jones III collection.*

Lt. Albert L. Norris, Fort Brown post surgeon, 114th U.S. Colored Troops. Surgeon Norris examined William Gardiner's body and testified at the court martial of Pvt. Robert Rodgers. *Carte de visite* attributed to Louis de Planque or R. H. Wallis, ca. 1866. *Lawrence T. Jones III collection.*

time. Among the rarest of these is a series of images depicting two different executions by hanging in Brownsville, and they are the only known copies to date. The hanging of Pvt. Robert Rodgers of the Seventy-seventh Ohio Volunteer Infantry was the first of the two executions. His story was a melodrama not soon forgotten in Brownsville or Matamoros for many years. Were it not for the documentation, the Robert Rodgers episode would seem incredulous.

Rodgers was an eighteen-year-old laborer from Marietta, Ohio, when he enlisted in Company B, Seventy-seventh Ohio on December 27, 1861.[130] A man who consumed too much whiskey for his own good, he was in trouble with the law almost from the beginning of his enlistment. In January 1862 he was arrested and convicted of stabbing a Marietta store owner after being caught stealing. "Whiskey is chargeable for this transaction," a local newspaper wrote in describing Private Rodgers and his crime.[131] Rodgers was imprisoned at Marietta for ten months before he was released from custody to return to his regiment. The troubled young private saw combat with the Seventy-seventh Ohio Infantry, primarily in Tennessee and Arkansas. Ironically, Rodgers was present when his regiment guarded the Confederate military prison camp at Alton, Illinois, from September 1862 to August 1863.[132] In June 1865 Rodgers was still with the Seventy-seventh Ohio when the regiment was sent to the Lone Star State.

It was at Brownsville that the incredible story of Rodgers reached a dramatic conclusion. Early in the evening of February 21, 1866, Rodgers and members of his company were sitting around their tents. Rodgers, who was frequently drunk, was busily drinking when an intoxicated civilian, William A. Gardiner, strolled into camp. Gardiner was an army veteran, having served earlier during the war as a surgeon with the Eighty-first Pennsylvania Infantry. From the time of his enlistment in September 1861, the surgeon was said to be in a "constant state of intoxication" and was verbally abusive towards others in his regiment. He was soon court-martialed but allowed to resign in August 1862.[133]

After the war, Gardiner made his way to the Lower Rio Grande Valley, working as a sutler with the Federal occupation troops. When he came into the camp of the Seventy-seventh Ohio that February evening looking for whiskey, he found trouble. A member of Company B told Private Rodgers to give Gardiner a drink. Rodgers, resenting the suggestion because Gardiner owed him money for previous liquor purchases, struck Gardiner in the face with an uncorked whiskey bottle and knocked him backward, spilling whiskey all over him.[134] Several men in his company quickly restrained Rodgers, and Gardiner was told to leave. As Gardiner walked away, however, Rodgers cursed him and picked up a three-foot-long wooden club and began to chase after him, striking Gardiner on the shoulder and then on the arm. The second blow was so hard that the club flew out of Rodgers's hand. Becoming even more enraged, Rodgers picked up the club with both hands and struck Gardiner on the head, fracturing his skull and killing him instantly. Rodgers was immediately placed under arrest. "When I strike a man, I strike to kill," he cried out as he was dragged away.[135]

One week after the murder, a general court-martial was convened at Fort Brown. Individuals testifying included Dr. Albert L. Norris, post surgeon, who was assigned to the 114th United States Colored Infantry. Norris recalled how Gardiner was already dead by the time he examined him. The court-martial was brief, and Rodgers was found guilty of murder and intent to commit murder and sentenced by the court to be hanged on Friday, April, 27, 1866.[136]

Incarcerated in an upstairs cell of the brick military prison at Fort Brown with barely thirty days before he was scheduled to die, Rodgers implemented an elaborate escape plan. In a part of his cell wall covered by tiers of sleeping bunks, at the top of the eight-foot-high ceiling where one of the supporting cross-timbers rested, Rodgers began to scrape out a hole. From this small hole, which was only visible from the top bunk, he crawled through and descended by a "mysteriously procured" rope fifty feet into a side yard of the prison that was invisible to the prison guards. A prison wall still blocked him from completing his escape, so Rodgers began digging a tunnel, his only tool being the split side-half of a canteen. He worked only at night. As each morning approached, he climbed back up the rope and returned to his cell so that he would be visible to guards during daylight hours. For every night for a month prior to his execution, the condemned man vigorously labored on his escape tunnel. On the night before he was to be hanged, he had not completed his tunnel so he went into it and remained there. His "escape" was not discovered until the following morning, and outraged military authorities had no clue as to his disappearance. Some of the prison guards were even arrested and charged with aiding in the escape. When no evidence against them could be found, all charges were dropped. It was presumed that Rodgers had crossed the Rio Grande to the safety of Mexico. Rumors persisted in Matamoros that he had even joined the Contra-Guerrillas.

Increasingly desperate, Rodgers hid in the tunnel for the next four weeks, digging away day and night. He came out of the ground only in the dead of night to receive food and water saved for him by other prisoners, who hoped to escape themselves. While everybody thought he had escaped to Matamoros, Rodgers was "patiently, quietly, perseveringly" digging his way to freedom.[137]

After passing under the prison wall, Rodgers kept burrowing until he thought he had gone far enough. Over four weeks after permanently descending into the tunnel, Rogers decided to surface under a house. The day before he emerged, the woman under whose house he mysteriously appeared was washing clothes in her backyard when she and her daughter noticed the earth moving. Believing this was nothing more than rat trails and rat holes, she poured a tub of soapsuds into a small hole that had appeared. About nine o'clock that same night, the woman and her children were startled by an inexplicable noise coming from under the back room of the house. She decided to remove a couple of planks from the floor and was surprised to see a man crawl "slowly out of the ground."[138] Discerning quickly that the man must be an escaped prisoner, nearby sentries were immediately summoned, and the unknown man was taken into custody. When the "human mole" was identified as Rodgers, there was general astonishment in both Brownsville and Matamoros.

When the tunnel was examined, it was found to be neatly dug, three feet from the surface and with a flat bottom and arched roof. It was roomy enough for a large man to crawl through easily and was a remarkable eighty to ninety feet in length. The tunnel ran under a Brownsville street, and, fearing the street would collapse, troops were immediately put to work filling the tunnel. Realizing his last chance to escape the hangman's noose was gone, Rogers watched the work forlornly from his new upstairs cell. His extraordinary feat and near escape made him an instant folk hero on both sides of the border, and many people hoped he would be pardoned. A little over two weeks after his re-arrest, the military court set a new execution date for June 11, 1866, and carpenters began constructing a new gallows on "the prairie east of the city."[139]

As the day set for his hanging approached, Rodgers grew sullen and morose. Having come so close to escaping, the prospect of his imminent death weighed heavily on him. A day or two before his execution, Rodgers allowed one unidentified local photographer to take his likeness. In this image, he is seen wearing the shirt and jacket he was wearing when he was hanged. The seriousness of Rodgers's countenance is an indication of the dire situation in which he found himself.

If Rodgers felt bad the day his photograph was taken, he felt even worse on the day of his hanging. Terrified and grief stricken, he was barely able to walk, and a little before 3 P.M. he was dragged from his cell. Attended by two clergymen, he was placed in a cart with his arms securely pinioned and made to sit atop his coffin. He cried and moaned during the entire ride to the execution site. Upon seeing the gallows for the first time, "he trembled and groaned in the utmost agony." He had to be assisted to the top of the scaffold, but once there "fell down and gave himself up to the noisiest and most wretched paroxysms of grief, crying and sobbing like any child."[140] Rodgers was so mortified that he was unable to deliver his intended final speech. One of the clergymen then stepped forward and uttered a few words on his behalf. After a short prayer and the quick reading of the death warrant the noose was placed around his neck and Rodgers was forced to step on the trap door, which was sprung immediately. He fell four

Portrait of Juan Vela taken in his Fort Brown prison cell shortly before his execution, June 1866. Because of the poor light in the cell, the photograph was heavily retouched to show Vela's hair and beard. *Carte de visite* attributed to Louis de Planque or R. H. Wallis. *Lawrence T. Jones III collection.*

Portrait of *Cortinista* Vicente García taken in his prison cell at Fort Brown shortly before his execution on the same gallows from which Robert Rodgers had been hanged eleven days earlier in June 1866. *Carte de visite* attributed to Louis de Planque or R. H. Wallis. *Lawrence T. Jones III collection.*

Florencio Garza was the third man to have his portrait taken shortly before his execution on June 22, 1866. The photographs of the three condemned *Cortinistas* are the only known images of these men. *Carte de visite* attributed to Louis de Planque or R. H. Wallis. *Lawrence T. Jones III collection.*

feet, quivered two or three times, and was dead. "Poor Rodgers!" a newspaper reported. "He will kill no more men and will dig no more holes."[141]

The hanging of Private Rodgers was not the first in Brownsville. In the months before the Civil War, one of Cortina's 1859 raiders, Evaristo Rómulo, had been caught on the wrong side of the Rio Grande and hanged.[142] The hangings that generated the most interest, however, came in the summer of 1866. Fortunately for the historian, the men were photographed in their jail cells and at the time of their hanging. The rarest of these images shows the execution of three *Cortinistas*, condemned for murder during Cortina's 1859 raid on Brownsville. This 1866 *carte de visite* is the earliest known photographic image of a hanging in Texas. It is certainly among the earliest, if not the earliest, such photograph in the southern United

States. The execution of three of Cortina's men on the same gallows eleven days after Rodgers in 1866, however, was a truly sensational event that left a much deeper and lasting impression on the citizens of Brownsville and Matamoros. Three *Cortinistas*, Vicente García, Juan Vela and Florencio Garza, like Rómulo, had been with Cortina during his deadly Brownsville raid, and all had been indicted by a Cameron County grand jury for murder. Apprehended in early 1866, Juan Vela was convicted in the Brownsville District Court on May 15, 1866, and Vicente García and Florencio Garza four days later. District Judge Franklin Cummings sentenced all three to be publicly hanged on June 22.[143]

Even though their murder convictions were under the criminal laws of the state of Texas, the three doomed men were held in the same military

Standing on the gallows only seconds before the trap door is sprung are, from left to right, Vicente García, Juan Vela, and Florencio Garza. Father Parisot waits below, just to the right rear of the gallows, and a battalion of mounted U.S. cavalrymen stand guard in the background. *Carte de visite* attributed to Louis de Planque or R. H. Wallis. *Lawrence T. Jones III collection.*

prison as was Rodgers. From early morning on the day they were scheduled to die, a large crowd of citizens from both sides of the border assembled "as near as possible" to the prison.[144] Many of the spectators were sullen and unruly, so much so that the Cameron County sheriff was forced to deputize two hundred local men to prevent potential mob violence. As more and more Mexicans poured across the border toward the prison, it soon became apparent that a possible attempt to rescue the men might be made. The situation was so tense that the sheriff appealed to Gen. George Getty for military assistance. General Getty immediately called out the entire garrison at Fort Brown to prevent the possibility of any civil disturbances.

As the hour for their execution approached, P. F. Parisot, the Texas Catholic missionary in Brownsville, took the confessions of the three men.[145] The condemned trio had been kept in leg irons since their convictions. With the execution set for 3 P.M., the same time Rodgers had been hanged, a blacksmith was brought to their cells at two to remove their manacles. He worked awkwardly with a cold chisel and severely gashed the ankles of all three men. The prisoners, accompanied by Father Parisot, then limped from their cells and, like Rodgers, were escorted to a waiting cart. Well-armed deputies and a contingent of the Ninth U.S. Colored Troops with bayoneted rifles surrounded them.

On the cart were three coffins, on which the condemned men were forced to sit as they slowly rolled toward the gallows in the 100-degree heat and stifling humidity. There, Father Parisot guided them in the recitation of the Rosary. One of the prisoners shouted that he knew he was going to die, but that it was all right because Cortina would have the blood of every individual responsible for his death.[146] All three men displayed coolness and bravado as they nimbly mounted the ten steps to the top of the scaffold. Before their arms were bound, García and Vela waved their hats at the large multitude that had gathered.

An entire regiment of black troops surrounded the gallows on two sides. In the rear of the gallows was a battalion of mounted cavalry. Four pieces of artillery were placed on the front side, facing away from the gallows toward the civilians. On the front side were at least two photographers, probably Louis de Planque and R. H. Wallis, with their apparatus and portable darkrooms on carts. When the men's arms and legs had been bound and the nooses adjusted around their necks, one of the condemned men bellowed out an allusion to Rodgers, who had died such a cowardly death a few days earlier on the same scaffold. "When Americans come to be hung, they cry and behave like babies. Mexicans die like men and I intend to show it."[147] After a final prayer by Father Parisot, the death warrants were read, and the photographers were allowed to take a photograph of the prisoners just before the trap door was sprung.

The men fell four feet when the "drop" was released. Vicente García and Juan Vela died quickly and easily, but Florencio Garza struck the edge of the platform as he fell, which caused the jerk of the rope to be weakened. Since their hands had not been tied at the wrist and they were secured only at the elbows, Garza made a superhuman effort and raised one hand and then the other to the rope above his head, slowly lifting himself up as the throng of onlookers groaned and gasped. The executioner was forced to lie down on his stomach on the platform, reach down, and, after a severe struggle, wrench the dying Garza's hands from the rope. He literally pulled Garza up, readjusted the noose, and then let him drop again. It took another minute or two for Garza to die.

Chapter Six

IMPERIAL DREAMS
AND REPUBLICAN TRIUMPHS

The continued struggle for power south of the border generally overshadowed events on the north bank. On the evening of January 25, 1866, without a shot being fired, a combined force of Contra-Guerrillas, French marines, 120 Austrians, 100 *rurales*, and 300 Mexican lancers, some traveling on the *Camargo* and *Antonia* under the command of Lt. Col. Rodolien, were able to enter Bagdad.[1] The town was

found to be "completely empty and pillaged, abandoned both by the enemy as well as by all its inhabitants." The entire population of the town, perhaps as many as seven thousand citizens four weeks earlier, had dwindled to only "six or eight people." The Imperial occupiers began constructing what became a "splendid little redoubt," christened Fort Carlotta. Despite the protests of a number of Liberals, the *Imperialistas* even persuaded the Americans in Clarksville to return some of the plunder that had been taken in the previous raid and reestablish the stagecoach connection to Matamoros. On March 23, 1866, however, the Imperial force was battered by high winds that swept over the town from the southeast, demolishing the army's two-story barracks and frightening the citizenry.[2]

A week later in Matamoros, a grand review was held on the esplanade at which time the Austrian Corps, the Mejía Division, the Rural Militia, and Contra-Guerrillas paraded and formed in line of battle. Thousands of citizens poured forth to witness the "grand and imposing spectacle," at which time General Mejía was presented with the Grand Cross of the Order of the Mexican Eagle by a representative of the Emperor Maximilian.[3]

Imperial hopes for holding Matamoros heightened as the Liberal forces were unable to obtain any unity of command. In a region with a long history of failed federalism, the national interest of the Republican government was plagued by the virtual autonomy of the various generals in Tamaulipas, many of whom were jealous of each other. Isolated from the central government, they remained irresolute and uncooperative. Certainly Cortina was one of the most intrepid fighters, but he was seen as an outcast, more for having served in the Imperial army than for his fierce independence. Cortina even attacked but was badly beaten by the forces of Servando Canales, who then proclaimed his brother, Tristan, as governor of Tamaulipas. On the north bank, the large United States military presence, numbering as many as ten thousand troops, began to clamp down on Cortina's unquestioned use of Texas soil to launch raids into Mexico. The Federals even seized three of his cannon that had been secreted in the dense chaparral upriver from Brownsville.[4] The military was forced to take action following the killing of a captain and severe wounding of another officer in the Ninth Maryland U.S. Colored Troops a few miles above Brownsville as well as the murder of a courier on his way from Brownsville to Brazos Santiago.[5]

On April 30, 1866, Gen. Rafael Olvera, commanding the Imperial cavalry, was able to rout Cortina at Palo Blanco, thirty miles above Matamoros. Cortina's pickets were taken before they could sound the alarm, and Cortina's encampment in a dense thicket was overrun. Most of the *Cortinistas* were said to be "lying around, sleeping, smoking, and card playing," when the attack was made.[6] While running for their lives, many of the *Cortinistas* were shot and sabered by the pursuing Imperialists. Cortina himself narrowly escaped capture by mounting a bareback horse and racing away in a hail of bullets. In the camp, Cortina's personal effects, consisting of his horse, saddle, pocket book, watch, and money, along with his official correspondence and a sword that General McClernand had presented him, were all seized, along with a small silver bugle.[7] With cathedral bells ringing and thousands of citizens crowding the streets and rooftops, 118 *Cortinistas* were paraded through the streets of Matamoros. The prisoners were in wretched condition, "dirty, ragged—some more than half naked—bareheaded, barefooted, and really looking as if they felt it would be a kindness to shoot them at once, and put them out of their misery," a correspondent recorded.[8]

Although May 1866 was relatively quiet in Matamoros, June would bring the undoing of General Mejía's Imperial forces on the Rio Grande. At daylight on June 7 a huge column stretching for more than six miles and consisting of two hundred large wagons containing $3 million in merchandise pulled by two thousand mules departed Matamoros for Monterrey under the command of General Olvera. The column consisted of 290 Austrians and 1,110 Mexicans, including cavalry, a company of Contra-Guerillas, a company of *rurales*, engineers, and eight pieces of artillery. Moving through the thick chaparral without adequate water, the march became a nightmare. On

Gen. Tomás Mejia, Imperial Mexican army and commander of Imperial forces in Matamoros. General Mejía was executed with Maximilian. *Carte de visite* by Louis de Planque, ca. 1865. *Lawrence T. Jones III collection.*

the first day out, five men died of sunstroke in the heat and stifling dust. Three more succumbed on the second day. To quench their intense thirst, the men began eating the *tunas* of the prickly pear cactus and, as a result, fell sick with violent diarrhea and began to vomit profusely.[9] To complicate matters, *Juaristas* under Gen. Jerónimo Treviño, the Philip Sheridan of Mexico, harassed the column from both sides of the narrow road, although

Gen. Jerónimo Treviño was commander of cavalry, Mexican Republican Army of the North. *Carte de visite* by Louis de Planque, ca. 1867. *La Retama Public Library, Corpus Christi, Texas.*

Gen. Mariano Escobedo, commander of the Republican Army of the North. *Carte de visite* by Louis de Planque, ca. 1865–1866. *La Retama Public Library, Corpus Christi, Texas.*

rounds of grapeshot fired into the dense chaparral by the Imperial artillery frequently sent the guerrillas scurrying for cover. Slowing the column even more was the fact that deep arroyos had to be filled in by the Mexican engineering company.

Learning that the convoy was scheduled to depart Matamoros and that a large force would be moving from Monterrey to join them, Gen. Mariano Escobedo, commanding the *Juarista* Army of the North, ordered his badly scattered armies into action. From his headquarters at Linares, Escobedo positioned a division of infantry at China, a cavalry brigade at Paso del Zacate, and another cavalry brigade on the road between Monterrey and Cerralvo. At the same time, Gen. Jerónimo Treviño was sent to impede the column of French and Mexicans leaving Monterrey. Treviño threw up obstacles and poisoned or filled the watering holes with rotting debris. Although the column from Monterrey reached Cerralvo on June

12, Escobedo learned from a captured messenger that the French would not move again until the column from Matamoros reached Mier. As a result he changed plans and ordered his scattered armies to undertake a forced march for Camargo. By June 15 Escobedo was in position southeast of Camargo, just west of the Mesa de Santa Gertrudis, along the Camargo–Monterrey Road.[10] Here he bivouacked his army, blocking the *Imperialistas'* access to water. As advance scouts for both the *Imperialistas* and the *Juaristas* came in contact, both armies camped for the night. Austrian Lt. Ernst Pitner remembered being "greeted with a veritable volley from the shrubberies running alongside the camp." Hungry and without water, many of the men in the Imperial army slept with their arms. To quench their burning thirst, some were given wine, which made their dehydration even worse. Many realized their peril. A veteran officer, Captain Alvárez warned Lieutenant Pitner:

"Tomorrow there will be confusion the like of which one will not often witness."[11]

Escobedo arranged his army into five attacking columns with a sixth column in reserve. At 4 A.M. in the early morning darkness of June 16, the Imperial column was on the move, with the two Austrian Rifle Companies in the advance and the wagons driven in groups of four in the middle. Sighting the *Juaristas* on the horizon, General Olvera sent his two Austrian companies forward in columns with part of the artillery in between. He then brought up a company of Mexican *Zapadores*, then the cavalry, with the Contra-Guerrillas in the rear. For more than half an hour, the Imperial army slowly advanced, the artillery frequently unlimbering to fire at the retreating *Juaristas*. Finally the advance of the Imperial army reached the crest of the Mesa de la Santa Gertrudis.

On the opposite side of the mesa Escobedo had concealed his cavalry in a thicket of mesquite trees and ordered his infantry to lay flat on the ground. The *Juaristas* waited until the Imperial forces were within rifle shot and then ordered a frontal attack. "The enemy," Lieutenant Pitner wrote, "broke out of a woodlands and in close order advanced offensively towards us." Just as the Imperial forces advanced on the *Juarista* left, Escobedo ordered General Treviño's cavalry into action. With the rattle of spurs, Treviño's horsemen were able to completely turn the Imperial flank, driving back the Imperial cavalry, who retreated at a gallop. At this point much of the fighting became hand-to-hand. "It was a moment of the most frightful small-arms fire, and the men in their ranks fell down dead in droves," Lieutenant Pitner recalled.[12] With little alternative, the Austrians fixed bayonets and with the cry of "hurrah" gallantly charged into the *Juarista* infantry only to be attacked by a second column of Escobedo's infantry with the Liberal battle cry of "Viva la libertad!" With half their men killed or wounded, and supported only by a company of Mexican *Zapadores*, the Austrians ran for the safety of the wagons. Surrounded by both infantry and cavalry and realizing their situation to be hopeless, 350 men of the Sierra Gorda Imperial infantry stuck their rifles in the ground with the point of their bayonets and began to cry "Viva la libertad" as they surrendered.

"The combat with side-arms was of short duration, having ended at seven in the morning with the complete destruction of the austrio-traitor forces," General Escobedo wrote.[13] Besides capturing millions of dollars in valuable goods, Escobedo's gallant *Juaristas* seized more than a thousand muskets, eight pieces of Imperial artillery, and a huge amount of ammunition and military equipment, including gun carriages, lances, and sabers. Even the Imperial band and their cornets, clarinets, and drums were taken. The Imperial army was decimated. In all, 165 men had been wounded, 396 killed, and hundreds taken prisoner. Only a few officers in the Imperial Mexican cavalry escaped. The "miserable cowards,"

BATTLE OF SANTA GERTRUDIS: JUNE 16, 1866

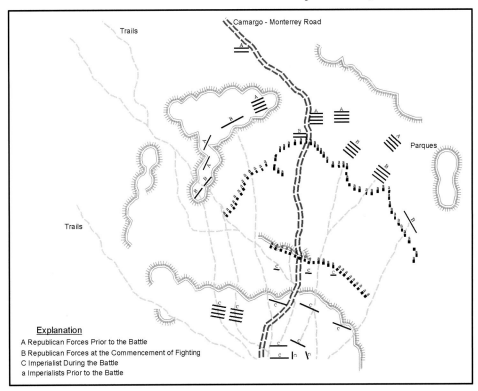

Trails

Camargo - Monterrey Road

Parques

Trails

Explanation
A Republican Forces Prior to the Battle
B Republican Forces at the Commencement of Fighting
C Imperialist During the Battle
a Imperialists Prior to the Battle

Col. Servando Canales. After General Mejía fled from Matamoros in August 1866, Canales took control of Matamoros and proclaimed himself military governor. *Carte de visite* by Louis de Planque, ca. 1866. *Brownsville Historical Association.*

Escobedo wrote, "had not the courage to brave death on the field of battle, but trusted their lives and safety to the fleetness of their horses."[14] In the Republican army, Escobedo lost 155 men killed.[15] "The fighting was very severe and the slaughter fearful on both sides," the American commercial agent in Matamoros recorded.[16] Shortly after the battle, a few of the Mexican Imperial officers were singled out as having previously ordered the execution of *Juaristas*, and they were taken away and shot, especially those in the Contra-Guerrillas. The hundreds of wounded from both sides were hauled in wagons to Camargo to a makeshift hospital. Lying on mud and stone floors in the oppressive heat and with little medical care, many expired within days.

The battle of Santa Gertrudis proved to be the Waterloo of the Imperial army in northern Mexico. The disaster was, the *Brownsville Daily Ranchero* wrote, "a death blow to the reign of [the] Empire in Northern Mexico."[17] "The national arms are once more crowned with glory," Escobedo wrote in triumph. "Let us hasten onward, fellow soldiers and capture Matamoros; then we can have time to rest."[18] Across the mountains and deserts of northern Mexico the tide of battle began to change. Fed by mounting support from the north, long the hotbed of republican rule in Mexico, *Juaristas* everywhere gathered momentum. The war, which had been seen by many as a dispute between conservative and liberal Mexican parties, increasingly became a war against the foreigner.

Receiving news of the disaster at Santa Gertrudis, General Mejía evacuated Bagdad on the night of June 18. With his garrison in Matamoros reduced to six hundred men and facing a growing number of desertions, Mejía was forced to conclude that the city could no longer be held. Only six days after the disaster at Santa Gertrudis, he concluded an agreement with the newly proclaimed governor of Tamaulipas, José María Jesús Carbajal.[19] Mejía would evacuate Matamoros within forty-eight hours providing the Imperial army would be allowed to leave the city by land and by river to Bagdad without being molested.[20] In a meeting with Gen. George Washington Getty, commanding the District of the Rio Grande, it was agreed that Mejía could even use steamers flying the American flag to depart the city. With flags flying and drums beating, the Imperial army marched out with their arms, ammunition, baggage, and two 6-pounder artillery pieces and embarked on the *Colonel Holcomb*, *Eugenia*, and *Colonel Benedict*. No sooner were the men on board than church bells rang out and citizens rushed into the streets to celebrate.[21] With the evacuation of Matamoros, no Imperial armies remained on the Rio Grande frontier.

General Escobedo was furious when he learned that General Mejía had been allowed to escape unscathed. From distant Chihuahua, President

Col. Servando Canales. Another portrait of Canales shows him wearing a different jacket and without his hat. *Carte de visite* by Louis de Planque, ca. 1866. *Enrique Guerra collection.*

General Servanda Cannales, Commanding Corps, Armies of Mexico.

Juárez declared the actions of Carbajal "null and of no force, because those who made it on the part of the republican government had not the proper authority."[22] Moreover, Carbajal and his chief lieutenant, Juan José de la Garza, were ordered to be court-martialed. To complicate matters, Cortina issued a *pronunciamiento* at Camargo on August 21, once again proclaiming himself governor.[23] Before General Escobedo could reach the heroic city, Col. Servando Canales, assisted by Gen. Pedro Hinojosa, proclaimed himself military governor on August 12, deposing Carbajal, who was "not fit to govern," in a bloodless *coup d'état*. Carbajal, along with Lew Wallace, who was consistently involved in Mexican affairs, as were several other Americans, fled to Brownsville. Hoping to solidify power in the city, Canales issued a *pronunciamiento* promising "independence and liberty" and to lay all "animosities aside."[24] Hearing of the chaos in Matamoros, Foreign Secretary Sebastián Lerdo de Tejada, reflecting the thoughts of President Juárez, nullified Canales's actions. Moreover, Gen. Santiago Tapia, a loyal Liberal, was proclaimed military governor, and Canales and Hinojosa were immediately ordered to Chihuahua "to answer for their actions." No hope for the "salvation of the country can be entertained, if a stop is not put to military revolts," Lerdo de Tejada concluded.[25]

Thirsting for power in Tamaulipas and influenced by the Matamoros merchant elite, Canales was not about to give up Matamoros or report to Chihuahua. Said to have been even more ruthless than Cortina, he was determined to hold the city at all costs. When one of the garrisons manning one of the forts protecting the city declared against him, he had the garrison subdued and six of the

Constant & Stephen,   Matamoras.

A group of Austrian soldiers of the Mexican Imperial army in Matamoros. *Carte de visite* by Constant and Stephen, ca. 1865. *Lawrence
T. Jones III collection.*

Monterrey and then assaulted the fortified
Casa Mata near the Plaza de Independencia and the northwestern gates to the city.
Canales, however, was able to reinforce the
garrison, and the *Cortinistas* were driven
off.[28] Yet by late November Escobedo was
in front of the city with several thousand
men demanding that Canales surrender.

After enjoying breakfast in Matamoros
with the leading merchants, many of them
American, Col. Thomas D. Sedgwick, commanding the garrison at Fort Brown, was
persuaded to intervene. Sedgwick was
encouraged by rumors that Canales could
no longer pay his troops and was preparing
to turn them loose on the city. Despite
explicit written instructions not to intervene in Mexican affairs, on November 23,
1866, Sedgwick sent 118 men of Companies E and I of the black Fourth U.S. Cavalry, under the command of J. G. Perkins,
across the river. Officially, the men were to
protect "American citizens and their property" and "guard the city and prevent
bloodshed between the two contending
parties."[29] The next day in Brownsville,
several small boats were hauled to the foot
of Thirteenth Street and gently slid into the
Rio Grande. Floated down the river to the
ferry landing at Fourteenth Street and
anchored, a pontoon bridge, or what the
newspapers called "Sedgwick's Bridge,"
was hastily thrown up connecting the ferry
landing in Brownsville with Santa Cruz on
the Mexican side of the river.

When Perkins fell ill, Sedgwick replaced
him with Col. A. M. Randall of the First
Artillery. Within hours, the American troopers had
occupied the Plaza de Hidalgo and the Stars and
Stripes was floating over Matamoros.[30] The next
day Canales agreed to surrender the city, under the
condition that his men could retain their weapons
and continue to hold the city's defenses. In hopes
of avoiding bloodshed, while at the same time protecting the merchants and their hardware, Sedgwick was able to persuade Canales to visit with
Escobedo. Arriving at Escobedo's camp in the
early evening, Escobedo refused to see Canales for

men hanged.[26] Men were frequently whipped for
minor disciplinary discretions and threatened with
execution if they were caught deserting. To avoid
such revolts, Canales paid his men daily and
organized a large and loyal bodyguard.[27] As
Canales attempted to solidify power, Cortina continued to lurk in the chaparral, cutting all communications and consistently threatening to attack
the city. Able to pay his troops from a forced loan,
or *prestamos*, on the merchants who had returned
to Bagdad, Cortina feigned an attack on Fort

over an hour, swearing "like a Turk" in the process.[31] Finally acquiescing, the two men met in the corner of a room. Voices were raised and the two men became so angry that observers thought the two were about to fight. When their tempers calmed slightly, Canales offered to negotiate the surrender of the city, providing that Escobedo compensated the merchants for the funds previously advanced to Canales, said to be as much as $600,000.[32] Escobedo refused, and the meeting ended in "bickering and recrimination"; nothing was accomplished.

Before daylight on the morning of November 27, 1866, Escobedo, with fifteen hundred men, ordered an all-out attack on the city. While Cortina feigned an assault on the southern and eastern defenses, Escobedo launched a ferocious attack on the north. Forts Guadalupe, San Fernando, Freeport, and Monterrey all fell under heavy artillery fire. But the fourteen guns guarding the forts and Casa Mata took a terrible toll on Escobedo's men. At Fort Monterrey, in particular, the fighting was fierce. One thousand men at double-quick time approached within thirty yards before the defenders opened fire. One company of Austrians, who had joined the Liberals after the disaster at Santa Gertrudis, were said to have lost half their men in the attack. One observer thought Escobedo's men were close to carrying the fortifications when reinforcements appeared and the charging columns began to waiver. Both "the infantry and cavalry joined in the firing, and the columns of Escobedo were rolled back, leaving the ground strewn with the dead and dying."[33] In the assault, many of the bridges constructed to span the moat proved to be too short and scaling ladders were not available. Once the attack faltered, Canales, who commanded Fort Monterrey in person, ordered his infantry and cavalry in pursuit. About five hundred yards from the fort at a spot where a lagoon could only be crossed by a narrow bridge, fighting was hand-to-hand. In ten minutes Escobedo lost

Capt. R. C. Lorin of General Mejía's staff. *Carte de visite* by Louis de Planque, ca. 1866. *Martin L. Callahan collection.*

250 men killed and 150 taken prisoner. One of those killed in the bloody pursuit was Canales's brother, Modesto, who fell by Canales's side.[34]

At Fort San Fernando on the eastern outskirts of the city, Cortina's Tamaulipas Brigade, too, formed in a long line, much in the European tradition, and marched on the fortifications. Certain that they would carry the works, the men were given the watchword of "Oaxaca" and the countersign of "Durango." Without uniforms and to prevent being confused with the defenders, the

Gen. Felipe Berriozábal (seated, center) and his staff in the courtyard at Louis de Planque's Matamoros gallery, April 1867. This particular photograph is mentioned in the April 5, 1867, *Brownsville Daily Ranchero*: "That Prince of Photographers Senor Du (sic) Planque has left at our office the picture of a group composed of Gen. Berriozábal and staff. . . . There are twenty-three all told persons represented, with foreheads high which indicates talent sufficient to rule all of Mexico." *Carte de visite* by Louis de Planque. *Brownsville Historical Association.*

Cortinistas were ordered to wear "a green leaf of any kind of plant."[35] Here also, Canales's defenders waited until the advancing column was within twenty yards before opening a devastating rifle and artillery fire. "No set of men ever made a more gallant display of valor, and no set of men were ever more suddenly defeated, dispersed, annihilated," an American officer observed.[36] Retreating with heavy losses, Cortina's men fell back into the chaparral. Several unsuccessful attacks were also made on Fort Paredes on the river, opposite Freeport, but the fighting there was not as severe as elsewhere.

About 11 A.M. at Fort Zaragoza, for example, Escobedo's gallant attackers advanced across a bridge spanning a lagoon near the fort and were easily repulsed. Eight of those advancing were killed or wounded. Many of the officers who were wounded were carried across the river for medical care in Brownsville. Falling back, Escobedo promised to renew the attack. In three hours of bloody fighting Escobedo lost several hundred killed, as many as four hundred wounded, and between three hundred and four hundred taken prisoners, while Canales lost seventy-five killed.[37]

During this time, the Americans continued to occupy Plaza de Hidalgo and the ferry at Santa Cruz. Orders were given that the forces of Escobedo were not to be fired on should they enter the city. By prior arrangement the Americans were to withdraw, leaving only a small provost guard behind.[38] To assure their safety during the withdrawal, Sedgwick ordered a battery of the First U.S. Artillery to occupy the Brownsville bank near the ferry.

In the midst of the fighting Colonel Randall sent a flag of truce to Escobedo. If Escobedo carried the defenses, Randall asked him not to fire on the American troops in Matamoros. Escobedo responded by inquiring what Randall's intentions were in occupying the city. The American colonel responded that his forces were under orders not to

Gen. Felipe Berriozábal. General Berriozábal was adjutant to Gen. Mariano Escobedo, Mexican Republican Army of the North. *Carte de visite* attributed to Louis de Planque, ca. 1867. *Brownsville Historical Association.*

Santiago Vidaurri, governor of Tamaulipas. As one of the most powerful men in Mexico, Vidaurri was later executed by the *Juaristas* in Mexico City on July 8, 1867. *Carte de visite* by Louis de Planque, ca. 1865–1866. *La Retama Public Library, Corpus Christi, Texas.*

fire on either side, that his intentions were to protect Americans and their property. When Escobedo refused to give Randall any information, Sedgwick placed all the American forces on the north bank in a state of readiness to cross the river should Escobedo carry the works and the Americans come under fire. In addition, 250 men under "Rip" Ford were hastily organized in Brownsville, including Confederate and Union Civil War veterans, citizens, and even "strangers."[39]

No sooner were the Americans in position than Sedgwick received a telegram from General Sheridan from New Orleans ordering him to withdraw. The pontoon bridge connecting Brownsville with

Santa Cruz was dismantled just as quickly as it had been constructed. Leaving fifty men to guard the plaza and a small guard at the ferry, the Americans re-crossed the river to Brownsville. "The object of the occupation," General Sheridan wrote Gen. Ulysses S. Grant, "was for the alleged purpose of protecting American citizens, but the real facts are that he was made the cat's-paw of shrewd merchants of Matamoros, who wanted to secure the liabilities which were due to them from Canales before he was obliged to give up the city to the liberal forces."[40] In Sheridan's mind, there was little doubt that the Matamoros "merchants were at the bottom of all the troubles over

City police captain, Matamoros. *Carte de visite* by Louis de Planque, ca. 1866. *Lawrence T. Jones III collection.*

to Brownsville. Arriving on the Rio Grande on the early morning of December 6, 1866, Sheridan concluded that although the American intervention was "unauthorized," it had essentially been "harmless," and with Escobedo's occupation of the city, a "very good condition of affairs . . . existed in Matamoros."[44] Sheridan, along with Lewis D. Campbell, United States minister to Mexico, crossed the river to meet with Escobedo, who asked that Sedgwick be released from arrest. Sedgwick returned to his regiment in early February.[45]

Although badly battered and demoralized, Escobedo retreated, only to reappear and begin digging parallel trenches in front of Forts Monterrey and Zaragoza. Cortina's Tamaulipas Brigade began to also entrench in the chaparral in front of Fort San Fernando.[46] Learning that Gen. Jerónimo Treviño would be arriving in a few days from Monterrey to reinforce Escobedo, Canales realized his hold on Matamoros was slipping, and he immediately entered into discussions with Colonel Sedgwick as to the possibilities of surrendering to the

there."[41] Colonel Sedgwick was not a "strong man" and he had "been simply outwitted by a combination of military and civil influences, the latter mostly of American nationality," the Brownsville *Rio Grande Courier* concluded.[42] Secretary of War Edwin Stanton ordered Sedgwick relieved of command and placed under arrest.[43]

General Sheridan, after meeting with Gen. William T. Sherman at Brazos Santiago, hurried on

American forces with his men crossing the river as prisoners of war. Since the United States and Mexico were not at war, however, it was difficult to see how his men could be classified as prisoners of war. In the end, negotiations were renewed with Escobedo, and, despite the bloodletting in the preceding days, the two combatants were able to agree on a compromise. Escobedo would march into the city, and the two would unite their forces to fight the *Imperialistas* else-where. "The terms of surrender are unconditional and still conditional," the *Ranchero* remarked. Without resistance, early on the morning of December 1, 1866, Escobedo and Cortina and their men slowly moved into the city and took possession of the upper forts. Always popular with the people of Matamoros, Cortina was widely cheered by many in the city. "The troops of both armies are now parading through the town . . . and apparently upon the most friendly terms," it was said.[47]

Although Escobedo now held the upper hand in Matamoros, the *Juarista caudillos*, with their designs on the lucrative proceeds of the Matamoros customhouse, continued to jockey for power. Escobedo contemplated calling for elections, but knew Cortina would emerge the victor because of his popularity in Matamoros. Carbajal hoped to become governor, but he was unpopular and few trusted him. It was also rumored that Canales, who was still under orders to report to Juárez, would insist on his aging father, Antonio Canales, as governor. Disregarding both Canales and Cortina, Escobedo left his trusted adjutant, Felipe Berriozábal, in command at Matamoros and struck out for Monterrey and central Mexico and the epic events that would unfold at Querétaro. Cortina and Canales were ordered to follow, but the two, with no money to pay their men, hesitated. Claiming that he would obey Escobedo but not Berriozábal, Cortina eventually moved upriver to occupy Reynosa, Camargo, Mier, and even Guerrero, recruiting and levying *prestamos*, or

Mexican mother preparing to follow her husband in the army. In Mexico it was not uncommon for a wife to accompany her husband on the march. This scene shows a mother, loaded with supplies and her children, as she prepares to leave and join her husband's military command. *Carte de visite* by Louis de Planque, ca. 1866. *Lawrence T. Jones III collection.*

forcing loans, as well as circulating a petition that called on Juárez to appoint him governor of Tamaulipas.[48] When he returned to the Lower Valley, Cortina lingered about Matamoros and proclaimed himself loyal to Juárez, but still threatened to attack the city. With General Berriozábal outnumbered two to one, many on the border speculated that Cortina would take Matamoros by storm. Finally able to raise enough money from the merchants in Matamoros to appease the *Cortinistas*, Cortina, too, marched off to the south and destiny at Querétaro.[49]

By the spring of 1867, with Napoleon III ordering the French army out of Mexico, Emperor Maximilian was left to the mercy of Juárez and the Liberals. On June 19, 1867, following the defeat of what remained of the Mexican Imperial army, the emperor, along with Gen. Tomás Mejía and Miguel Miramón, was executed on El Cerro de la Campanas outside Querétaro. Three weeks later, on July 8, the once powerful Santiago Vidaurri, who had served as Maximilian's minister of finance, was found hiding in a house in Mexico City. Dragged into the streets and beaten, he was executed by firing squad in a dung heap as several hundred citizens cheered and bands played.[50] The collapse of the empire, however, did not end the political intrigue nor violence in Mexico.

Complicating matters on the Rio Grande was the vain and personally ambitious Jesús González Ortega, who claimed to be the constitutionally elected president of Mexico. Rumors persisted that Cortina or Canales were preparing to swear allegiance to Ortega and attack Escobedo.[51] Although he was said to have a large following in northern Mexico and Brownsville, Ortega feared that he would be detained south of the border. He crossed to the north bank, where he was hoping to travel to New York to enlist American volunteers, but was arrested by the U.S. Army on the evening of November 3, 1866, while on board the steamship *St. Mary.*[52] Ortega was taken to New Orleans but released and sent to Mexico City. In the capital he issued a *pronunciamiento* asserting his claim to the presidency and protesting his treatment in the United States, only to be arrested and imprisoned.[53] Historical transformation was again the order of the day on the Rio Grande.

Chapter Seven

THE GREAT STORM OF 1867 AND THE END OF AN ERA

On January 2, 1867, a rare South Texas snowstorm swept over the Lower Valley, leaving as much as three inches of snow on the streets of Matamoros and Brownsville. With the thermometer at twenty-four degrees, citizens streamed into the streets for snowball fights. In Brownsville, parties hooked animals to makeshift sleds and scampered "through town as though a pack of Laplanders." One group constructed a "Yankee" made of snow on the banks of the river overlooking Matamoros.[1]

A yellow fever epidemic raged along the Texas coast well into the summer of 1867, killing thousands and taking a terrible toll on civilians in Galveston, Houston, Indianola, Corpus Christi, and in the army in military camps in Victoria, Huntsville, and San Antonio. Although a self-imposed quarantine temporarily devastated the local economy, Brownsville and the Rio Grande Valley largely escaped the deadly pestilence.[2]

The climatic abnormalities of early January 1867 would pale in comparison to what happened in October of that year. Friday and Saturday, October 4 and 5, proved to be unseasonably warm. On October 6 a few citizens noticed that the barometer fell dramatically. Yet few could envision what was to happen in the next forty-eight-hours. At first citizens noticed a gentle, northerly breeze, "cool, fresh and bracing, having a momentum of no more than twenty-five or thirty miles per hour." By late afternoon the winds had accelerated; by nightfall rain began to fall in torrents, and residents realized they were in the fearful grasp of a hurricane. Well into the early evening the storm raged, dark gloomy clouds descending as gust after gust swept over the twin cities, each time with increasing violence and velocity. "Trees began to be dismembered and crushed, buildings began to rock to and fro with every blast, and the rain came in sheets and dashes, like the breaking of furious seas over the brow of a stranded vessel," the *Ranchero* reported. Roofs were ripped off houses, and the structures crashed to earth as frightened citizens scurried for safety. Tin roofs in particular went flying and banging through the streets. Residents watched as "planks, timbers, and all sorts of loose and shattered fragments were falling thick and fast."[3] A local physician's yard fence, constructed of three hundred wooden barrels, two deep and two high, went bouncing "over house tops . . . up and down alleys . . . rolled, tumbled and jumped from side to side of the streets [and] went to pieces and the separated staves went rolling on."[4]

As the hurricane hissed and roared and the destruction escalated, panic-stricken citizens fled into the streets, hoping to find refuge in secure buildings. Others huddled in prayer. By 10 P.M. the awful storm seemed only to intensify. With a com-

Men stand and sit atop a pile of bricks from a collapsed building in Matamoros after the hurricane of October 7, 1867. *Carte de visite* by Louis de Planque. *Brownsville Historical Association.*

bined population of thirty thousand, both Brownsville and Matamoros "were converted into a howling earthly hell."[5] Suddenly, as if by divine intervention, the bellowing winds ceased, the rain stopped, and an ominous lull set in. A full moon lent a pale, eerie appearance to the ruins as shocked citizens by the thousands, assuming the hurricane was over, flooded into the moonlit streets to survey the damage and help the distressed and injured. Within an hour, however, winds with a deafening roar, even more intense than before, swept out of the southwest, causing many citizens to think they had now become victims of a tornado. In reality, the two cities had been in the eye of the storm.[6] With the winds increasing to an ever frightening velocity, even sturdy brick structures began to collapse. Lightning flashed about as the shrieking winds muted the thunder. One resident compared the deafening noise overhead to "a thousand trains of cars passing over a thousand bridges at full speed." Wood buildings, including stores and residences, were

tossed into the air and "wretched into a thousand fragments, and then dashed back upon the city with fearful violence." Citizens who lost their homes and were unable to find refuge clung to street posts. One family literally had their clothing blown from their bodies and were totally naked upon reaching safety.[7] Timbers were driven through brick walls as if they had been fired from a cannon. The Presbyterian and Episcopal churches in Brownsville were destroyed. The ornate and gothic Immaculate Concepción Cathedral suffered serious damage. The Catholic convent collapsed and thirteen young women were killed.[8] The Cameron County Courthouse was destroyed. So was the Cameron County jail, and inmates fled into the night. At the corner of Elizabeth and Thirteenth streets, only a block from the Matamoros ferry, Henry Miller's hotel and adjacent billiard parlor were badly damaged.[9] The three-story building that housed the *Brownsville Daily Ranchero* collapsed, and the newspaper was suspended for six weeks. Somers Kinney, one of the *Ranchero* editors, had his leg broken.[10] The office of the *Rio Grande Courier* also was damaged, and on Elizabeth Street the post office was blown away. Even the sturdy Market House suffered structural damage. In one business, a four-feet-tall safe weighing 1,600 pounds was blown against a door. The storm blasted the door off the building, and the safe was found turned on its side.[11] Streets and alleys were clogged with debris. In all, fourteen buildings were destroyed along Levee Street, twenty buildings along Elizabeth Street, twelve on Washington Street, and hundreds of other homes and buildings throughout the city.[12] One of the few prominent structures in the city that survived unscathed was the two-and one-half story St. Joseph's College.[13] Three thousand Brownsville families were said to have lost everything. Perhaps hardest hit were the poorer residents, many of whom lived in simple one- or two-room *jacales* with thatched roofs, who watched in horror as their homes were swept away in the darkness. "As we sander amid the crumbling ruins of fallen walls," the *Rio Grande Courier* reported, "and see the crowds of homeless poor, we feel

incapable to give the merest conception of that night of terrors." In "the midst of life we are in death," the newspaper continued.[14]

Matamoros was also devastated in the "Great Storm of 1867." More than fifteen hundred homes were seriously damaged or destroyed, and losses were placed at five million dollars.[15] The entire block of buildings bounded by Seventh, Eighth, Herrera, and Bustamante streets was flattened while the block bounded by Sixth, Seventh, Guerrero, and Caesar streets was destroyed. The cathedral was badly damaged, although the buildings around the Plaza de la Independencia largely survived the storm. The houses on the Plaza de Hidalgo, however, were badly damaged.[16] At the ferry crossing at Santa Cruz, nothing was left standing. The customhouse and two large ice-houses were flattened, ten people were killed, and twenty injured.[17]

Several of King and Kenedy's steamboats, anchored along Levee Street in Brownsville, were sent crashing about and the *Camargo* and *Sandusky* sank. The *Colonel Bennett, San Roman*, and *Tamaulipas No. 1* were seriously damaged and

Matamoros after the hurricane of October 7, 1867. *Carte de visite* by Louis de Planque. *Brownsville Historical Association.*

their paddle wheels destroyed. The *Matamoros* was swept down the river and wrecked. Only the *Tamaulipas No. 2* escaped serious damage. The loss to King and Kenedy was said to be over $200,000.[18] "What became of King & Kenedy's steamers?" a gentleman later asked. "They are scattered all over the country; some are in the chaparral, some are on the prairie, some on the bottom and some on top of the river, and some were blown entirely away. Most of them went bodily to kingdom come. Any one who wants a steamboat now, can get it at his own price," the *Brownsville Daily Ranchero* reported, half in jest.[19]

It was later learned that the storm, eighty miles wide and dealing death and destruction everywhere it went, had come roaring off the Gulf of Mexico after raking the Texas coast. It struck the Mexican coast fifteen miles south of Bagdad before bearing down on Brownsville and Matamoros. The situation on Brazos Island and in Bagdad, Clarksville, Point Isabel, and La Burrita was even worse than in Brownsville and Matamoros.

On Brazos Island the storm sent waves entirely over the island, sweeping away every house but two. The United States customhouse, including furniture and records, was swept away.[20] Residents and the black garrison on the island fled in panic. Taking only what possessions they could carry, most of the 150 residents sought refuge half a mile away in the sand dunes near the lighthouse. The loss of life on the island would have been far greater, however, had not many of the women and children found safety on the schooner *Volumnia*, which was anchored at the port when the storm struck.[21]

On Brazos Island, in the "midst of floating roofs, ambulance beds, and bales of hay," three men sought safety in a small skiff. When the boat capsized, two of the men were drowned, and the lone survivor, J. T. Sayles, was knocked unconscious. Revived and clinging to the small boat, he was swept several miles out to sea before being washed ashore ten miles to the north on Padre Island. Surviving on sand crabs and a piece of can-

Mexican soldiers and civilians, including the ex-Confederate at right who still wears his Texas star two-piece belt buckle, examine a damaged house in Matamoros. *Carte de visite* by Louis de Planque, October 1867. *Martin L. Callahan collection.*

This view of hurricane damage was taken not far from Louis de Planque's gallery on Abasolo Street. *Carte de visite* by Louis de Planque, October 1867. *Brownsville Historical Association.*

dle, the badly injured Sayles made his way north along Padre Island to finally reach Corpus Christi.[22] One family known to be living on the southern end of Padre Island was never seen again.

After the storm had subsided on Brazos Island, pillagers commenced their dastardly work at what had once been a thriving community. Although the army placed guards around what little property remained and one looter was shot, some of the black soldiers were accused of participating in the plunder themselves.[23] For days after the storm, the survivors sifted through the wreckage for anything eatable, erecting cooking stoves and cooking whatever they could salvage.

At Clarksville, as the tide rolled through the town, several citizens drowned, and only a few houses were left standing. Across the river at Bagdad, more than one hundred citizens were killed, and only four houses survived. As the Gulf boiled over, water fourteen feet deep went crashing through Bagdad and poured inland as far as La Burrita.[24] Several schooners and lighters were swept inland and wrecked. Ninety frightened citizens who sought refuge on the *Antonia* watched as the steamer was swept five miles inland. The boat was later found on the Texas side of the river, several hundred yards from the Rio Grande.[25] Another steamer, the *Rio Grande,* went aground

half a mile from the river. For days after the storm, victims continued to be found in the wreckage or buried in the sand. A few were never found. On October 15 alone, thirty persons were buried.[26] "We are in the greatest distress," one citizen wrote, "everything is lost; nothing saved; not even provisions."[27] In the isolated communities on the coast in the days following the storm, hunger became a serious problem. More than 140 residents of Bagdad, Clarksville, and Brazos Santiago were reported to be in a wretched condition when the *Tamaulipas No. 2* arrived to transport them safely to Brownsville.[28]

Killing cattle and destroying houses, the "Great Storm of 1867" swept inland, passing north of Edinburg. Continuing into northern Starr and Zapata counties, even a brick residence on the Laredo–Corpus Christi road was blown down. The hurricane, the worst in the recorded history of South Texas, did not play out until far into the interior. Those who had survived would never forget the killing winds and torrential rains of October 1867.

Always offering pointed and barbed opinions on the tumultuous events at Matamoros and Brownsville and throughout the United States and Mexico was the *Daily Ranchero*, a rabid pro-Maximilian, anti-Juárez, anti-Washington, anti-

In the aftermath of the hurricane, wagons began the slow delivery of food and water to Matamoros citizens. *Carte de visite* by Louis de Planque, October 1867. *Brownsville Historical Association.*

African American troublesome periodical that used the "basest language" when referring to Federal authority in Texas. The fact that General Mejía allowed a "Rebel newspaper" to function in Matamoros long after the end of the American Civil War did much to poison relations with army commanders in Brownsville.[29] Black soldiers stationed on the Rio Grande hated the *Ranchero*, and when the newspaper was moved to Brownsville they probably would have destroyed it had their officers not prevented them from doing so.[30] Because of the *Ranchero*'s never-ending criticism of the Federal army on the border, the War Department advised officers in Brownsville to watch for disloyal articles. Edited by Henry Maltby, the newspaper had its origins in Corpus Christi in 1859. The Ohio-born Maltby had moved to Texas in 1851, where he became mayor of Corpus Christi but resigned in 1857 to raise a company of filibusters in the seaside community for the ill-fated imperialistic William Walker in Nicaragua. Following the Union occupation of the Texas coast in 1863, Maltby took the *Ranchero* and fled into the brush country to the Santa Margarita crossing on the Nueces River and then to Matamoros. After Maltby published several sensitive orders from Confederate authorities in Texas,

General Bee threatened to draft the fiery publisher into the Confederate army and was only prohibited from doing so by the fact that General Magruder had given Maltby "a special exemption." Maltby "is a nuisance, and seeks to do all the harm he can, and it is my desire to put a stop to the evil, by putting him in the army, where he can be of some use," Bee wrote.[31]

In Matamoros Maltby took on a new crusade. No publication did more to sustain the Empire in Northern Mexico than the *Matamoros Ranchero,* a newspaper in San Luis Potosi editoralized.[32] "The force and weight with which the *Ranchero* sustained the Imperial cause, gave that power much respectability abroad," the *Galveston News* wrote.[33] Often publishing sections and entire issues in French and Spanish, Maltby was indeed a powerful voice for the Imperial cause as he persistently abused many of the leading Liberals. Following the fall of Matamoros to the *Juaristas* in the summer of 1866, Kinney and Maltby, who by this time were publishing a daily, tri-weekly, and a weekly edition, took the *Ranchero* back to Brownsville, where they established offices in the only three-story building in the city on Elizabeth Street. Maltby was so abusive toward the Liberals that General Berriozábal prohibited the distribution of the newspaper in Mexico and tried to pressure General Sheridan into closing the *Ranchero*. Maltby, the self-proclaimed "fighting editor," asserted that the real reason Berriozábal was out to get him was because of the *Ranchero's* persistent criticism of the general for flaunting his mistress in public.[34] Maltby took great pride in learning that individuals were smuggling the newspaper into the country.

Maltby vilified all "carpetbaggers" and consistently quarreled with the editor of the Brownsville *Rio Grande Courier*, Emile P. Claudon, until he purchased the *Courier* in August 1868. He was equally despised by army officials because of his disdain of Reconstruction. In late 1867 Col. Ranald Slidell Mackenzie, in command of the black Twenty-fourth Infantry at Fort Brown, ordered the *Ranchero* closed and Maltby arrested, alleging that the *Ranchero* had insulted Northern women in an excitable editorial. Mackenzie drafted an apology for Maltby to publish in the *Ranchero*: "My attention having been called to

certain indecent publications in reference to Northern women in my issue of the 8th inst., I have to state that they are false, that I knew them to be false when published, and now greatly regret having published them. In [the] future, I propose conducting my paper with less scurrility than heretofore."[35]

Obstinate and defiant, Maltby refused to comply with Mackenzie's order. Instead, before Mackenzie could act himself, Maltby closed the newspaper, placed black crepe on the door of the *Ranchero* office, and announced that the newspaper had died "of miscegenation." Moreover, he caught a steamer for New Orleans to appeal to military authorities in the Crescent City. The rival yet sympathetic *Rio Grande Courier* remarked that the *Ranchero* had really died "by a visitation of a certain M.D., otherwise Military Despotism."[36] Kinney claimed the real reason for the closing of the *Ranchero* was the fact that Maltby had published a letter from Cruse Carson, who had been banished to Mexico, which criticized the

This photograph, taken from the Mexican side of the flooded Rio Grande at the Santa Cruz ferry crossing, shows the devastation on Levee Street in Brownsville after the October 1867 hurricane. *Carte de visite* attributed to Louis de Planque. *University of Texas at Brownsville, courtesy Institute of Texan Cultures at San Antonio, no. 73-830.*

Left homeless by the great storm, a Mexican woman grinds corn and prepares tortillas for her husband and children in the midst of hurricane debris. *Carte de visite* attributed to Louis de Planque, October 1867. *William L. Schaeffer collection.*

his criticism of the military on the border.[38]

General Sheridan remained generally unsympathetic to the complaints of conservative Texas Democrats, and he frequently imposed the will of the Radical Republicans at gunpoint. In July 1867 Sheridan removed Gov. James W. Throckmorton, arguing that he had refused to cooperate in punishing individuals accused of committing outrages against Unionists and blacks. In his place, Sheridan appointed former governor Elisha M. Pease. On November 1, 1867, he also removed more than four hundred county officials in fifty-seven counties across the state, including several counties on the Rio Grande frontier. In Washington, bitter debate extended for weeks, centered around a Radical Republican objective to carve Texas into several states and create a new state, West Texas, from the area west and south of the Colorado River, including all of South Texas. The Radicals went as far as to draft a constitution for the proposed new state with San Antonio as the capital. Led by Edmund J. Davis, the Texas Radicals rushed to Washington to persuade Congress to approve the new state. Only when the moderates, led by Andrew Jackson Hamilton, testified against the new state did Congress ignore the proposition and the proposal failed. The Davis Radicals also pushed a Texas ordinance that disfranchised anyone who had voluntarily aided or abetted the Confederacy.

The violence and lawlessness on the Rio Grande continued unabated throughout 1868. Late on the evening of December 18, 1868, twelve masked bandits riding out of Mexico plundered what remained of the village of Clarksville. Shouting "Kill the d—n Yankee son of a b—s," the raiders left two customhouse officers, William H. Phelps and George F. Hammond, dead before townsmen and the Bagdad police were able to restore order.[39]

But life on the border often featured the finer aspects of life. In addition to the *dieciséis de septiembre* and the Fourth of July celebrations, by

military in Brownsville.[37] In New Orleans in late December, Gen. Winfield Scott Hancock overruled Colonel Mackenzie and directed Gen. Joseph Jones Reynolds, commanding the District of Texas, to allow Maltby to reopen the *Ranchero*: "You will permit the publication of the *Ranchero* to be resumed and continued unconditionally." Proclaiming that civil law had triumphed over military despotism and that freedom of the press and the Constitution had prevailed, Maltby continued

Matamoros citizens left homeless in the aftermath of the hurricane lived in makeshift huts until permanent housing could be constructed. *Carte de visite* attributed to Louis de Planque, October 1867. *Lawrence T. Jones III collection.*

1869 Brownsville and Laredo had begun to commemorate George Washington's birthday with festive dinners and celebrations.[40] At Miller's Billiard Hall in late January 1868, the Royal Theatre of Dublin and Manchaster performed "Readings from Shakespeare," including *Henry VIII, Julius Caesar, Macbeth, Othello*, and *Richard III*.[41] Baseball, which had been played at Fort Brown as early as 1860, proved to be a pleasant distraction from the endemic violence. By 1868 at least three clubs were playing baseball in Brownsville and Matamoros. The Robert E. Lee and Rio Grande clubs had been organized in Brownsville while the Union Club represented Matamoros. After Rio Grande defeated the R. E. Lee Club, 46 to 22, on Christmas Day 1868, the Rio Grande Club squared off against the Union Club before a "great many ladies and gentlemen," for the "championship of the border," but was defeated 49 to 22. After the game, the two teams retired "to a sumptuous repast furnished by the Rio Grande Club."[42] By the summer of 1869 teams had also been formed by the military at Fort Brown. The Sheridan Club was made up of soldiers from the Fourth Cavalry while the McClellan Club was composed of men from the Tenth Infantry. In their final game the infantry won by a score of 49 to 18 and then went on to defeat the Rio Grande Club, 73 to 30, when the latter took the field with only seven players.

There was not a team in the United States that needed more practice than the men and boys of the Rio Grande Club, the *Ranchero* commented.[43]

In Mexico Juárez was able to pacify large regions of the country, but areas in the north remained under control of regional *caudillos* and defiant *caciques*. Tamaulipas, in particular, fell into chaos and a state of utter anarchy. After assisting the government defeat bandit gangs and brigands in central Mexico, Cortina, at the head of his Tamaulipas Brigade, returned to the border. In Tamaulipas the *Cortinistas* were instrumental in helping to crush roving revolutionary chieftains such as Braulio Vargas and help Gov. Juan José de la Garza restore some semblance of law and order.[44] On June 9, 1870, a defiant Gen. Pedro Martinez occupied Matamoros, saying that he came to "wage war on the dictatorship of Don Benito Juárez."[45] Urging all "good sons of Tamaulipas" to rally to the defense of the government, Cortina chased General Martinez out of Matamoros and marched triumphantly into the city in the third week of September 1870.[46] Even the American press acclaimed a return to law and order and hoped that Cortina would end the cattle rustling on the border.[47] A number of Texas citizens, including many of Cortina's old enemies in Brownsville, even attempted to secure a pardon for him in Texas.[48] Sen. Albert J. Fountain, representing the Rio Grande frontier, went as far as to introduce a joint resolution in the Texas legislature for the "relief" of Cortina. But public opinion would quickly change as many of the stock raisers began to suspect that Cortina was responsible for the wide-scale cattle rustling.

In time, Cortina would be accused by American authorities of masterminding the theft of thousands of head of cattle in South. Texas. Some of Cortina's men raided as far north as Nuecestown near Corpus Christi.[49] In retaliation for such raids, Texas Rangers invaded Mexico, burned, plundered, and indiscriminately hanged Mexicans.[50] Border violence threatened to drag the two republics into war, and both countries sent commissions of investigation to the region. Although the U.S. commission amassed a mountain of incriminating evidence against Cortina, the Mexican commission largely exonerated him.[51] William Steele, Texas adjutant general, was convinced that Cortina was in control of a border army of no fewer than two thousand "armed adherents." Steele told Gov. Richard Coke that Cortina was "the recognized head and protector of all of the cattle thieves and murderers from Camargo to the mouth of the Rio Grande."[52] In Mexico City John W. Foster, United States minister to Mexico, pressured José María Lafragua, Mexican minister of foreign affairs, to remove Cortina to some remote part of the Mexican republic. "His removal," Foster told Lafragua, "would have a very salutatory effect upon the frontier and be accepted as an act of conciliation and peace toward the United States."[53] Pres. Sebastián Lerdo de Tejada, who became president when Juárez died in 1872, ordered Cortina arrested and taken under armed guard to Mexico City and placed in Santiago Tlatelolco prison. Later released, but under house arrest, Cortina defiantly announced his support of Gen. Porfirio Díaz and fled for the border. Recruiting men, he drove the federal forces from Reynosa, Camargo, and Mier, and, with another revolutionary general, Miguel Blanco, he triumphantly entered Matamoros. But Cortina's stay on the border would be brief. With the United States continuing to withhold diplomatic recognition of the Díaz regime until the Mexican government could put an end to the cattle raids on the border, Díaz ordered Cortina arrested. Narrowly escaping a firing squad, Cortina was again taken to Mexico City and placed in a dark cell in Santiago Tlatelolco prison.[54] In bad health, Cortina was released. He died in the village of Azcapotzalco outside Mexico City on October 30, 1894.

In Texas on April 16, 1870, civil government was finally restored. Nine years after Texas seceded, the Lone Star State was back in the Union. Both banks of the Lower Rio Grande Valley had somehow survived secession, endless political intrigues, civil war, bloody revolution, misguided foreign intervention, deadly pestilence, genocidal guerrilla warfare, killer hurricanes, and unbounded and indiscriminate violence. Undeniably, the period from 1861 to 1870 had been one of the most eventful and turbulent periods in the history of the Rio Grande frontier.

NOTES

INTRODUCTION
THE PHOTOGRAPHERS

[1] In 1983 the National Historical Society published a massive and important six-volume Civil War photographic history, *The Image of War, 1861–1865*. Among the many images reproduced in Volume V, *The South Besieged*, in a chapter entitled, "The Forgotten War: The West" are six *carte de visite* photographs taken in Brownsville and Matamoros in 1865 and 1866. Five of the six are misidentified and completely misinterpreted, causing confusion to this date. One photograph purports to show the November 6, 1863, Confederate evacuation of Brownsville but is really a postwar view of Elizabeth Street looking west. Even today, Elizabeth Street is considered the main downtown street in Brownsville.

The second photograph shows a typical Mexican *jacal* or hut. The third photograph is described as showing men helping evacuate large supplies of Confederate stores and cotton at Brownsville. This photograph actually depicts a group of Mexican water carriers. The water carrier or *barrilero* was an omnipresent part of daily life in Brownsville and Matamoros and the subject of many photographs in the towns and villages all along the border well into the next century. They were a colorful and integral part of commerce as they delivered their rolling barrels of water to their customers. The ox-drawn wagons behind them are the large freight-hauling carts or *carretas* common to Mexico and South Texas at the time.

The fourth photograph purports to show the bustling Brownsville riverfront during the Confederate evacuation with "many people even loading their furniture to take it with them in the evacuation." In reality, the photograph is a postwar view of the daily activity along busy Levee Street, the thoroughfare in Brownsville that runs along the Rio Grande. The fifth misidentified photograph is of a Federal army pontoon bridge that was constructed during the brief American military occupation of Matamoros in 1864, certainly not a bridge that was used during the Confederate evacuation of Brownsville. The shore in the background of this view is Mexico.

The sixth and final view is also misinterpreted as "the bustle and confusion of the evacuation." In fact, the photograph is of a second and different Federal army pontoon bridge from the one mentioned above but looking in the opposite direction toward Brownsville. This bridge was constructed between Brownsville and Matamoros during the postwar Federal occupation of Brownsville. See William C. Davis (ed.), *The South Besieged: The Image of War, 1861–1865* (Garden City, N.J.: Doubleday & Co., 1983), 434–437.

[2] David Haynes, *Catching Shadows: A Directory of Nineteenth-Century Texas Photographers* (Austin: Texas State Historical Association, 1993), 117. Two of these photographs are of Capt. Durant Duponte and Capt. E. P. Turner, officers on the staff of General Magruder. They are in the Louisiana and Lower Mississippi Valley Collection of the Hill Memorial Library, Louisiana State University, Baton Rouge, Louisiana. The image of General Magruder is in the Lawrence T. Jones III collection, Austin, Texas.

[3] See note 1.

[4] Margaret Denton Smith and Mary Louise Tucker, *Photography in New Orleans: The Early Years, 1840–1865* (Baton Rouge: Louisiana State University Press, 1982), 155, 108. His first name is thought to have been Anton, but this is far from certain.

[5] *El Ranchero Diario* (Matamoros), Apr. 3, 1866, William C. and Patricia Cisneros Young collection (Brownsville, Texas); Arthur W. Bergeron Jr., *Guide to Louisiana Confederate Military Units, 1861–1865* (Baton Rouge: Louisiana State University Press, 1996), 124.

[6] Peter E. Palmquist, Thomas R. Kailbourn, and Martha A. Sandweiss, *Pioneer Photographers of the Far West: A Biographical Dictionary, 1840–1864* (Palo Alto, Calif.: Stanford University Press, 2004); *carte de visite* in the collection of Lawrence T. Jones III.

[7] *Brownsville Daily Ranchero*, Dec. 4, 1866; Robert O. Brown, *Collector's Guide to 19th Century U.S. Traveling Photographers* (Forest Grove, Ore.: Brown-Spath and Associates, 2002), 208.

[8] Smith and Tucker overlooked Wallis/Wallace in their book on early New Orleans photography. This recently discovered information is courtesy of Peter E. Palmquist and Thomas R. Kailbourn, independent researchers and authors of *Pioneer Photographers of the Far West: A Biographical Dictionary, 1840–1865*. Also see Haynes, *Catching Shadows*, 115.

[9] Wallis appears on the tax rolls in Brownsville from 1866 through 1870. He continued his business in Brownsville through the decade of the 1870s and is listed in the *Texas Business Directory, 1878–79* as "R. H. Wallis."

[10] Haynes, *Catching Shadows*, 115.

[11] *Matamoros Daily Ranchero*, Nov. 2, 1866.

[12] In *Catching Shadows* de Planque's date of birth is given as 1837. His obituary in the *Corpus Christi Caller* states that he died on May 1, 1898, "aged 56 years and 14 days," thus making his date of birth 1842. *Corpus Christi Caller*, May 6, 1898.

[13] European photo-historian Steven Joseph of Belgium could find no record of de Planque in any of the major directories of nineteenth-century European photographers. Steven Joseph to Lawrence T. Jones III, Mar. 26, 2000, e-mail. De Planque is listed on the 1880 Nueces County census along with his wife and two children, Louis E., age eleven, and Marie, nine. Tenth Census (1880), Nueces County, Texas (National Archives, Washington, D.C.; hereafter cited as NA).

[14] The exact site is easy to locate today because the street numbers in Matamoros are much the same as they were during the 1860s. As of 2003 a small parking lot sits on the site of his gallery. About half a block away is a small photography shop managed by an elderly couple.

[15] The Corpus Christi Museum of Science and History has a copy of a studio portrait *carte de visite* taken around 1875 with an imprint that reads, "Mrs. E. de Planque, Corpus Christi, Texas."

[16] *Matamoros Daily Ranchero*, Apr. 12, 1867.

[17] *Brownsville Daily Ranchero*, Nov. 15, 1867. An unidentified photographer took several photographs of the flood damage that occurred in Galveston as a result of this same storm. Four of these *cartes de visite* are in the collection of the Rosenberg Library in Galveston, and three are in the Lawrence T. Jones III collection.

[18] *Corpus Christi Caller*, May 6, 1898. Two children, a son, Louis, and a daughter, Marie, were born in Corpus Christi.

[19] Brownson Malsch, *Indianola: The Mother of Western Texas* (Austin: State House Press, 1988), 235–236. Today, a storm of that strength would be referred to as a "Category 5" hurricane, the strongest rating allowable.

[20] Louis de Planque, "A Photographer's Narrow Escape," *Philadelphia Photographer*, 12 (Dec., 1875),

358–359.

[21] Michael A. Howell, "Old Bayview–Not Just Another Cemetery," *Journal of South Texas*, 15 (Fall, 2002), 11.

MATAMOROS

[1] Milo Kearney and Anthony Knopp, *Boom and Bust: The Historical Cycles of Matamoros and Brownsville* (Austin: Eakin Press, 1991), 31.

[2] Leonard Pierce to William Seward, Mar. 1, 1862, *The War of the Rebellion: A Compilation of the Official Records of the Union and Confederate Armies* (Washington, D.C.: Government Printing Office, 1889), ser. I, vol. 9, 674.

[3] Ibid.

[4] Ernst Pitner, *Maximilian's Lieutenant: A Personal History of the Mexican Campaign, 1864–7*, trans. and ed. by Gordon Etherington-Smith (Albuquerque: University of New Mexico Press, 1993), 107.

[5] *Brownsville Daily Ranchero*, Dec. 16, 1866.

[6] James Irby, *Backdoor to Bagdad* (El Paso: Texas Western Press, 1977), 9.

[7] James W. Daddysman, *The Matamoros Trade: Confederate Commerce, Diplomacy and Intrigue* (Newark: University of Delaware Press, 1984), 34.

[8] Pitner, *Maximilian's Lieutenant*, 107.

[9] Ibid., 121.

BROWNSVILLE

[1] Jerry Thompson, *Palo Alto Battlefield National Historic Site* (Tucson: Southwest Parks and Monuments Association, 2001), 6.

[2] Kearney and Knopp, *Boom and Bust*, 68. See also Kearney and Knopp, *Border Cuates: A History of the U.S.–Mexican Twin Cities* (Austin: Eakin Press, 1995), 74–75.

[3] Alicia A. Garza and Christopher Long, "Brownsville," in Ron Tyler, Douglas E. Barnett, Roy R. Barkley, Penelope C. Anderson, and Mark F. Odintz (eds.), *The New Handbook of Texas* (6 vols.; Austin: Texas State Historical Association, 1996), I, 776–777.

[4] Kearney and Knopp, *Boom and Bust*, 67.

[5] Minutebook I (1850–1859), Brownsville City Council (City Secretary's Office, Brownsville, Texas), 1–69, quotation on 19.

[6] R. B. Marcy to Nellie Marcy, Nov. 15, 1856, George B. McClellan Papers (Library of Congress, Washington, D.C.).

Chapter 1: Secession and Civil War

[1] *Corpus Christi Ranchero*, Jan. 12, 1861.

[2] *Texas State Gazette* (Austin), Jan. 12, 1861. This article reports that Edmund Jackson Davis also was elected to the state convention. Various other sources state, however, that Davis was unsuccessful in his bid to become a member of the secession convention. Davis certainly is not listed as among those attending. Others in attendance at the Cameron County convention included the more influential members of the community, none of them Hispanic, including W. W. Nelson, F. W. Campbell, E. E. Scarborough, Henry Miller, George Dye, Alexander Werbiski, A. W. Allen, R. B. Kingsbury, Edward Downey, W. B. Thomas, James G. Brown, Mifflin Kenedy, and William Johnson. Marcus J. Wright (comp.), *Texas in the War, 1861–1865*, ed. Harold B. Simpson (Hillsboro: Hill College Press, 1965), 162, 175–182.

[3] Wright, *Texas in the War*, 175–180.

[4] Dale Baum, *The Shattering of Texas Unionism: Politics in the Lone Star State during the Civil War Era* (Baton Rouge: Louisiana State University Press, 1998), 79.

[5] Quoted in Ralph A. Wooster, *Texas and Texans in the Civil War* (Austin: Eakin Press, 1995), 17–18. See also Russell Brown, "An Old Woman with a Broomstick: General David E. Twiggs and the Surrender in Texas, 1861," *Military Affairs*, 48 (Apr., 1984), 57–61.

[6] Douglas Southall Freeman, *R. E. Lee: A Biography* (3 vols.; New York: Charles Scribner's Sons, 1934), I, 427; Samuel Peter Heintzelman Journal, Mar. 5, 25, 1861, manuscript division (Library of Congress, Washington, D.C.; hereafter cited as LC).

[7] C. C. Sibley to W. A. Nichols, Mar. 11, 1861, *The War of the Rebellion: A Compilation of the Official Records of the Union and Confederate Armies* (Washington, D.C.: Government Printing Office, 1889), ser. I, vol. 1, 534–545. Hereafter referred to as *OR* by series, volume, part, and page.

[8] O. L. Shepherd to S. Cooper, Mar. 20, 1861, *OR*, I, 1, 561,

[9] Order no. 5, February 1861, *OR*, I, 1, 537; James Thompson to L.G. Bailey, Feb. 22, 1861, *OR*, I, 1, 537–558; *Texas State Gazette* (Austin), Mar. 2, 9, 1861.

[10] John S. Ford, *Rip Ford's Texas*, ed. Stephen B. Oates (Austin: University of Texas Press, 1963), 319 (1st and 3rd quotations), 321 (2nd quotation).

[11] E. Backus to S. Cooper, Mar. 30, 1861, *OR*, I, 1, 560–561; Ford, *Rip Ford's Texas*, 321 (quotation).

[12] Jerry Thompson, *Juan Cortina and the Texas–Mexico Frontier, 1859–1877* (El Paso: Texas Western Press, 1994), 11–12; Jerry Thompson (ed.), *Fifty Miles and a Fight: Major Samuel Peter Heintzelman's Journal of Texas and the Cortina War* (Austin: Texas State Historical Association, 1998), 155–156.

[13] John S. Ford to Edward Clark, Apr. 16, 1861 (McAllen Ranch Archives, Linn, Texas).

[14] Virgil N. Lott and Mercurio Martinez, *The Kingdom of Zapata* (Austin: Eakin Press, 1983), 42–43.

[15] Gardner W. Pierce to [John Z. Leyendecker], June 1, 1861, John Z. Leyendecker Papers (Center for American History, University of Texas at Austin; hereafter cited as CAH). See also Baum, *The Shattering of Texas Unionism*, 75–76.

[16] *Corpus Christi Ranchero*, Apr. 20, 1861.

[17] Gardner W. Pierce to [John Z. Leyendecker], June 1, 1861, Leyendecker Papers, (CAH).

[18] *Corpus Christi Ranchero*, Apr. 20, 1861.

[19] Henry Redmond to John S. Ford, Apr. 12, 1861, Edward Clark Papers (Texas State Archives, Austin, Texas; hereafter cited as TSA). Also John D. Mussett to Captain Brown, Oct. 18, 1861, Letters Received, Confederate District of Texas, New Mexico, and Arizona, RG 109 (NA).

[20] Eighth Census (1860), Zapata County, Texas (NA).

[21] *Corpus Christi Ranchero*, Apr. 27, 1861. As a result of his service during the Mexican War, Nolan had become known in South Texas as the "Boy Bugler of the Battle of Cerro Gordo." In the years after the Mexican War Nolan joined Capt. John S. Ford's company of Rangers in the Nueces Strip as a bugler. Later he was elected sheriff of Nueces County. Nolan was murdered in Corpus Christi on December 22, 1864. See Bill Walraven, *Corpus Christi: The History of a Texas Seaport* (Woodland Hills, Calif.: Windsor Publications, 1982), 53.

[22] Gardner Pierce to [John Z. Leyendecker], June 1, 1861, Leyendecker Papers (CAH); *Corpus Christi Ranchero*, Apr. 27, 1861. Santiago Vela, fifty-seven, a victim of "*una armada de aquel estado*," was buried in Guerrero at 10 A.M. on the same day, April 15, 1861. Registro Civil de Guerrero, "Libro de Defunciones, 1860–1861," 26–27 (Nuevo Guerrero Archives, Nuevo Guerrero, Tamaulipas; hereafter cited as NGA).

[23] *Reports of the Committee of Investigation Sent in 1873 by the Mexican Government to the Frontier of Texas* (New York: Baker and Godwin Publishers, 1875), 66. For a more detailed study of the turmoil in Zapata County, see Jerry Thompson, *Vaqueros in Blue and Gray* (Austin: State House Press, 2000), 15–23, and Jerry Thompson, *Mexican Texans in the Union Army* (El Paso: Texas Western Press, 1986), 1–7.

[24] Henry Redmond to John S. Ford, May 14, 1861, John S. Ford Papers (TSA); *Texas State Gazette* (Austin), June 8, 1861.

25 Ysidro Vela to Colonel Ford, May 14, 1861, Ford Papers (TSA).

26 [Juan G. Garza] to Gefe Politico del Distrito del Norte, May 19, 1861, Correspondencia del Alcalde de Guerrero (NGA); [Juan G. Garza] to Santos Benavides, May 18, 1861, Correspondencia del Alcalde de Guerrero (NGA).

27 Gardner W. Pierce to [John Z. Leyendecker], June 1, 1861, Leyendecker Papers (CAH).

28 Henry Redmond to John S. Ford, May 23, 1861, broadside file (TSA).

29 Gardner W. Pierce to [John Z. Leyendecker], June 1, 1861, Leyendecker Papers (CAH). Also see *Texas State Gazette* (Austin), June 15, 1861.

30 Santos Benavides to John S. Ford, May 14, 1861, Ford Papers (TSA); *Corpus Christi Ranchero*, June 1, 8, 1861. Benavides told José María Hinojosa that ten of Cortina's "men were left dead on the field and that the others were dispersed in all directions." [Juan G. Garza] to Gefe Politico del Distrito del Norte, May 22, 1861, Correspondencia del Alcalde de Guerrero (NGA). Yet in a letter to his friend Santiago Vidaurri, Benavides said seven *Cortinistas* were killed. Santos Benavides to Santiago Vidaurri, June 10, 1861, Correspondencia de Santiago Vidaurri (Archivo General del Estado de Nuevo León, Monterrey, Nuevo León).

31 [Juan G. Garza] to Santos Benavides and Cristobal Benavides, May 31, 1861, Correspondencia del Alcalde de Guerrero (NGA).

32 John S. Ford to Edward Clark, July 14, 1861, Clark Papers (TSA). On December 8, 1866, Davis accidentally shot and killed himself with a shotgun near Rio Grande City while riding in a carriage on a hunting expedition with several officers from Ringgold Barracks. *New Orleans Daily Crescent*, Dec. 22, 1866; *Brownsville Daily Ranchero*, Dec. 12, 1866.

33 M. Capistran to [John S. Ford ?], Oct. 19, 1861, Letters Received, District of Texas, New Mexico, and Arizona, RG 109 (NA).

34 Wallace E. Oakes to Edward Clark, Aug. 27, 1861, Clark Papers (TSA).

35 L. E. Daniell, *Types of Successful Men of Texas* (Austin: n.p., 1890), 327.

36 Ford, *Rip Ford's Texas*, 327.

37 F. J. Parker to A. Buchel, Dec. 20, 1861; H. Willke to P. N. Luckett, Dec. 31, 1861; P. N. Luckett to A. Yager, Dec. 31, 1861; P. S. Buquor to P. N. Luckett, Dec. 31, 1861; all in Letters Received, District of Texas, New Mexico, and Arizona, RG 109 (NA).

38 M. Capistran to [John S. Ford], Oct. 13, 1861, Letters Received, District of Texas, New Mexico, and Arizona, RG 109 (NA); Milo Kearney and Anthony Knopp,

Boom and Bust: The Historical Cycles of Matamoros and Brownsville (Austin: Eakin Press, 1991), 123.

39 John S. Ford to Macedonio Capistran, Oct. 21, 1861, Letters Received, District of Texas, New Mexico, and Arizona, RG 109 (NA).

40 P. O. Hébert to Judah P. Benjamin, Oct. 31, 1861, *OR*, I, 4, 130–131. See also James W. Daddysman, *The Matamoros Trade: Confederate Commerce, Diplomacy and Intrigue* (Newark: University of Delaware Press, 1984), 31; and Wooster, *Texas and Texans in the Civil War*, 44–45.

41 Leonard Pierce Jr. to [William H. Seward], Apr. 15, 1863, Consular Dispatches, Matamoros, Mexico, Records of the United States Department of State, RG 59 (NA).

42 Daddysman, *The Matamoros Trade*, 30–31; Ford, *Rip Ford's Texas*, 329 (quotation).

43 John Warren Hunter, "The Fall of Brownsville on the Rio Grande, November 1863," typescript, 4–5 (CAH). See also John Warren Hunter, *Heel-Fly Time in Texas* (Bandera, Texas: Frontier Times, 1931), 11–12; and Ronnie C. Tyler, "Cotton on the Border, 1861–1865," *Southwestern Historical Quarterly*, 73 (Apr., 1970), 456.

44 Hunter, "Fall of Brownsville," 4–5 (1st quotation); Leonard Pierce to William Seward, Mar. 1, 1862, *OR*, I, 9, 674 (2nd quotation). Some of the larger firms operating on the Rio Grande included Droege, Oetling and Company; Brown, Fleming and Company; Harding, Pullin and Company of London; Lloyd's of London; Treviño Brothers; Oliver Brothers of Monterrey; Attrill and Lacosta; and Marks and Company. See Daddysman, *The Matamoros Trade*, 31. For an excellent account of Matamoros during the war, see Robert W. Delaney, "Matamoros: Port for Texas during the Civil War," *Southwestern Historical Quarterly*, 58 (Apr., 1955), 473–487.

45 Ed. J. Allen to John Price, January 12, 1866, Letters Received, Adjutant General's Office, RG 94 (NA).

46 James Irby, *Backdoor to Bagdad* (El Paso: Texas Western Press, 1977), 9.

47 The best study of Confederate diplomacy remains Frank Lawrence Owsley, *King Cotton Diplomacy: Foreign Relations of the Confederate States of America* (Chicago: University of Chicago Press, 1959). See also James M. Callahan, *The Diplomatic History of the Southern Confederacy* (Baltimore: Johns Hopkins University Press, 1901).

48 Wooster, *Texas and Texans in the Civil War*, 120; Daddysman, *The Matamoros Trade*, 35; J. Fred Rippy, *The United States and Mexico* (New York: Alfred A. Knopf, 1926), 238.

49 Hunter, *Heel-Fly Time in Texas*, 19.

50 Wooster, *Texas and Texans in the Civil War*, 119.

51 H. P. Bee to A. M. Hobby, Mar. 29, 1863, and A. M.

Hobby to James A. Ware, Apr. 11, 1863; both in Letters Received, District of Texas, New Mexico, and Arizona, RG 109 (NA).

52 S. Hart to Lieutenant Phillips, May 29, 1863, Letters Received, District of Texas, New Mexico, and Arizona, RG 109 (NA).

53 S. Hart to J. E. Slaughter, Mar. 7, 1864, Letters Received, District of Texas, New Mexico, and Arizona, RG 109 (NA).

54 Eliza Moore McHatton-Ripley, *From Flag to Flag: A Woman's Adventures and Experiences in the South during the War, in Mexico, and in Cuba* (New York: D. Appleton, 1889), 95–96.

55 Daddysman, *The Matamoros Trade*, 33; Theodorus Bailey to Gideon Welles, Apr. 2, 1863, *Official Records of the Union and Confederate Navies in the War of the Rebellion* (30 vols.; Washington, D.C.: Government Printing Office, 1894–1927), I, 17, 403. Hereafter referred to as *ORN* by series and volume. See also *Brownsville Daily Ranchero*, Dec. 16, 1866.

56 *Matamoros Daily Ranchero*, Jan. 18, 1866; *New York Herald*, July 2, 1865.

57 *New York Herald*, July 29, 1865.

58 Arthur James Lyon Fremantle, *The Fremantle Diary: Being the Journal of Lieutenant Colonel Arthur James Lyon Fremantle, Coldstream Guards, on His Three Months in the Southern States*, ed. Walter Lord (London: Andre Deutsch, 1856), 6.

59 P. F. Parisot, *Reminiscences of a Texas Missionary* (San Antonio: St. Mary's Church, 1899), 56.

60 Pitner, *Maximilian's Lieutenant*, 102.

61 *Brownsville Weekly Ranchero*, June 15, 1867.

62 William Watson, *Adventures of a Blockade Runner, Or, Trade in Time of War* (London: Unwin, 1892), 26.

63 John C. Rayburn and Virginia Kemp Rayburn (eds.), *Century of Conflict, 1821–1913: Incidents in the Lives of William Neale and William A. Neale, Early Settlers in South Texas* (Waco: Texian Press, 1966), 83. See also Ronnie C. Tyler, *Santiago Vidaurri and the Southern Confederacy* (Austin: Texas State Historical Association, 1973), 106–108.

64 *New York Herald*, July 2, 1865. Clarksville began as a temporary camp of the United States Army during the Mexican War when a civilian, William H. Clark, established a store at the site.

65 Tyler, *Santiago Vidaurri and the Southern Confederacy*, 34.

66 Tyler, "Cotton on the Border," 458.

67 José A. Quintero to William M. Browne, n.d., John T. Pickett Papers, manuscript division (LC).

68 José Quintero to R. M. T. Hunter, Aug. 17, 1861, Pickett Papers (LC).

69 José Quintero to R. M. T. Hunter, Aug. 19, 1861, Pickett Papers (LC).

70 William M. Browne to José Quintero, Sept. 3, 1861, in James D. Richardson (ed.), *A Compilation of the Messages and Papers of the Confederacy* (8 vols.; Nashville: United States Publishing Company, 1906), II, 77–80; Daddysman, *The Matamoros Trade*, 69.

71 Daddysman, *The Matamoros Trade*, 51, 53.

72 José Quintero to R. M. T. Hunter, Nov. 11, 1861, Pickett Papers (LC); Tyler, "Cotton on the Border," 459.

73 José Quintero to William M. Browne, Sept. 9, 1861, Pickett Papers (LC).

74 *Fort Brown Flag* (Brownsville), Apr. 17, 1862. The raid was said to have been led by Texas revolutionary hero Juan N. Seguín. Seguín at this time, however, was in central Mexico with Gen. Ignacio Zaragoza. J. F. de la Teja to Jerry Thompson, Jan. 26, 2002, e-mail (printed copy in possession of the authors).

75 Gilberto Miguel Hinojosa, *A Borderlands Town in Transition: Laredo, 1755–1870* (College Station: Texas A&M University Press, 1983), 83.

76 *Bandera Americana* (Brownsville), Feb. 2, 1863, quoted in the *Boletin Oficial* (Monterrey), n.d., copy in Pickett Papers (LC).

77 Journal of James Hampton Kuykendall, Dec. 27, 28, 1863 (CAH).

78 *Fort Brown Flag* (Brownsville), Feb. 2, 1863, quoted in the *Corpus Christi Ranchero*, Jan. 22, 1863; *Bandera Americana* (Brownsville), Feb. 2, 1863, quoted in the *Boletin Oficial* (Monterrey), n.d., copy in Pickett Papers (LC).

79 Hamilton P. Bee to Albino López, Feb. 25, 1863, *OR*, I, 15, 967.

80 *Reports of the Committee of Investigation Sent in 1873*, 69; H. P. Bee to Albino López, Apr. 22, 1863, *OR*, I, 15, 1,051–1,053.

81 *Corpus Christi Ranchero*, Jan. 15, 23, Feb. 5, 1863; *Houston Tri-Weekly Telegraph*, Feb. 2, 1863; *Confederate Veteran* (1922), 473.

82 H. P. Bee to Albino López, Mar. 19, 1863; Albino López to [H. P. Bee], Mar. 20, 1863, *OR*, I, 15, pt. 1, 133; Octaviano Zapata to Antonio Pérez, July 24, 1863, Correspondencia de Santiago Vidaurri (Archivo General del Estado de Nuevo León, Nuevo León). At this time, Leonard Pierce Jr., the American consul in Matamoros, reported that he had three hundred muskets in his possession. It is probable these arms were intended for Zapata's guerrillas. L. Pierce Jr. to W. H. Seward, Apr. 10, 1863, Matamoros Consular Dispatches, RG 59 (NA).

83 Hamilton P. Bee to Manuel Ruiz, Sept. 7, 1863, Bee Letterbook, Library (United States Military Academy,

West Point, New York; hereafter cited as USMA).

84 Ibid.

85 Santos Benavides to William O. Yager, Sept. 3, 1863, *OR*, I, 14, 285; *Reports of the Committee of Investigation Sent in 1873*, 200–203; *Corpus Christi Ranchero*, Sept. 17, 1863.

86 Hamilton P. Bee to E. P. Turner, Sept. 11, 1863, Bee Letterbook, Library (USMA).

87 Jerry Thompson, *Warm Weather and Bad Whiskey* (El Paso: Texas Western Press, 1991), 16–19; Election Returns, City of Laredo, microfilm roll 15, Laredo Archives (St. Mary's University, San Antonio, Texas); Ronald Norman Gray, "Edmund J. Davis: Radical Republican and Reconstruction Governor of Texas" (Ph.D. diss., Texas Tech University, 1976), 54–55; Carl Moneyhon, "Edmund Jackson Davis," in Ron Tyler, Douglas E. Barnett, Roy R. Barkley, Penelope C. Anderson, and Mark F. Odintz (eds.), *The New Handbook of Texas* (6 vols.; Austin: Texas State Historical Association, 1996), I, 83–87.

88 Gray, "Edmund J. Davis: Radical Republican and Reconstruction Governor of Texas," 13–15; Election Returns, 1851–1856, Webb County, Records of the Secretary of State, RG 307 (TSA).

89 Vicki Betts, "'Private and Amateur Hangings': The Lynching of W. W. Montgomery, March 15, 1863," *Southwestern Historical Quarterly*, 88 (Oct., 1984), 147.

90 G. D. Kingsbury to Brother Milton, Mar. 13, 1863, Gilbert D. Kingsbury Papers (CAH). The overly optimistic Kingsbury predicted that "half the troops on the Rio Grande line would be in the Federal lines" within weeks.

91 Betts, "Lynching of W. W. Montgomery," 148.

92 Ibid.

93 R. H. Williams, *With the Border Ruffians, Memories of the Far West, 1852–1868*, ed. E. W. Williams (Lincoln: University of Nebraska Press, 1982), 294.

94 Ibid., 296.

95 Betts, "Lynching of W. W. Montgomery," 149.

96 Williams, *With the Border Ruffians*, 297.

97 Hamilton P. Bee to Dickinson, Mar. 15, 1863, *OR*, I, 15, 1,017.

98 Fremantle, *Fremantle Diary*, 8.

99 Hamilton P. Bee to Dickinson, Mar. 15, 1863, *OR*, I, 15, 1,017.

100 Fremantle, *Fremantle Diary*, 8.

101 Betts, "Lynching of W. W. Montgomery," 154; [G. D. Kingsbury] to Mariah McMahon, Apr. 26, 1863, Kingsbury Papers (CAH).

102 [G. D. Kingsbury] to Mariah McMahon, Apr. 26, 1863, Kingsbury Papers (CAH).

103 Leonard Pierce to W. H. Seward, Mar. 1, 1862, Matamoros Consular Dispatches, Matamoros, Mexico,

Records of the United States Department of State, RG 59 (NA).

104 Thompson, *Mexican Texans in the Union Army*, 13.

105 L. Pierce Jr. to W. H. Seward, Mar. 21, 1862, and L. Pierce Jr. to W. H. Seward, Aug. 26, 1862, both in Matamoros Consular Dispatches, RG 59 (NA).

106 *Dallas Herald* quoted in James Marten, "True to the Union: Texans in the U.S. Army," *North and South: The Magazine of the Civil War Conflict*, 3 (Nov., 1999), 83.

107 William Huster to E. J. Davis, Dec. 12, 1863, William Huster, Compiled Service Record (hereafter cited as CSR), United States Department of War, RG 94 (NA). For the Nueces Massacre see Rodman L. Underwood, *Death on the Nueces: German Texans, Treue der Union* (Austin: Eakin Press, 2000); Robert W. Shook, "The Battle of the Nueces, August 10, 1862," *Southwestern Historical Quarterly*, 66 (July, 1962), 31–42; John W. Sansom, "The Desperate Battle of the Nueces River, August 10, 186[2]," *Hunter's Magazine*, 1 (Sept., 1911), 22–24. See also Leonard Pierce Jr. to W. H. Seward, Sept. 22, 1862, Matamoros Consular Dispatches, RG 59 (NA). For the flight of Texas Unionists to Mexico see L. Pierce Jr. to W. H. Seward, Mar. 1, 21, 24, Apr. 8, 21, 22, 30, May 5, Aug. 26, and Sept. 21, 22, 1862, Monterrey Consular Dispatches, RG 59 (NA). For accounts of Texas refugees arriving in Monterrey, see Caleb B. H. Blood to William H. Seward, May 23, 1862, M. M. Kimmey to Wm. H. Seward, Oct. 29, Nov. 21, 1862, Apr. 7, 17, June 4, Sept. 21, 28, 1863, and May 21, 1864, Monterrey Consular Dispatches, RG 59 (NA).

108 Williams, *With the Border Ruffians*, 167; Marten, "True to the Union," 83.

109 L. Pierce Jr. to W. H. Seward, Mar. 8, 1864, Matamoros Consular Dispatches, RG 59 (NA).

110 L. Pierce Jr. to W. H. Seward, Dec. 8, 1864, Matamoros Consular Dispatches, RG 59 (NA).

111 Thompson, *Mexican Texans in the Civil War*, 13.

112 F. J. Herron to Ch[arles] P. Stone, Feb. 2, 1864, Matamoros Consular Dispatches, RG 59 (NA). "All of them," Herron wrote in reference to the refugees, "are entirely destitute of money and in many cases have nothing but the clothing they wear, which after the rough journey they are compelled to make to get here, is badly worn."

113 E. Dorsey Etchinson to W. A. Pile, Dec. 7, 1864, Matamoros Consular Dispatches, RG 59 (NA).

114 Stephen Yancey to Hamilton P. Bee, Sept. 1, 1863, Bee Letterbook, Library (USMA).

115 Santos Benavides to E. J. Gray, Mar. 13, 1863, Cotton Bureau Records, Confederate Department of the Treasury, RG 395 (NA).

116 Ibid.

117 Ibid.

118 Albino López to Hamilton P. Bee, Mar. 15, 1863, *OR*, I, 4, 1,129.

119 Hamilton P. Bee to Albino López, Mar. 22, 1863, *OR*, I, 4, 1,135.

120 Juan Cortina to Miguel Negrete, May 15, 1864, in Alberto María Carreño (ed.), *Archivo del General Porfirio Díaz: Memorias y Documentos* (Mexico City: Editorial "Elede," 1949), 3, 302–303.

CHAPTER 2: BLUECOATS ON THE RIO GRANDE

1 *Harper's Weekly*, Nov. 28, 1863. A severe storm was encountered off Aransas Pass, forcing some of the men to throw several of their mules overboard as well as wagons and forage for their animals.

2 Nathaniel P. Banks to Abraham Lincoln, Nov. 3, 1863, *OR*, I, 26, pt. 1, 396. Also see Nathaniel P. Banks to H. W. Halleck, Nov. 4, 1863, *OR*, I, 25, pt. 1, 397–398; Nathaniel P. Banks to H. W. Halleck, Nov. 6, 1863, *OR*, I, 26, pt. 1, 399–400.

3 *Harper's Weekly*, Nov. 28, 1863.

4 Ibid.

5 Thompson, *Mexican Texans in the Union Army*, 10–15.

6 Edmund J. Davis to [N. P. Banks], n.d., John L. Haynes, CSR, RG 94 (NA).

7 John L. Haynes to N. P. Banks, Aug. 26, 1863, John L. Haynes, CSR, RG 94 (NA).

8 Juan N. Cortina to John L. Haynes, Sept. 12, 1863, letter in private collection.

9 A. Lincoln to Edwin M. Stanton, Aug. 4, 1862, *The Collected Works of Abraham Lincoln*, ed. Roy P. Basler (9 vols.; New Brunswick, N.J.: Rutgers University Press, 1953), V, 357.

10 "Rebel Plan," n.d., John L. Haynes Papers (CAH); "Various Propositions Submitted to the War Department by E. J. Davis and J. L. Haynes, 1862," Heintzelman Papers (LC). Also Edmund J. Davis to S. P. Heintzelman, Aug. 8, 1862, Heintzelman Papers (LC).

11 Heintzelman Journal, Sept. 6, 1863, Manuscript Division (LC).

12 *New Orleans Picayune*, Apr. 27, 1864; John L. Waller, *Colossal Hamilton of Texas: A Biography of Andrew Jackson Hamilton, Militant Unionist and Reconstruction Governor* (El Paso: Texas Western Press, 1968), 52–53.

13 H. P. Bee to Manuel Ruiz, Sept. 12, 1863, *OR*, I, 26, pt. 2, 222.

14 Edmund P. Turner to H. P. Bee, June 5, 1863, *OR*, I, 26, pt. 2, 37.

15 H. P. Bee to E. P. Turner, April 27, 1863, Letters Received, District of Texas, New Mexico, and Arizona, RG 109 (NA).

16 Hamilton P. Bee to E. P. Turner, Aug. 15, 1863, Bee Letterbook, Library (USMA).

17 Hamilton P. Bee to E. P. Turner, Aug. 24, 1863, ibid.

18 Hamilton P. Bee and James Slaughter to E. P. Turner, Sept. 14, 1863, ibid.

19 Hamilton P. Bee to E. P. Turner, Aug. 14, 1863, ibid.

20 Hamilton P. Bee to E. P. Turner, Aug. 24, 1863, ibid.

21 Henry T. Davis to George W. Caldwell, Nov. 11, 1863, *OR*, I, 26, pt. 1, 444–445. The bluecoats had come to the Rio Grande frontier "to enlist the Mexicans and arm the negroes as they march through Texas," Bee wrote. H. P. Bee to Edmund J. Turner, Nov. 15, 1863, *OR*, I, 26, pt. 2, 414.

22 Hamilton P. Bee to Edmund P. Turner, Nov. 5, 1863, *OR*, I, 26, pt. 1, 433.

23 R. Taylor to James Duff, Nov. 3, 1863, *OR*, I, 26, 1, 443–444.

24 *Houston Tri-Weekly Telegraph*, Nov. 12, 1863, quoting the *Fort Brown Flag* (Brownsville), Oct. 30, 1863.

25 James Duff to E. R. Tarver, Nov. 11, 1863, *OR*, I, 26, pt. 1, 439–443; Hamilton P. Bee to Edmund P. Turner, Oct. 28, 1863, *OR*, I, 26, pt. 1, 448–449; and Adrián J. Vidal, CSR (Union), RG 54 (NA).

26 Thompson, *Vaqueros in Blue and Gray*, 71–74. Also *Houston Tri-Weekly Telegraph*, Nov. 12, 1863, quoting the *Fort Brown Flag* (Brownsville), Oct. 30, 1863.

27 James Duff to E. R. Tarver, Nov. 11, 1863, *OR*, I, 26, pt. 1, 439–444. Also Williams, *With the Border Ruffians*, 201.

28 James Duff to E. R. Tarver, Nov. 11, 1863, *OR*, I, 26, pt. 1, 439–443.

29 *Houston Tri-Weekly Telegraph*, Nov. 12, 1863, quoting the *Fort Brown Flag* (Brownsville), Oct. 30, 1863.

30 Several of Vidal's men were later arrested for murders committed in Mexico and were executed by firing squad in Matamoros in January 1867. *Brownsville Daily Ranchero*, Jan. 18, 1867.

31 Hamilton P. Bee to Manuel Ruiz, Oct. 28, 1863, *OR*, I, 26, pt. 1, 450.

32 Manuel Ruiz to Hamilton P. Bee, Oct. 28, 1863, *OR*, I, 26, pt. 1, 450.

33 *Houston Tri-Weekly Telegraph*, Nov. 12, 1863, quoting the *Fort Brown Flag* (Brownsville), Oct. 30, 1863.

34 Hamilton P. Bee to Edmund P. Turner, Nov. 8, 1863, *OR*, I, 26, pt. 1, 434.

35 Ibid., 434–435.

36 Kearney and Knopp, *Boom and Bust*, 128.

37 N. P. Banks to H. W. Halleck, Nov. 6, 1863, *OR*, I, 26, pt. 1, 399–400.

38 Thompson, *Juan Cortina*, 30. Also H. P. Bee to A. G.

Dickinson, Mar. 3, 1863, Letters Received, District of Texas, New Mexico, and Arizona, RG 109 (NA).

[39] N. P. Banks to H. W. Halleck, Nov. 9, 1863, *OR*, I, 26, pt. 1, 404.

[40] Post Returns, Brazos Santiago, May 1864, Records of the Adjutant General's Office, RG 393 (NA). The Eighty-seventh and Ninety-fifth regiments were later combined to form the Eighty-first U.S. Colored Troops.

[41] General Order no. 16, Brownsville, Feb. 19, 1864. Copy in Kingsbury Papers (CAH).

[42] Kearney and Knopp, *Boom and Bust*, 127–128.

[43] José María Cobos to his Companions in Arms, Nov. 6, 1863, *OR*, I, 26, pt. 1, 401.

[44] Leonard Pierce Jr. to [William H. Seward], Jan. 16, 1864, Matamoros Consular Dispatches, RG 59 (NA).

[45] Juan Nepomuceno [Cortina] to the Public, Nov. 8, 1863, *OR*, I, 26, pt. 1, 406–407; N. P. Banks to H. W. Halleck, Nov. 6, 1863, *OR*, I, 26, pt. 1, 399–400. Also see Nannie M. Tilley (ed.), *Federals on the Frontier: The Diary of Benjamin F. McIntyre, 1862–1864* (Austin: University of Texas Press, 1963), 388–389; Santiago Vidaurri to Benito Juárez, Nov. 7, 1863, *Benito Juárez: Documentos, Discursos y Correspondencia* (15 vols.; Mexico City: Secretaria del Patrimonio Nacional, 1964–1969), VIII, 315 (hereafter cited as *Correspondencia de Juárez*); Daddysman, *The Matamoros Trade*, 94–95. Bee was under the impression that Cobos had been executed on the main plaza in Matamoros. Edmund J. Turner to H. P. Bee, Nov. 15, 1863, *OR*, I, 26, pt. 2, 415.

[46] N. P. Banks to H. W. Halleck, Nov. 7, 1863, *OR*, I, 26, pt. 1, 403.

[47] N. P. Banks to L. Pierce, Nov. 7, 1863, *OR*, I, 26, pt. 1, 405.

[48] Manuel Ruiz to the Citizens of Matamoros, Nov. 7, 1963, *OR*, I, 26, pt. 1, 402.

[49] N. P. Banks to H. W. Halleck, Nov. 6, 1863, *OR*, I, 26, pt. 1, 399–400. Also see Thompson, *Juan Cortina*, 31.

[50] F. J. Herron to Charles P. Stone, Jan. 16, 1864, *OR*, I, 34, pt. 2, 92–93; Juan N. Cortina to Santiago Vidaurri, Dec. 28, 1863, Correspondencia de Santiago Vidaurri (Archivo General del Estado de Nuevo León). Vidaurri had previously sent a small number of men to assist Cortina while asking for armaments, especially rifles, which Cortina was unable to deliver.

[51] N. J. T. Dana to Charles P. Stone, Dec. 11, 1863, *OR*, I, 26, pt. 1, 843–844 (quotation); N. J. T. Dana to Charles P. Stone, Dec. 18, 1863, *OR*, I, 26, pt. 1, 864–865.

[52] Tilley, *Federals on the Frontier*, 290.

[53] F. J. Herron to Charles P. Stone, Jan. 16, 1864, *OR*, I, 34, pt. 2, 92. Also see Daddysman, *The Matamoros Trade*, 96.

[54] Tilley, *Federals on the Frontier*, 290; Manuel Ruiz to

Benito Juárez, Jan. 12, 1864, *Correspondencia de Juárez*, VIII, 533–534.

[55] Tilley, *Federals on the Frontier*, 290.

[56] Ibid. Also see F. J. Herron to Charles P. Stone, Jan. 16, 1864, *OR*, I, 34, pt. 2, 92; and Manuel Ruiz to F. J. Herron, Jan. 15, 1864, *Correspondencia de Juárez*, VIII, 543.

[57] *Frank Leslie's Illustrated Newspaper*, Feb. 20, 1864; F. J. Herron to Charles P. Stone, Jan. 15, 1864, *OR*, I, 34, pt. 1, 84; *Houston Tri-Weekly Telegraph*, Feb. 1, 1864.

[58] L. Pierce Jr. to F. J. Herron, Jan. 12, 1864, *OR*, I, 34, pt. 1, 81.

[59] Manuel Ruiz to F. J. Herron, Jan. 15, 1864, *Correspondencia de Juárez*, VIII, 535. This same letter is in *OR*, I, 34, pt. 1, 82. Also see *Harper's Weekly*, Feb. 6, 1864, and F. J. Herron to Charles P. Stone, Jan. 15, 1864, *OR*, I, 34, pt. 1, 82.

[60] F. J. Herron to Manuel Ruiz, Jan. 12, 1864, *OR*, I, 34, pt. 1, 83. This letter is reprinted in *Correspondencia de Juárez*, VIII, 535–536.

[61] H. Bertram to [F. J.] Herron, Jan. 12 [13], 1864, *OR*, I, 34, pt. 1, 83.

[62] Tilley, *Federals on the Frontier*, 292.

[63] Manuel Ruiz to Benito Juárez, Jan. 14, 1864, *Correspondencia de Juárez*, VIII, 536–537; F. J. Herron to Charles P. Stone, Jan. 15, 1864, *OR*, I, 34, pt. 1, 84.

[64] Manuel Ruiz to Benito Juárez, Jan. 14, 1864, *Correspondencia de Juárez*, VIII, 536–537.

[65] Juan N. Cortina to the Inhabitants [of Matamoros], Jan. 14, 1865, *Correspondencia de Juárez*, VIII, 538–539; M. M. Kimmey to William H. Seward, May 21, 1864, *OR*, I, 34, pt. 4, 166–167.

[66] *Matamoros Daily Ranchero*, Feb. 1, 1866. In May 1866 a Cameron County grand jury indicted Gen. Francis J. Herron for kidnapping. *New Orleans Daily Crescent*, May 23, 1866; *Brownsville Daily Ranchero*, Mar. 17, 1868, and Sept. 21, 1869.

[67] John A. McClernand to Juan N. Cortina, Apr. 7, 1864, *OR*, I, 34, pt. 3, 73.

[68] John A. McClernand to Juan N. Cortina, Apr. 8, 1864, *OR*, I, 34, pt. 3, 87.

[69] J. B. Magruder to John Slidell, Apr. 27, 1864, *OR*, I, 34, pt. 3, 796.

[70] J. B. Magruder to Juan N. Cortina, May 22, 1864, *OR*, I, 34, pt. 3, 835.

[71] M. M. Kimmey to William H. Seward, May 21, 1864, *OR*, I, 34, pt. 4, 467.

[72] Ibid. For Bee praising Benavides, see H. P. Bee to Edmund P. Turner, Nov. 15, 1863, *OR*, I, 26, pt. 2, 414–415.

[73] J. Bankhead Magruder to W. R. Boggs, Jan. 6, 1864, *OR*, I, 34, pt. 2, 834.

74 Edmund P. Turner to [Hamilton P.] Bee, Dec. 5, 1863, *OR*, I, 26, pt. 2, 483.

75 J. Bankhead Magruder to W. R. Boggs, Jan. 6, 1864, *OR*, I, 34, pt. 2, 834.

76 Thompson, *Mexican Texans in the Civil War*, 15.

77 N. J. T. Dana to Charles P. Stone, Dec. 2, 1863, *OR*, I, 26, pt. 1, 840. Also see Muster Roll of Vidal's Partisan Rangers, Adjutant General's Records (TSA). Muster rolls of the First and Second Texas Cavalry were reprinted in *Adjutant General's Report, 1873* (Austin, 1875), 111–112.

78 N. P. Banks to J. L. Haynes, Nov. 5, 1863, Seb Wilcox Papers (St. Mary's University Library, San Antonio, Texas).

79 Recruiting handbill signed by Antonio Abad Días, John S. Ford Papers (Confederate Research Center, Hill College, Hillsboro, Texas).

80 "Sketch of the Life of Matias S. Garza and Matianita Ramirez de Garza," document in possession of Elena F. Barrera, Mission, Texas.

81 Gil Treviño to Jerry Thompson, Sept. 20, 2001, interview.

82 *Brownsville Daily Ranchero and Republican*, Sept. 19, 1871.

83 Thompson, *Mexican Texans in the Union Army*, 17–19, 21.

84 *Houston Tri-Weekly Telegraph*, Jan. 20, Feb. 1, 1864; Tom Lea, *The King Ranch* (2 vols.; Boston: Little, Brown and Co., 1957), I, 215–218; James Speed, CSR, RG 94 (NA).

85 Ford, *Rip Ford's Texas*, 638–639; John S. Ford "Memoirs," 1,058 (CAH).

86 Ford, *Rip Ford's Texas*, 355.

87 In 2001 Homero Vera, editor of *Los Mesteños* and a resident of Premont, after much effort, located what is thought to be the site of Los Patricios twelve miles northwest of Premont.

88 Mat Nolan to John S. Ford, Mar. 15, 1864, *OR*, I, 34, pt. 1, 642–643; *Corpus Christi Caller*, Nov. 22, Dec. 6, 1976.

89 Ford, *Rip Ford's Texas*, 357.

90 Santos Benavides to John S. Ford, Mar. 21, 1864, *OR*, I, 34, pt. 1, 648; Thomas A. Dwyer to John S. Ford, Mar. 21, 1864, Ford Papers; Jerry Thompson, "A Stand Along the Border: Santos Benavides and the Battle for Laredo," *Civil War Times Illustrated*, 26 (Aug., 1980), 26–33; Thompson, *Vaqueros in Blue and Gray*, 107–110. The Union version of the battle, if it exists, was lost or has yet to be found.

91 Santos Benavides to John S. Ford, Mar. 21, 1864, *OR*, I, 34, pt. 1, 648; Thompson, *Mexican Texans in the Civil War*, 24.

92 F. J. Herron to Charles P. Stone, Jan. 15, 1864, *OR*, I, 34, pt. 2, 84–87.

93 T. P. McManus to N. J. T. Dana, Feb. 13, 1864, *OR*, I, 34, pt. 2, 316–320.

94 J. R. West to Nathaniel P. Banks, Dec. 17, 1863, *OR*, I, 34, pt. 2, 219.

95 H. P. Bee to A. G. Dickinson, Nov. 13, 1863, *OR*, I, 26, pt. 2, 413.

96 F. J. Herron to William Dwight, July 2, 1864, *OR*, I, 34, pt. 1, 1,054.

97 J. B. Weyman to E. P. Turner, Apr. 5, 1864, *OR*, I, 34, pt. 3, 736.

99 James A. Ware to Bart J. DeWitt, June 20, 1864, *OR*, I, 34, pt. 1, 1,034.

100 Entry of John L. Haynes, Dec. 26, 1863, "Record Book of the Second Texas Cavalry, 1863–1864," Adjutant General's Office (TSA).

101 McIntyre, *Federals on the Frontier*, 346–347.

102 Thompson, *Mexican Texans in the Civil War*, 25.

103 A. J. Vidal to H. Clamp [*sic*], May 30, 1864, Adrián J. Vidal, CSR, RG 94 (NA).

104 Thompson, *Mexican Texans in the Civil War*, 27.

105 Thompson, *Vaqueros in Blue and Gray*, 204; Court-Martial of Pedro García, Court-Martial Case Files, File no. 2228, Records of the Judge Advocate General's Office, RG 153 (NA), cited hereafter as JAGO.

106 Testimony of John Tuscana and Calletano Molina, Court-Martial of Pedro García, JAGO.

107 Testimony of A. B. Slaughter, Court-Martial of Pedro García, JAGO.

108 Court-Martial of Pedro García, JAGO.

109 Parisot, *Reminiscences of a Texas Missionary*, 108.

110 McIntyre, *Federals on the Frontier*, 353–354.

111 Ibid.

112 Parisot, *Reminiscences of a Texas Missionary*, 108.

113 McIntyre, *Federals on the Frontier*, 354.

CHAPTER 3: CONFEDERATE CAVALRY OF THE WEST

1 Ford, *Rip Ford's Texas*, 344.

2 Edmund P. Turner to John S. Ford, Dec. 22, 1863, *OR*, I, 26, pt. 2, 525–526.

3 Ford, *Rip Ford's Texas*, 347.

4 One was Maj. Anton Felix Hans Hellmuth von Blücher. The grand-nephew of Field Marshal Gerhard Leberecht von Blücher of the Prussian Army and Waterloo fame, he was fluent in Spanish and several other languages. Moreover, he had surveyed much of the area between the Nueces and the Rio Grande in the years before the war and was thoroughly acquainted with the geography and topography of the area. Ford, *Rip Ford's Texas*, 350. By

the time of the Civil War Blücher had shortened his name to Felix Blücher.

[5] Ford, *Rip Ford's Texas*, 351.

[6] John S. Ford to E. P. Turner, Dec. 25, 1863, Letters Received, District of Texas, New Mexico, and Arizona, RG 109 (NA).

[7] Jerry Thompson, "Drama in the Desert: The Hunt for Henry Skillman in the Trans–Pecos, 1862–1864," *Password*, 3 (Fall, 1992), 107–126.

[8] John S. Ford to Maj. Gen. Magruder, Feb. 9, 1864, Letters Received, District of Texas, New Mexico, and Arizona, RG 109 (NA).

[9] John S. Ford to E. P. Turner, Feb. 21, 1864, Letters Received, District of Texas, New Mexico, and Arizona, RG 109 (NA).

[10] "Reconstruction of Past Drought across the Coterminous United States from a Network of Climatically Sensitive Tree-Ring Data," National Oceanic and Atmospheric Administration, United States Department of Commerce, www.ngdc.noaa.gov/paleo,pdsiyear.html. With the exception of 1861, when the rainfall was normal in South Texas, precipitation was from two to three inches below normal every year from 1859 to 1864. Not until 1865 was the drought in the Lower Valley broken by adequate rainfall.

[11] Rodgers quoted in Ford, *Rip Ford's Texas*, 347–348.

[12] John S. Ford to S. Benavides, Captain Ware, and Captain Giddings, Feb. 4, 1864, Letters Received, District of Texas, New Mexico, and Arizona, RG 109 (NA).

[13] Ford, *Rip Ford's Texas*, 350.

[14] John S. Ford to Mat Nolan, Mar. 5, 1864, Letters Received, District of Texas, New Mexico, and Arizona, RG 109 (NA). Also see John S. Ford to Santos Benavides, Mar. 5, 1864; John S. Ford to G. H. Giddings, Mar. 5, 1864; John S. Ford to E. P. Turner, Mar. 6, 1864, all in ibid. Ford's letters can be found at the Harold B. Simpson Research Center, Hill College, Hillsboro, Texas, and copies of the same are at the Texas State Archives in Austin.

[15] Nolan was later murdered in Corpus Christi on December 19, 1864. *Houston Tri-Weekly Telegraph*, Jan. 6, 1865.

[16] John S. Ford to E. P. Turner, Apr. 9, 1964, *OR*, I, 34, pt. 3, 754.

[17] John S. Ford to E. P. Turner, Apr. 17, 1864, *OR*, I, 53, 980–981.

[18] Ford, *Rip Ford's Texas*, 359, 360.

[19] J. B. Weyman to E. P. Turner, Apr. 5, 1864, *OR*, I, 34, pt. 3, 736.

[20] Thompson, *Vaqueros in Blue and Gray*, 112.

[21] J. María García Villarreal to John S. Ford, June 11, 1864, Letters Received, District of Texas, New Mexico, and Arizona, RG 109 (NA).

[22] John S. Ford to J. E. Slaughter, June 5, 1864, Letters Received, District of Texas, New Mexico, and Arizona, RG 109 (NA).

[23] Thompson, *Vaqueros in Blue and Gray*, 112.

[24] Undated, unsigned document in Letters Received, District of Texas, New Mexico, and Arizona, RG 109 (NA); George Pfeuffer to [Santos] Benavides, Feb. 22, 1864, Letters Received, District of Texas, New Mexico, and Arizona, RG 109 (NA).

[25] John S. Ford to E. P. Turner, May 5, 1864, *OR*, I, 34, pt. 3, 808.

[26] John S. Ford to J. E. Slaughter, June 20, 1864, *OR*, I, 34, pt. 4, 684–685.

[27] Thompson, *Vaqueros in Blue and Gray*, 362.

[28] John S. Ford to J. E. Slaughter, June 20, 1864, *OR*, I, 34, pt. 4, 685.

[29] John S. Ford to J. E. Slaughter, July 2, 1864, *OR*, I, 34, pt. 1, 1,055.

[30] Thompson, *Mexican Texans in the Union Army*, 30.

[31] Killed and Wounded at Las Rucias, [Texas], June 25, 1864, Confederate Army Casualties and Narrative Reports, RG 109 (NA). See also Frank Wilson Kiel (ed.), "'Wir waren unser 20 mann gegen 150' ('We were 20 men against 150'): The Battle of Las Rucias: A Civil War Letter from a German–Texan Soldier in the 1864 Union Invasion of the Lower Rio Grande Valley," *Southwestern Historical Quarterly*, 105 (Jan., 2002), 465–478.

[32] John S. Ford to J. E. Slaughter, July 2, 1864, *OR*, I, 34, pt. 1, 1,055.

[33] General Herron reported the Union losses at "15 to 20 killed and wounded." Francis J. Herron to William Dwight, June 26, 1864, *OR*, I, 34, pt. 1, 1,055–1,056.

[34] John S. Ford to J. E. Slaughter, July 2, 1864, *OR*, I, 34, pt. 1, 1,056.

[35] Ibid., 1,055.

[36] Hunt, "History of the First Texas Cavalry," John L. Haynes Papers (CAH).

[37] Ford, *Rip Ford's Texas*, 365–366.

CHAPTER 4: LONG ROAD TO PALMITO RANCH

[1] *New York Herald*, July 2, 1865.

[2] As of May 1864 the artillery overlooking Boca Chica and on the south end of Brazos Santiago consisted of both light and heavy artillery, including two 20-pounder Parrots, two 30-pounders, one 24-pounder brass howitzer, one 24-pounder smoothbore, one 18-pounder smoothbore, and three 12-pounders. Post Returns, Brazos Santiago, August 1864, RG 393, Adjutant General's Office (NA).

[3] Henry M. Day to George B. Drake, Aug. 15, 1864,

OR, I, 41, pt. 1, 211–212.

⁴ John S. Ford to W. Kearny, Aug. 16, 1864, *OR*, I, 42, pt. 2, 1,069.

⁵ Post Returns, Brazos Santiago, Nov. 1864, RG 393, Adjutant General's Office (NA).

⁶ Henry M. Day to George B. Drake, Sept. 8, 1864, *OR*, I, 41, pt. 1, 742.

⁷ Charles Allen Smart, *Viva Juárez: A Biography* (New York: J. B. Lippincott, 1964), 277; Ralph Roeder, *Juárez and His Mexico* (New York: Viking Press, 1947), 512–513.

⁸ J. A. Quintero to J. P. Benjamin, Jan. 25, 1864, Pickett Papers (LC); Tyler, *Santiago Vidaurri and the Southern Confederacy*, 137.

⁹ Juan N. Cortina to Benito Juárez, Jan. 21, 1864, *Correspondencia de Juárez*, VIII, 549.

¹⁰ Smart, *Viva Juárez*, 303; Tyler, *Santiago Vidaurri and the Southern Confederacy*, 139.

¹¹ J. E. Slaughter to [Santos Benavides], Mar. 24, 1864, *OR*, I, 34, pt. 2, 1,079.

¹² Santos Benavides to James E. Slaughter, Apr. 10, 1864, *OR*, I, 53, 980–981.

¹³ Tyler, *Santiago Vidaurri and the Southern Confederacy*, 139.

¹⁴ L. Pierce Jr. to [William H. Seward], Sept. 1, 1864, Matamoros Consular Dispatches, RG 59 (NA).

¹⁵ John S. Ford to the Officer in Command of the French Forces on the Rio Grande near Boca del Rio, Aug. 24, 1864, *OR*, I, 42, pt. 2, 1,089.

¹⁶ A. Veron to the Colonel Commanding the Confederate Forces on the Rio Grande, [Aug. 25, 1864], *OR*, I, 42, pt. 2, 1,089–1,090.

¹⁷ Ford, *Rip Ford's Texas*, 369.

¹⁸ Ibid., 375.

¹⁹ John S. Ford to J. E. Dwyer, Sept. 3, 1864, *OR*, I, 41, pt. 3, 909.

²⁰ Ford, *Rip Ford's Texas*, 375.

²¹ Ibid., 370, 372.

²² Ibid., 371, 373.

²³ Ibid., 376. Colonel Canales was allowed, however, to take his army back across the river, where he rearmed and again took up the cause of the republic.

²⁴ L. Pierce to F. J. Herron, Sept. 8, 1864, *OR*, I, 41, pt. 3, 101; L. Pierce Jr. to [William H. Seward], Sept. 1, 1864, Matamoros Consular Dispatches, RG 59 (NA).

²⁵ H. M. Day to George B. Drake, Sept. 14, 1864, *OR*, I, 41, pt. 3, 184. Also see *Matamoros Daily Ranchero*, Aug. 12, 1865.

²⁶ Ford, *Rip Ford's Texas*, 374.

²⁷ H. M. Day to George B. Drake, Sept. 14, 1864, *OR*, I, 41, pt. 3, 184.

²⁸ Ford, *Rip Ford's Texas*, 375.

²⁹ A. Veron to [H. M. Day], Sept. 7, 1964, *OR*, I, 41, pt. 3, 100.

³⁰ J. G. Walker to J. E. Slaughter, Oct. 1, 1864, *OR*, I, 41, pt. 3, 972.

³¹ John S. Ford to Commanding Officer, U.S. Forces, Sept. 12, 1864, *OR*, I, 41, pt. 3, 947.

³² H. M. Day to J. S. Ford, Sept. 13, 1864, *OR*, I, 41, pt. 3, 947. Lt. Col. H. S. Smith of the Ninety-first Illinois allowed Ford's couriers to proceed to the Union headquarters on the north end of the island without being blindfolded, thus enabling the Confederates "to see the exact number and position of our guns and to form a fair estimate of the number of our troops." As a result Day ordered Smith arrested and preferred charges against him.

³³ H. M. Day to George B. Drake, Oct. 9, 1864, *OR*, I, 41, pt. 3, 721.

³⁴ Thos. F. Drayton to J. G. Walker, Sept. 26, 1864, enclosing statements of Juan N. Cortina (Sept. 23, 1864), Thomas F. Drayton (Sept. 22, 1864), Thos. F. Drayton to Juan N. Cortina (Sept. 23, 1864), and agreement of Juan N. Cortina, J. S. Espiundola, and Thos. F. Drayton (Sept. 23, 1864), *OR*, I, 41, pt. 3, 958–959.

³⁵ Ford, *Rip Ford's Texas*, 376.

³⁶ H. M. Day to George B. Drake, Oct. 9, 1864, *OR*, I, 41, 3, 721.

³⁷ *Brownsville Daily Ranchero*, Sept. 24, 1870; Thompson, *Juan Cortina*, 48, 59.

³⁸ Geo. F. Emmons to W. H. Seward, Mar. 8, 1865, Matamoros Consular Dispatches, RG 59 (NA).

³⁹ Thos. F. Drayton to Thomas [*sic*] Mejía, Sept. 28, 1864, *OR*, I, 41, pt. 3, 973.

⁴⁰ Ford, *Rip Ford's Texas*, 383.

⁴¹ Pitner, *Maximilian's Lieutenant*, 119.

⁴² H. M. Day to George B. Drake, Oct. 21, 1864, *OR*, I, 41, pt. 1, 888.

⁴³ Robert L. Kerby, *Kirby Smith's Confederacy: The Trans–Mississippi South, 1863–1865* (New York: Columbia University Press, 1972), 1.

⁴⁴ Robert E. Morsberger and Katherine M. Morsberger, *Lew Wallace, Militant Romantic: The Colorful Life of America's Foremost Literary Adventurer* (New York: McGraw Hill, 1980), 159.

⁴⁵ Lew Wallace, *An Autobiography* (2 vols.; New York: Harper and Brothers, 1906), II, 814.

⁴⁶ Lew Wallace to [Ulysses S. Grant], Mar. 14, 1865, *OR*, I, 48, pt. 1, 1,277.

⁴⁷ Morsberger and Morsberger, *Lew Wallace*, 161.

⁴⁸ Lew Wallace to [Ulysses S. Grant], Mar. 14, 1865, *OR*, I, 48, pt. 1, 1,277.

⁴⁹ Lew Wallace to J. E. Slaughter and J. S. Ford, Mar. 12, 1865, *OR*, I, 48, pt. 1, 1,280–1,281.

⁵⁰ Lew Wallace to [Ulysses S. Grant], Mar. 14, 1865,

OR, I, 48, 1, pt. 1, 277.

51 J. G. Walker to [Lew] Wallace, Mar. 27, 1865, *OR*, I, 48, pt. 1, 1,275.

52 Richard King to Green Hall, Apr. 26, 1865 (King Ranch Archives, Kingsville, Texas).

53 L. G. Aldrich to George Patrick, May 20, 1865, in *New York Tribune*, July 2, 1865.

54 *New York Tribune*, July 2, 1865.

55 William L. Richter, *The Army in Texas during Reconstruction, 1865–1870* (College Station: Texas A&M University Press, 1987), 13.

56 Ford, *Rip Ford's Texas*, 396.

57 *New York Herald*, July 2, 1865.

58 Testimony of Col. Theodore H. Barrett, Court-Martial Records in the Case of Robert G. Morrison, July 21–Aug. 29, 1865, JAGO.

59 Ibid.

60 Eight companies of the Thirty-fourth Indiana Infantry had arrived on Brazos Santiago three days before Christmas 1864, replacing the Ninety-first Illinois Infantry, which embarked for New Orleans on the *Clinton*. Post Returns, Brazos Santiago, December 1864, RG 393, Adjutant General's Office (NA).

61 Theodore H. Barrett to L. Thomas, Aug. 10, 1865, *OR*, I, 48, pt. 1, 266.

62 Ford, *Rip Ford's Texas*, 390, 391.

63 Theodore H. Barrett to L. Thomas, Aug. 10, 1865, *OR*, I, 48, pt. 1, 266.

64 Ibid.

65 John R. Smith Testimony, Morrison Court-Martial, JAGO.

66 George W. Burns Testimony, Morrison Court-Martial, JAGO.

67 David Branson Testimony, Morrison Court-Martial, JAGO.

68 Charles A. Jones Testimony, Morrison Court-Martial, JAGO.

69 Barrett Testimony, Morrison Court-Martial, JAGO.

70 Jones Testimony, Morrison Court-Martial, JAGO.

71 Ford, *Rip Ford's Texas*, 392.

72 Barrett Testimony, Morrison Court-Martial, JAGO.

73 Testimony of Capt. W. C. Dukee, Morrison Court-Martial, JAGO.

74 Ford, *Rip Ford's Texas*, 391.

75 L. G. Aldrich to John S. Ford, Oct. 21, 1890, in Ford, *Rip Ford's Texas*, 394–395.

76 Theodore Barrett to L. Thomas, Aug. 10, 1865, *OR*, I, 48, pt. 1, 267.

77 Noah Andre Trudeau, "The Last Gun Had Been Fired," *Civil War Times Illustrated*, 29 (July–Aug., 1990), 63.

78 Theodore Barrett to L. Thomas, Aug. 10, 1865, *OR*,

I, 48, pt. 1, 267. Also see Noah Andre Trudeau, *Out of the Storm: The End of the Civil War, April–June 1865* (Baton Rouge: Louisiana State University Press, 1994), 309–310. From the various testimony in the court-martial case of Lt. Col. Robert G. Morrison, along with the Post Returns for Brazos Santiago, it appears the casualties amounted to two men killed (one of those mortally wounded was Bill Redman) and four wounded from the Sixty-second U.S. Colored Infantry; seventy-seven men and two officers captured, one wounded and one killed (John Jefferson Williams) from the Thirty-fourth Indiana Infantry; and twenty men and two officers (1st Lt. J. W. Hancock and 2nd Lt. Thomas A. James) captured, seven wounded, and one killed in the Second U.S. Texas Cavalry. The behavior of the Thirty-fourth Indiana, a veteran regiment that had fought at Port Gibson and Champion's Hill, Mississippi, in May 1863, was blamed on the lax discipline and lack of leadership in the regiment. See Post Returns, Brazos Santiago, May 1865, RG 393, Adjutant General's Office (NA). For a detailed discussion of the confusion over determining the casualties at Palmito Ranch see Phillip Thomas Tucker, *The Final Fury: Palmito Ranch, the Last Battle of the Civil War* (Mechanicsburg, Pa.: Stackpole Books, 2001), 156–163. For an excellent and comprehensive study of the battle see Jeffrey Wm. Hunt, *The Last Battle of the Civil War: Palmetto Ranch* (Austin: University of Texas Press, 2002).

79 John Markle testimony, Morrison Court-Martial, JAGO. Also see Hunt, *Last Battle of the Civil War*, 131.

80 Ford, *Rip Ford's Texas*, 393.

81 Hunt, *Last Battle of the Civil War*, 132.

82 Ford, *Rip Ford's Texas*, 396. Also see *Matamoros Ranchero*, May 24, 1865; and *Matamoros Daily Ranchero*, May 31, 1865.

83 Ford, *Rip Ford's Texas*, 387.

84 J. E. Slaughter to Commanding Officer, U.S. Forces on the March, May 29, 1865, Letters Received, Adjutant General's Office, RG 94 (NA).

85 E. G. Brown to J. E. Slaughter, May 30, 1865, Letters Received, Adjutant General's Office, RG 94 (NA).

86 D. Finley to John Price, Jan. 13, 1866; William Griffin to Price, Jan. 13, 1866; Ed. J. Allen to Price, Jan. 12, 1866; all in Letters Received, Adjutant General's Office, RG 94 (NA).

87 E. B. Brown to J. Schuyler Crosby, May 28, June 2, 1865, Letters Received, Adjutant General's Office, RG 94 (NA).

88 *Matamoros Daily Ranchero*, May 31, 1865.

89 Ed. J. Allen to John Price, Jan. 12, 1866, Letters Received, Adjutant General's Office, RG 94 (NA).

90 E. B. Brown to J. Schuyler Crosby, May 30, 1865, Letters Received, Adjutant General's Office, RG 94 (NA).

91 F. Steele to P. H. Sheridan, June 10, 1865, Letters Received, Adjutant General's Office, RG 94 (NA).

92 W. G. Wiley to Headquarters, Military District of the Gulf, June 13, 1865, Letters Received, Adjutant General's Office, RG 94 (NA).

93 Santos Benavides to John Z. Leyendecker, May 16, 1865, John Z. Leyendecker Papers (CAH).

CHAPTER 5: BLOODY SIEGES AND BORDER RAIDS

1 Ben Z. Grant, "A Texas Governor Buried in Mexico," *Marshall News Messenger*, Jan. 3, 1999; Ben Z. Grant, "Finding Governor Murrah," *Marshall News Messenger*, Mar. 14, 1999.

2 Edwin Adams Davis, *Fallen Guidon: The Saga of Confederate General Jo Shelby's March to Mexico* (College Station: Texas A&M University Press, 1995), 71.

3 *Brownsville Daily Ranchero*, July 28, 1865, and Dec. 11, 1867; Richard and James Owen, *Generals at Rest: The Grave Sites of the 425 Official Confederate Generals* (Shippensburg, Pa.: White Mane, 1997), 335.

4 *New York Herald*, July 2, 1865.

5 *New York Tribune*, Oct. 27, 1865. Also see P. H. Sheridan to F. Steele, June 9, 1865; F. Steele to P. H. Sheridan, June 10, 1965; both in Letters Received, Adjutant General's Office, RG 94 (NA).

6 *Brownsville Daily Ranchero*, Dec. 1, 1866.

7 *New Orleans Daily Picayune*, Sept. 6, 1865.

8 [Lester Haines], "Tracing the Remains of Sheridan's Railroad Today," *Journal of Texas Shortline Railroads and Transportation* (Aug.–Oct., 1996), 2, 11–13.

9 *Brownsville Daily Ranchero*, Oct. 16, 1868.

10 *Matamoros Daily Ranchero*, June 2, 1865.

11 *New York Tribune*, Sept. 1, 1865.

12 After the regular army evacuated Fort Brown in 1861 and forces of the state of Texas assumed control, as recalled earlier, the post was turned over to Confederate authorities. In December 1863 the Federal army occupied the Lower Valley, followed by the Confederate reoccupation and the return of the Union army in May 1865.

13 *Matamoros Daily Ranchero*, June 9, 1865.

14 Richter, *Army in Texas during Reconstruction*, 17.

15 *New York Tribune*, Sept. 1, 1865.

16 Post Returns, Fort Ringgold, July 1865, Adjutant General's Office, RG 393 (NA). The Irish-born Jackson was a dedicated officer and combat veteran who had risen in the antebellum army from private to brigadier general during the Civil War.

17 Post Returns, Fort Ringgold, October 1865, Adjutant General's Office (NA).

18 Post Returns, Fort Ringgold, August 1866, Adjutant General's Office (NA).

19 Post Returns, Fort McIntosh, October 1865, Adjutant General's Office (NA).

20 Post Returns, Fort McIntosh, March 1866, Adjutant General's Office (NA).

21 Nathaniel Prime, Order no. 3, May 23, 1869, Letters Received, Department of Texas, Adjutant General's Office, RG 393 (NA).

22 *New York Tribune*, Sept. 1, 1865.

23 Post Returns, Fort Brown, February 1869, Adjutant General's Office, RG 393 (NA). For plans for construction of the new barracks, see *Brownsville Daily Ranchero*, Mar. 11, 1868.

24 Richter, *Army in Texas during Reconstruction*, 82. At Fort Brown the soldier was bucked and gagged as punishment.

25 *Brownsville Daily Ranchero*, Jan. 16, 1867.

26 Richter, *Army in Texas during Reconstruction*, 133.

27 *Galveston Tri-Weekly News*, Feb. 9, 1867.

28 *Brownsville Daily Ranchero*, Jan. 16, 1869.

29 E. B. Brown to J. S. Crosby, May 26, 1865, Letters Received, Adjutant General's Office, RG 94 (NA).

30 E. B. Brown to Tomás Mejía, May 31, 1865, Letters Received, Adjutant General's Office, RG 94 (NA).

31 Genaro García (ed.), *Documentos inéditos o muy raros para la historia de México* (Mexico City: n.p., 1910), 30, 46–47; Michael G. Webster, "Texan Manifest Destiny and the Mexican Border Conflict, 1865–1880" (Ph.D. diss., Indiana University, 1972), 44.

32 Richter, *Army in Texas during Reconstruction*, 24.

33 *Matamoros Daily Ranchero*, June 18, 1865.

34 E. B. Brown to J. E. Slaughter, June 4, 1865, Letters Received, Adjutant General's Office, RG 94 (NA).

35 P. H. Sheridan to Gordon Granger, June 16, 1865; F. Steele to P. H. Sheridan, June 21, 1865; F. Steele to Tomás Mejía, June 28, 1865; F. Steele to P. H. Sheridan July 6, 1865; all in Letters Received, Adjutant General's Office, RG 94 (NA).

36 P. H. Sheridan to F. Steele, July 7, 1865, Letters Received, Adjutant General's Office, RG 94 (NA).

37 Tomás Mejía to E. B. Brown, July 6, 1865, Letters Received, Adjutant General's Office, RG 94 (NA).

38 P. H. Sheridan to F. Steele, July 13, Aug. 7, 1865, Letters Received, Adjutant General's Office, RG 94 (NA).

39 *New York Herald*, Aug. 8, 1865.

40 Paul Andrew Hutton, *Phil Sheridan and His Army* (Lincoln: University of Nebraska Press, 1985), 22.

41 *New York Herald*, July 17, 1865.

42 *New York Herald*, July 29, 1865.

43 *Matamoros Daily Ranchero*, June 11, 1865.

44 *El Orden* (Matamoros), Feb. 16, 1865.

45 *New York Herald*, Sept. 20, 1965; *Matamoros Daily Ranchero*, Sept. 26, 1865.

46 Pitner, *Maximilian's Lieutenant*, 102.

47 Kearney and Knopp, *Boom and Bust*, 138.

48 *Matamoros Daily Ranchero*, June 13, 1865.

49 Kearney and Knopp, *Boom and Bust*, 143.

50 Webster, "Texan Manifest Destiny," 44.

51 *New York Herald*, July 15, 1865; *Matamoros Daily Ranchero*, June 27, 29, 1865. Also F. Steele to F. C. Newhall, July 1, 1865, Letters Received, Adjutant General's Office, RG 94 (NA).

52 *Matamoros Daily Ranchero*, July 16, 1865.

53 Kearney and Knopp, *Boom and Bust*, 136.

54 F. Steele to F. C. Newhall, July 1, 1865, Letters Received, Adjutant General's Office, RG 94 (NA).

55 F. Steele to P. H. Sheridan, July 6, 1865, Letters Received, Adjutant General's Office, RG 94 (NA).

56 E. B. Brown to J. N. Cortina, July 7, 1865; E. B. Brown to F. Steele, July 7, 1865; J. B. Rush to N. Heading-ton, July 7, 1865; Charles Black to F. Steele, July 8, 1865; E. B. Brown to F. Steele, July 8, 1865; all in Letters Received, Adjutant General's Office, RG 94 (NA).

57 F. Steele to Tomás Mejía, Aug. 3, 1865, Letters Received, Adjutant General's Office, RG 94 (NA).

58 *Matamoros Daily Ranchero*, July 4, 5, and 26, 1865.

59 *Matamoros Daily Ranchero*, Oct. 14, 1865.

60 *New York Herald*, July 21, 1865. Also E. B. Brown to F. Steele, July 7, 1865, Letters Received, Adjutant General's Office, RG 94 (NA).

61 *New York Herald*, July 21, 26, 1865; *Matamoros Daily Ranchero*, July 23, 1865.

62 *Matamoros Daily Ranchero*, Sept. 19, 1865.

63 Count Emile de Kératry, *The Rise and Fall of the Emperor Maximilian: A Narrative of the Mexican Empire, 1861–67 from Authentic Documents with the Imperial Correspondence* (London: Sampson Low, Son, and Marston, 1868), 70.

64 Jack A. Dabbs, *The French Army in Mexico, 1861–1867: A Study in Military Government* (The Hague: Mouton and Company, 1963), 85.

65 Pedro Martinez to the Citizens of Galeana, Yturbide, and Rio Blanco, May 22, 1866, in *Conditions of Affairs in Mexico*, 39th Cong., 2nd sess. (1866–1867), no. 1294, 222–223.

66 A. Gonzales to Mariano Escobedo, May 30, 1866, in *Conditions of Affairs in Mexico*, 223–224.

67 *New York Herald*, Oct. 20, 1865.

68 *Houston Tri-Weekly Telegraph*, June 16, 1865. Also see Jerry Thompson, "Adrián J. Vidal: Soldier of Three Republics," *Hispanic Genealogical Journal*, 14 (1996), 74–84; Jerry Thompson, "Mutiny and Desertion on the Rio Grande: The Strange Saga of Captain Adrián J.

Vidal," *Military History of Texas and the Southwest*, 11, no. 3 (1975), 160–169.

69 M. Kenedy to John Wilson, June 10, 1865, Kenedy Letterbook (King Ranch Archives, Kingsville, Texas). A few years later Vidal's remains were moved to the Kenedy family plot in a dark corner of the old Brownsville Cemetery.

70 Weber, "Texan Manifest Destiny," 46.

71 Mariano Escobedo, General of the Mexican Republic and Commanding the Division of the North, to the Inhabitants of the State of Tamaulipas; Mariano Escobedo, General of the Mexican Republic, Commanding Division of the North, to his Subordinates; both dated Oct. 19, 1865, in *New York Herald*, Nov. 23, 1865.

72 *New York Herald*, Nov. 28, 1865.

73 Lucius Avery to [W. H. Seward], Oct. 26, 1865, Matamoros Consular Dispatches, RG 59 (NA).

74 *New York Herald*, Nov. 10, 16, 18, 20, 1865; *Matamoros Daily Ranchero*, Oct. 25, 1865. Also see Godfrey Weitzel to F. Steele, Oct. 25, 1865, Letters Received, Adjutant General's Office, RG 94 (NA).

75 D. de la Bedolliero to Godfrey Weitzel, Nov. 8, 1865, Letters Received, Adjutant General's Office, RG 94 (NA).

76 G. Clouse to [Godfrey Weitzel], Nov. 9, 1865; Tomás Mejía to [Godfrey Weitzel], Nov. 9, 1865; both in Letters Received, Adjutant General's Office, RG 94 (NA). Also *New York Herald*, Dec. 4, 1865.

77 Godfrey Weitzel to G. Clouse, Nov. 10, 1865, Letters Received, Adjutant General's Office, RG 94 (NA).

78 G. Clouse to [Godfrey Weitzel], Nov. 6, 1865, Letters Received, Adjutant General's Office, RG 94 (NA).

79 *New York Herald*, Oct. 27, 1865.

80 Godfrey Weitzel to H. G. Wright, Nov. 5, 1865; H. G. Wright to Godfrey Weitzel, Nov. 9, 1865; both in Letters Received, Adjutant General's Office, RG 94 (NA).

81 *Matamoros Daily Ranchero*, Oct. 25, 28, 1865.

82 *Matamoros Daily Ranchero*, Nov. 10, 1865.

83 *Monitor of the Frontier* (Matamoros), Dec. 16, 1865.

84 Statement of Wm. D. St. Clair, Nov. 7, 1865, Letters Received, Adjutant General's Office, RG 94 (NA).

85 Wm. D. St. Clair to Edmund De Buck, Nov. 6, 1865; Franz Benter to Edmund De Buck, Nov. 5, 1865; Edmund De Buck to D. D. Wheeler; R. Rico to [Edmund De Buck], Nov. 5, 1865; statement of Henry Edmonds (watchman on the *Rio Grande*), Nov. 14, 1865; all in Letters Received, Adjutant General's Office, RG 94 (NA).

86 Weber, "Texan Manifest Destiny," 47.

87 P. H. Sheridan to [U. S. Grant], Jan. 28, 1866; G. S. Dodge to R. Clay Crawford, Jan. 12 (two letters), 1866, Letters Received, Adjutant General's Office, RG 94 (NA). Yet to learn of the raid on Bagdad, Dodge told Crawford that three hundred filibusters could be recruited in Galve-

ston and that arms could be procured in New Orleans. Unfortunately, many of the letters in the Adjutant General's Records at the National Archives relevant to the raid on Bagdad have faded to the point of being unreadable.

88 E. D. Townsend endorsement, Jan. 18, 1866, quoting Court-Martial Order no. 43, Department of the Cumberland, June 14, 1865, on J. Hubley Ashton to Hamilton Fish, Jan. 18, 1866, Letters Received, Adjutant General's Office, RG 94 (NA). Other leaders implicated in the raid on Bagdad included Wm. D. St. Clair, Thomas D. Sears, Theodore Lamberton, Benjamin Shaw, Alexander McDonald, and Edgar McDonald.

89 R. Clay Crawford to Geo. P. Edgar, Dec. 18, 1865, Letters Received, Adjutant General's Office, RG 94 (NA).

90 *New York Herald*, July 2, 1865.

91 Testimony of Frank J. White, A. C. Decker, and Albert A. M. McGaffie, "Military Commission Appointed to Investigate and Report Upon the Facts Relative to the Capture of the Town of Bagdad on the Mexican Side of the Rio Grande on January 5, 1866," RG 393, Adjutant General's Office (NA). Hereafter referred to as Bagdad Commission Investigation.

92 A. F. Reed to R. Clay Crawford, Dec. 18, 1865, Letters Received, Adjutant General's Office, RG 94 (NA). This letter, along with a number of others, was found in Crawford's baggage when he was later arrested in New Orleans.

93 Reed to Crawford, Jan. 3, 1866, Letters Received, Adjutant General's Office, RG 94 (NA).

94 *Galveston Tri-Weekly News*, Jan. 24, 1866.

95 *Matamoros Daily Ranchero*, Jan. 6, 1866. Also J. D. Davis to R. M. Hall, Jan. 5, 1866, Letters Received, Adjutant General's Office, RG 94 (NA).

96 Pitner, *Maximilian's Lieutenant*, 106.

97 Testimony of Frank Benter, Bagdad Commission Investigation.

98 *Matamoros Daily Ranchero*, Jan. 7, 1866. Lucius Avery, United States Commercial Agent in Matamoros, felt many of the outrages that were reported in the Matamoros newspapers were greatly exaggerated. Lucius Avery to [W. H. Seward], Jan. 13, 1866, Matamoros Consular Dispatches, RG 59 (NA). Much of the plundering, Avery asserted a few days later, was by residents of Bagdad. Lucius Avery to W. H. Seward, Jan. 24, 1866, Matamoros Consular Dispatches, RG 59 (NA).

99 *New Orleans Daily Crescent*, Jan. 17, 1866.

100 Ibid.

101 Testimony of Edmund De Buck, Bagdad Commission Investigation.

102 Testimony of Reginold Musgrave, Bagdad Commission Investigation.

103 *Matamoros Daily Ranchero*, Jan. 10, 1866.

104 *Matamoros Daily Ranchero*, Jan. 27, 1866.

105 Testimony of Frank J. White, Bagdad Commission Investigation.

106 Mariano Escobedo to Godfrey Weitzel, Jan. 5, 1866, Letters Received, Adjutant General's Office, RG 94 (NA).

107 Francisco de León to J. D. Davis, Jan. 5, 1866, Exhibit A, Bagdad Commission Investigation. A copy of this letter is in Letters Received, Adjutant General's Office, RG 94 (NA).

108 *New Orleans Daily Crescent*, Jan. 17, 1866.

109 Ibid.

110 Frank J. White to W. D. Morrison, Jan. 22, 1866, Letters Received, Adjutant General's Office, RG 94 (NA).

111 Frank J. White to W. D. Munson, Exhibit E, Bagdad Commission Investigation. Also Frank J. White to W. D. Morrison, Jan. 22, 1866, Letters Received, Adjutant General's Office, RG 94 (NA).

112 *Matamoros Daily Ranchero*, Jan. 30, 1866.

113 *Galveston Tri-Weekly News*, Feb. 2, 1866.

114 P. H. Sheridan to U. S. Grant, Jan. 17 (two letters), 1866; and P. H. Sheridan to H. G. Wright, Jan. 17, 1866; all in Letters Received, Adjutant General's Office, RG 94 (NA).

115 Pitner, *Maximilian's Lieutenant*, 106.

116 *Galveston Tri-Weekly News*, Feb. 9, 1866. Also Special Orders no. 19, Jan. 21, 1866, Letters Received, Adjutant General's Office, RG 94 (NA).

117 *New Orleans Daily Crescent*, Jan. 27, 1866; *Matamoros Daily Ranchero*, Feb. 9, 1866; *Galveston Tri-Weekly News*, Jan. 26, 1866. In New Orleans Crawford was arrested by the military and confined at Fort Jackson, where he later escaped.

118 U. S. Grant endorsement on Commission Report, Mar. 1, 1866, Letters Received, Adjutant General's Office, RG 94 (NA).

119 Pitner, *Maximilian's Lieutenant*, 106.

120 H. G. Wright to W. T. Clark, Jan. 27, 1866: H. G. Wright to Geo. L. Hartsuff, Jan. 27, 1866; both in Letters Received, Adjutant General's Office, RG 94 (NA).

121 P. H. Sheridan to William H. Stanton, May 9, 1866, Letters Received, Adjutant General's Office, RG 94 (NA).

122 Enrique A. Mejía to Matias Romero, Mar. 6, 1866, Letters Received, Adjutant General's Office, RG 94 (NA).

123 M. Romero to [William H. Seward], Mar. 30, 1866, Letters Received, Adjutant General's Office, RG 94 (NA).

124 Gregory Weitzel to C. H. Whittlesey, Jan. 27, 1866, Letters Received, Adjutant General's Office, RG 94 (NA).

125 *Galveston Tri-Weekly News*, Feb. 2, 1866.

126 *Matamoros Daily Ranchero*, Jan. 23, 25, 1866.

127 *Matamoros Daily Ranchero*, Jan. 24, 1866.

128 *New Orleans Daily Picayune*, Dec. 11, 1866.

129 *New York Herald*, July 26, 1865.

130 Robert Rodgers, CSR, Seventy-seventh Ohio Volunteer Infantry, Adjutant General's Office, RG 94 (NA).

131 *Marietta Register*, Jan. 11, 1862.

132 Frederick H. Dyer, *A Compendium of the War of the Rebellion* (Dayton: Morningside Bookshop, 1978), 1,532. On April 25, 1864, Rodgers had been captured at the battle of Marks's Mills in southwest Arkansas. Paroled ten months later at Red River Landing, Louisiana, he rejoined the Seventy-seventh Ohio and was on duty at New Orleans and Mobile as the war wound down.

133 Court-Martial Records in the case of Robert Rodgers, JAGO.

134 William A. Gardiner, CSR, Eighty-first Pennsylvania Infantry, Adjutant General's Office, RG 94 (NA).

135 Court-Martial Records in the case of Robert Rodgers, JAGO.

136 Ibid.

137 *Matamoros Daily Ranchero*, May 26, 1866.

138 Ibid.

139 *New Orleans Daily Crescent*, July 10, 1866.

140 *New Orleans Daily Crescent*, June 23, 1866.

141 *Matamoros Daily Ranchero*, June 24, 1866.

142 Parisot, *Reminiscences of a Texas Missionary*, 102–103, 107; Kearney and Knopp, *Boom and Bust*, 162; Thompson, *Juan Cortina*, 101.

143 *Matamoros Daily Ranchero*, May 16, 22, 1866.

144 *New Orleans Daily Crescent*, July 10, 1866.

145 Parisot, *Reminiscences of a Texas Missionary*, 99–100.

146 *New Orleans Daily Crescent*, July 10, 1866.

147 Ibid.

Chapter 6: Imperial Dreams and Republican Triumphs

1 *New Orleans Daily Crescent*, Feb. 9, 1866; *Galveston Tri-Weekly News*, Feb. 2, 1866.

2 Pitner, *Maximilian's Lieutenant*, 110–111, 114, 116. Bagdad was again hit by a four-day storm in late July 1866, which inundated the town, damaged four vessels that were at anchor, and capsized several smaller craft. *New Orleans Daily Crescent*, Aug. 2, 1866.

3 *Matamoros Daily Ranchero*, Feb. 4, 1866.

4 *Matamoros Daily Ranchero*, Feb. 13, 1866.

5 *New Orleans Daily Crescent*, Feb. 26, 1866.

6 *New Orleans Daily Crescent*, May 15, 1866.

7 Ibid. Also *Galveston Daily News*, May 11, 1866.

8 *New Orleans Daily Crescent*, May 15, 1866.

9 *Matamoros Daily Ranchero*, June 14, 15, 1866; *New Orleans Daily Crescent*, June 21, 1866; Pitner, *Maximilian's Lieutenant*, 129–130; *Brownsville Daily Ranchero*, Sept. 26, 1866; Lucius Avery to William H. Seward, June 18, 1866, Matamoros Consular Dispatches, RG 59 (NA).

10 M. Escobedo to Minister of War and Marine, June 19, 1866; M. Escobedo to Minister of War and Marine, June 20, 1866, both in *Conditions of Affairs in Mexico*, 39th Cong., 2d sess., no. 1294, 226–229. Most of these letters and dispatches are also in Jesus de León Toral (ed.), *Historia Documental Militar de la Intgervencion Francesa en Mexico y El Denominado Segundo Imperio* (Mexico City: Secretaria de la Defensa Nacional, 1967), 516–535. Also Juan Fidel Zorrilla, *Governadores, Obispos y Rectores* (Ciudad Victoria: Universidad Autónoma de Tamaulipas, 1979), 22–23.

11 Pitner, *Maximilian's Lieutenant*, 130–131.

12 Ibid., 132–133.

13 M. Escobedo to Minister of War and Marine, June 19, 1866, *Conditions of Affairs in Mexico*, 228–229.

14 M. Escobedo to General of the Republic, June 16, 1866, in ibid., 227–228. Of the two hundred wagonloads of goods that were seized, twenty-seven were said to have been given to Canales as compensation for his part in the defeat of the Imperialists. What remained was returned to the owners upon their paying an export duty. *New Orleans Daily Crescent*, July 30, 1866.

15 Sostenes Rocha, list of killed, wounded, and prisoners at the battle of Santa Gertrudis, June 16, 1866, *Conditions of Affairs in Mexico*, 229–233.

16 Lucius Avery to William H. Seward, June 18, 1866, Matamoros Consular Dispatches, RG 59 (NA).

17 *Brownsville Daily Ranchero*, Sept. 26, 1866. Also *San Antonio Daily Herald*, July 6, 1866.

18 M. Escobedo to General of the Republic, June 16, 1866, *Conditions of Affairs in Mexico*, 227.

19 *Brownsville Daily Ranchero*, Sept. 26, 1866. "Sporting a huge moustache and huger whiskers," Carbajal had just arrived on the border from New York.

20 Tomás Mejía, José María J. Carbajal, et al., Agreement for the surrender of Matamoros, agreed to on June 22 and signed on June 23, *Conditions of Affairs in Mexico*, 233.

21 *Galveston Tri-Weekly Telegraph*, July 28, 1866; *San Antonio Daily Herald*, July 6, 1866.

22 [E. A.] Mejía to [Mariano] Escobedo, Aug. 4, 1866, *Conditions of Affairs in Mexico*, 240.

23 *Galveston Tri-Weekly News*, Sept. 10, 1866.

24 *Pronunciamiento*, Servando Canales, Aug. 13, 1866, *Conditions of Affairs in Mexico*, 242. Also Lucius Avery to William H. Seward, Aug. 13, 1866, Matamoros Consular Dispatches, RG 59 (NA).

25 Sebastián Lerdo de Tejada to Santiago Tapia, Sept. 12, 1862, *Conditions of Affairs in Mexico*, 242–243.

[26] *Brownsville Daily Ranchero*, Oct. 12, 1866.

[27] *Brownsville Daily Ranchero*, Oct. 24, 1866.

[28] *Brownsville Daily Ranchero*, Nov. 15, 1866.

[29] Post Returns, Fort Brown, December 1866, Adjutant General's Office, RG 393 (NA).

[30] *New Orleans Daily Crescent*, Dec. 9, 1866; *New Orleans Daily Picayune*, Dec. 6, 7, 8, 1866.

[31] *Brownsville Daily Ranchero*, Nov. 27, 1866.

[32] P. H. Sheridan to J. A. Rawlings, Dec. 11, 1866, *Conditions of Affairs in Mexico*, 487.

[33] *Brownsville Daily Ranchero*, Nov. 28, 1866.

[34] Ibid. Also *Brownsville Daily Ranchero*, Nov. 29, 1866.

[35] *Brownsville Daily Ranchero*, Nov. 29, 1866.

[36] *Brownsville Daily Ranchero*, Nov. 28, 1866.

[37] Ibid. Also *New York World*, Dec. 6, 1866; *San Antonio Daily Herald*, Dec. 9, 1866.

[38] For exchange of notes between Canales, Escobedo, and Sedgwick, see *New Orleans Daily Crescent*, Dec. 8, 1866. See also *Brownsville Daily Ranchero*, Jan. 23, 13, 1867.

[39] *Galveston Tri-Weekly News*, Dec. 5, 1866; *Brownsville Daily Ranchero*, Nov. 28, 1866.

[40] P. H. Sheridan to U. S. Grant, Dec. 10, 1866, *Conditions of Affairs in Mexico*, 545.

[41] P. H. Sheridan to U. S. Grant, Nov. 27, 1866, *Conditions of Affairs in Mexico*, 544.

[42] *Rio Grande Courier* (Brownsville), Dec. 7, 1866, quoted in *Conditions of Affairs in Mexico*, 488.

[43] *New Orleans Daily Picayune*, Dec. 11, 1866.

[44] P. H. Sheridan to J. A. Rawlins, Dec. 11, 1866, *Conditions of Affairs in Mexico*, 547.

[45] *Flake's Daily Galveston Bulletin*, Feb. 8, 1867.

[46] *Brownsville Daily Ranchero*, Dec. 1, 1866.

[47] *Brownsville Daily Ranchero*, Dec. 2, 1866.

[48] *Brownsville Daily Ranchero*, Jan. 25, 29; Feb. 2, 1867.

[49] *New Orleans Daily Picayune*, Jan. 18, 1867; *Flake's Daily Galveston Bulletin*, Jan. 18, 1867.

[50] For details of the execution, see *Brownsville Daily Ranchero*, Sept. 27, 1867. Also H. Montgomery Hyde, *Mexican Empire: The History of Maximilian and Carlota of Mexico* (London: Macmillan and Company, 1946), 311; J. J. Gallegos, "Santiago Vidaurri: Regional Power, Trade and Capital Formation in Northern Mexico," copy courtesy of the author.

[51] *Brownsville Daily Ranchero*, Dec. 20, 1866; *Flake's Daily Galveston Bulletin*, Jan. 12, 1867.

[52] *Daily Rio Grande Courier* (Brownsville), Nov. 8, 1866. Thomas D. Schoonover (ed. and trans.), *Mexican Lobby: Matías Romero in Washington, 1861–1867* (Lex-ington: University Press of Kentucky, 1986), 147.

[53] *Brownsville Daily Ranchero*, Sept. 25, 1867; Jan. 15, 1868; *New Orleans Daily Picayune*, Jan. 6, 1867.

Chapter 7: The Great Storm of 1867 and the End of an Era

[1] *New Orleans Daily Picayune*, Jan. 11, 1867.

[2] Yellow fever did strike Brownsville and Matamoros in November 1867, but the disease was of such a mild strain that there were few fatalities. *Brownsville Daily Ranchero*, Nov. 13, 1867; *New Orleans Times*, Aug. 10, 1867.

[3] *Brownsville Daily Ranchero*, Nov. 15, 1867.

[4] *Brownsville Daily Ranchero*, Jan. 5, 1868.

[5] *Brownsville Daily Ranchero*, Nov. 15, 1867.

[6] *Brownsville Daily Ranchero*, Dec. 3, 1867.

[7] *Brownsville Daily Ranchero*, Nov. 15, 1867.

[8] *New Orleans Crescent*, Oct. 29, 1867.

[9] The Miller Hotel, originally called the Cameron Hotel, was constructed by Henry Miller in 1848. With wide verandas, the two-story frame building contained a restaurant, barroom, and limited lodging for men only. After the storm Miller built an even larger structure on the site. A German immigrant from Hanover, Miller was known throughout the community for his kindness to the needy. It was said that no one was ever turned "away from the door of Henry Miller, hungry, weary or sleepy, because he had not the where with to pay his bill." A. A. Champion, "The Miller Hotel in the Antebellum Period," *More Studies in Brownsville History*, ed. Milo Kearney (Brownsville: Pan American University at Brownsville, 1989), 163–167; *La Bandera Americana* (Brownsville), Apr. 16, 1860.

[10] *Houston Tri-Weekly Telegraph*, Nov. 16, 1867.

[11] *Brownsville Daily Ranchero*, Jan. 7, 1868.

[12] For a detailed list of the buildings destroyed or damaged, see *Houston Tri-Weekly Telegraph*, Oct. 30, 1867.

[13] *Brownsville Daily Ranchero*, Jan. 27, 1869.

[14] *Rio Grande Courier* (Brownsville), n.d., quoted in the *New Orleans Daily Crescent*, Oct. 29, 1867.

[15] M. B. Marshall to William H. Seward, Oct. 12, 1867, Matamoros Consular Dispatches, RG 59 (NA).

[16] *New Orleans Crescent*, Oct. 29, 1869.

[17] *Houston Tri-Weekly Telegraph*, Oct. 30, 1867; *Galveston Daily News*, Oct. 19, 1867.

[18] *Houston Tri-Weekly Telegraph*, Oct. 30, 1867.

[19] *Brownsville Daily Ranchero*, Nov. 29, 1867.

[20] Report of J. S. Mansur, deputy collector of customs, n.d., typescript, A. A. Champion Papers (Brownsville Historical Society, Brownsville, Texas).

21 *Galveston Daily News,* Nov. 12, 1867.

22 *Galveston Daily News,* Oct. 29, 1867.

23 *Corpus Christi Advertiser*, Oct. 19, 1867, quoted in the *Galveston Daily News*, Oct. 29, 1867.

24 *New Orleans Crescent*, Oct. 29, 1867.

25 *New Orleans Crescent*, Oct. 31, 1867; Victor Egly, "Memorandom [*sic*] Book From tim[es] I comenced [*sic*] to Steamboadings [*sic*]," Oct. 7, 1867, photocopy, A. A. Champion Papers (Brownsville Historical Society, Brownsville, Texas).

26 *Galveston Daily News*, Nov. 12, 1867.

27 *New Orleans Crescent*, Oct. 31, 1867.

28 *Brownsville Daily Ranchero*, Nov. 17, 1867.

29 P. H. Sheridan to F. Steele, Aug. 15, 1865, Letters Received, Adjutant General's Office, RG 94 (NA).

30 Richter, *Army in Texas during Reconstruction*, 177.

31 H. P. Bee to E. P. Turner, June 29, 1863, Letters Received, District of Texas, New Mexico, and Arizona, RG 109 (NA).

32 *Brownsville Daily Ranchero*, Oct. 2, 1867.

33 *Galveston Daily News*, quoted in the *Brownsville Daily Ranchero*, Jan. 29, 1868.

34 Ibid.

35 *Galveston Daily News*, Dec. 27, 1867.

36 Ibid.

37 *Galveston Daily News*, Dec. 28, 1867. Many newspapers in Texas decried the lack of freedom of the press in Brownsville. The liberal *New York Tribune*, however, wrote that the "Ranchero has too often been convicted of forging documents and news." *Brownsville Daily Ranchero*, Sept. 22, 1866. One of the few southern newspapers critical of Maltby and the *Ranchero* was *Flake's Bulletin* (Galveston). The editor and owner of the newspaper, Ferdinand Flake, went as far as to strike the *Ranchero* from his exchange list. In turn, Maltby reciprocated by proclaiming *Flake's Bulletin* "niggerized." *Brownsville Daily Ranchero*, Feb. 2, 1868. See also A. A. Champion, "Papers and Personalities of Frontier Journalism (1830s to 1890s)," in *More Studies in Brownsville History*, ed. Milo Kearney, 113–161. Maltby was left as the sole editor of the *Ranchero* when Kinney established the *Houston Times* in August 1868. Ironically, Maltby sold the *Ranchero* to two Radical Republicans, Henry Haupt and B. S. Smith, in 1871.

38 *Brownsville Daily Ranchero*, Jan. 1, 1868. Reynolds had previously commanded the Subdistrict of the Rio Grande and was one of the more popular officers in Brownsville. Richter, *Army in Texas during Reconstruction*, 119.

39 *Brownsville Daily Ranchero* Dec. 20, 22, 23, 1868.

40 *Brownsville Daily Ranchero*, Feb. 17, 19, 1869; Jerry Thompson, *Laredo: A Pictorial History* (Norfolk: Donning Company, 1986), 195.

41 *Brownsville Daily Ranchero*, Jan. 21, 29, 1868.

42 *Brownsville Daily Ranchero*, Dec. 21, 27, 1868.

43 *Brownsville Daily Ranchero*, Aug. 17, Oct. 16, 23, Nov. 4, 6, 1869.

44 *Brownsville Daily Ranchero*, Mar. 4, 6, 9, July 15, 1869.

45 *Two Eagles* (Mexico City), June 25, 1870; *Brownsville Daily Ranchero*, May 27, 1870; Weber, "Texan Manifest Destiny," 71.

46 Thompson, *Juan Cortina*, 68. Also Thos. F. Wilson to Hamilton Fish, Sept. 1, 1870, Matamoros Despatches, RG 59 (NA).

47 *Brownsville Daily Ranchero*, Sept. 22, 1870.

48 Weber, "Texan Manifest Destiny," 71.

49 Leopold Morris, "The Mexican Raid of 1875 on Corpus Christi," *Quarterly of the Texas State Historical Association*, 4 (1900–1901), 128–139; William M. Hager, "The Nuecestown Raid of 1875: A Border Incident," *Arizona and the West*, 1 (Autumn, 1959), 258–270.

50 Walter Prescott Webb, *The Texas Rangers: A Century of Frontier Defense* (Austin: University of Texas Press, 1970), 255–290.

51 "Report of the United States Commissioners to Texas," *Depredations on the Frontiers of Texas*, 42nd Cong., 3rd sess., no. 39, 1–63; *Reports of the Mexican Committee of Investigation Sent in 1873 by the Mexican Government to the Frontier of Texas* (New York: Baker & Godwin, 1875), 127–163.

52 Wm. Steele to Richard Coke, July 1, 1875, *Texas Frontier Troubles*, 44th Cong., 1st sess., no. 343, 122.

53 John W. Foster to Hamilton Fish, May 4, 1875, *Texas Frontier Troubles*, 152.

54 Thompson, *Juan Cortina*, 93.

BIBLIOGRAPHY

Manuscripts and Archival Collections

"Amnesty Papers." Applications from Former Confederates for Presidential Pardons. Record Group 94, National Archives, Washington, D.C.

Bee, Hamilton P. Letterbook. Special Collections, Library, United States Military Academy, West Point, New York.

Bee, Hamilton P. Papers. Center for American History, University of Texas at Austin.

Broadside File. Texas State Archives, Austin, Texas.

Brown, Egbert B. Papers. New York Historical Society, New York, New York.

Clark, Edward. Papers. Texas State Archives, Austin, Texas.

Champion, A. A. Papers. Brownsville Historical Society, Brownsville, Texas.

Consular Dispatches, Matamoros, Mexico. Records of the United States Department of State. Record Group 59, National Archives, Washington, D.C.

Consular Dispatches, Monterrey, Mexico. Records of the United States Department of State. Record Group 59, National Archives, Washington, D.C.

Cotton Bureau Records. Confederate Department of the Treasury. Record Group 395, National Archives, Washington, D.C.

Correspondencia del Alcalde de Guerrero. Nuevo Guerrero Archives, Nuevo Guerrero, Tamaulipas.

Correspondencia de Santiago Vidaurri. Archivo General del Estado de Nuevo León, Monterrey, Nuevo León.

Court-Martial Records in the Case of Pedro García. Court-Martial Case Files. Records of the Judge Advocate General's Office. Record Group 153, National Archives, Washington, D.C.

Court-Martial Records in the Case of Robert G. Morrison. Court-Martial Case Files. Records of the Judge Advocate General's Office. Record Group 153, National Archives, Washington, D.C.

Court-Martial Records in the Case of Robert Rodgers. Court-Martial Case Files. Records of the Judge Advocate General's Office. Record Group 153, National Archives, Washington, D.C.

Davis, Edmund J. Papers. Texas State Archives, Austin, Texas.

Egly, Victor. "Memorandom [sic] Book From tim[es] I comenced [sic] to Steamboadings [sic]. Photocopy. A. A. Champion Papers. Brownsville Historical Society, Brownsville, Texas.

Eighth Census (1860), Zapata County, Texas. National Archives, Washington, D.C.

Eighth Census (1860), Cameron County, Texas. National Archives, Washington, D.C.

Election Returns. Laredo Archives. St. Mary's University Library, San Antonio, Texas.

Election Returns. Webb County, 1851–1856. Records of the Secretary of State, Record Group 307, Texas State Archives, Austin, Texas.

Ford, John S. Papers. Texas State Archives, Austin Texas.

Ford, John Salmon. "Memoirs of John Salmon Ford." 7 vols. Center for American History, University of Texas at Austin.

Ford, John S. Memoirs. Center for American History, University of Texas at Austin.

Gardiner, William A. Compiled Service Record. United States Department of War. Record Group 153, National Archives, Washington, D.C.

Hamilton, Andrew J. Papers. Texas State Archives, Austin, Texas.

Haynes, John L. Compiled Service Record. United States Department of War. Record Group 94, National Archives, Washington, D.C.

Haynes, John L. Papers. Center for American History, University of Texas at Austin.

Heintzelman, Samuel Peter. Papers. Library of Congress, Washington, D.C.

Herron, Francis J. Papers. New York Historical Society, New York, New York.

Huster, William. Compiled Service Record. United States Department of War. Record Group 94, National Archives, Washington, D.C.

Kenedy, Mifflin. Letterbook. King Ranch Archives, Kingsville, Texas.

Killed and Wounded at Las Rucias. Confederate Army Casualties and Narrative Reports. Record Group 109, National Archives, Washington, D.C.

King, Richard. Letters. King Ranch Archives, Kingsville, Texas.

Kingsbury, Gilbert D. Papers. Center for American History, University of Texas at Austin.

Kuykendall, James Hampton. Journal. Center for American History, University of Texas at Austin.

Letters Received. Confederate Adjutant General's Office. Records of the Confederate War Department. Record Group 109, National Archives, Washington, D.C.

Letters Received. Confederate Trans–Mississippi Department. Records of the Confederate War Department. Record Group 109, National Archives, Washington, D.C.

Letters Received. Confederate District of Texas, New Mexico, and Arizona. Records of the Confederate War Department. Record Group 109, National Archives, Washington, D.C.

Letters Received. Department of Texas. Record Group 393, National Archives, Washington, D.C.

Leyendecker, John Z. Papers. Center for American History, University of Texas at Austin.

Lubbock, Francis R. Papers. Texas State Archives, Austin, Texas.

Military Commission Appointed to Investigate and Report Upon the Facts Relative to the Capture of the Town of Bagdad on the Mexican Side of the Rio Grande on January 5, 1866. Records of the Adjutant General's Office. Record Group 393, National Archives, Washington, D.C.

Muster Roll. Vidal's Partisan Rangers. Adjutant General's Records. Texas State Archives, Austin, Texas.

Pickett, John T. Papers. Domestic Correspondence of the Confederacy. Office of the Secretary of State. Manuscript Division, Library of Congress, Washington, D.C.

Post Returns. Brazos Santiago. Records of the Adjutant General's Office. Record Group 393, National Archives, Washington, D.C.

Post Returns. Fort Brown. Records of the Adjutant General's Office. Record Group 393, National Archives, Washington, D.C.

Post Returns. Fort McIntosh. Records of the Adjutant General's Office. Record Group 393, National Archives, Washington, D.C.

Post Returns. Ringgold Barracks. Records of the Adjutant General's Office. Record Group 393, National Archives, Washington, D.C.

Record Book of the Second Texas Cavalry, 1863–1864. Adjutant General's Office. Texas State Archives, Austin, Texas.

Registro Civil de Guerrero, Nuevo Guerrero Archives, Nuevo Guerrero, Tamaulipas.

Robertson, George Lee. Papers. Center for American History, University of Texas at Austin.

Rodgers, Robert. Compiled Service Record. United States Department of War. Record Group 94, National Archives, Washington, D.C.

Speed, James. Compiled Service Record. United States Department of War. Record Group 94, National Archives, Washington, D.C.

Tenth Census (1880), Nueces County, Texas. National Archives, Washington, D.C.

Vidal, Adrián J. Compiled Service Record. United States Department of War. Record Group 94, National Archives, Washington, D.C.

Wilcox, Seb. Papers. St. Mary's University Library, San Antonio, Texas.

Newspapers

Southern Intelligencer (Austin)
Texas State Gazette (Austin)
Bandera Americana (Brownsville)
Boletin Extraordinario (Brownsville)
Brownsville Daily Ranchero
Brownsville Daily Ranchero and Republican
El Correo del Rio Grande (Brownsville)
Fort Brown Flag (Brownsville)
La Bandera (Brownsville)
Brownsville Herald Plus
Rio Grande Sentinel (Brownsville)
Union Journal (Brownsville)
Corpus Christi Advertiser
Corpus Christi Caller
Corpus Christi Ranchero
Dallas Herald
Flake's Daily Galveston Bulletin
Galveston Tri-Weekly News
Galveston Weekly News
Harper's Weekly
Houston Tri-Weekly Telegraph
Loyal National Union Journal
Marietta Register
Matamoros Daily Ranchero
El Orden (Matamoros)
Matamoros Ranchero
El Ranchero Diario (Matamoros)
Two Eagles (Mexico City)
Boletin Oficial (Monterrey)
New Orleans Daily Crescent
New Orleans Daily True Delta
New Orleans Daily Picayune
Tägliche Deutsche Zeitung (New Orleans)
New Orleans Times
New York Herald
New York Tribune
New York World
San Antonio Daily Herald
San Antonio Daily Ledger and Texan
San Antonio Weekly Herald

Books

Adjutant General's Report, 1873. Austin: n.p., 1875.

Bailey, Theodorus, and Gideon Welles, eds. *Official Records of the Union and Confederate Navies in the War of the Rebellion.* 30 vols. Washington, D.C.: Government Printing Office, 1894–1927.

Barney, Chester. *Recollections of Field Service with the Twentieth Iowa Infantry Volunteers.* Davenport: Gazette Job, 1865.

Barnett, Simeon. *A History of the Twenty-Second Regiment Iowa Volunteer Infantry.* Iowa City: N. H. Brainerd, 1865.

Basler, Roy P., ed. *The Collected Works of Abraham Lincoln.* 9 vols. New Brunswick, N.J.: Rutgers University Press, 1953.

Baum, Dale. *The Shattering of Texas Unionism: Politics in the Lone Star State during the Civil War Era.* Baton Rouge: Louisiana State University Press, 1998.

Benito Juárez: Documentos, Discursos y Correspondencia. Mexico City: Secretaria del Patrimonio Nacional, 1964–1969.

Bentley, W. H. *History of the Ninety-First Regiment Illinois Volunteer Infantry.* White Hall, Ill.: Pearce Printing Co., 1913.

Bergeron, Arthur W. Jr. *Guide to Louisiana Confederate Military Units, 1861–1865.* Baton Rouge: Louisiana State University Press, 1996.

Bowden, J. J. *The Exodus of Federal Forces from Texas, 1861.* Austin: Eakin Press, 1986.

Brown, Robert O. *Collector's Guide to 19th Century U.S. Traveling Photographers.* Forest Grove, Ore.: Brown-Spath and Associates, 2002.

Buenger, Walter L. *Secession and the Union in Texas.* Austin: University of Texas Press, 1984.

Callahan, James M. *The Diplomatic History of the Southern Confederacy.* Baltimore: Johns Hopkins University Press, 1901.

Carreño, Alberto María, ed. *Archivo del General Porfirio Díaz: Memorias y Documentos.* Mexico City: Editorial "Elede," 1949.

Conditions of Affairs in Mexico. 39th Cong., 2nd sess., no. 1294.

Cornish, Dudley Taylor. *The Sable Arm: Black*

Troops in the Union Army, 1861–1865. Lawrence: University Press of Kansas, 1987.

Cotham, Edward T. Jr. *Battle on the Bay: The Civil War Struggle for Galveston.* Austin: University of Texas Press, 1998.

Crooke, George. *The Twenty-First Regiment of Iowa Volunteer Infantry.* Milwaukee: King Fowle and Co., 1891.

Dabbs, Jack A. *The French Army in Mexico, 1861–1867: A Study in Military Government.* The Hague: Mouton and Company, 1963.

Daddysman, James W. *The Matamoros Trade: Confederate Commerce, Diplomacy and Intrigue.* Newark: University of Delaware Press, 1984.

Daniell, L. E. *Types of Successful Men of Texas.* Austin: n.p., 1890.

Davis, Edwin Adams. *Fallen Guidon: The Story of Confederate General Jo Shelby's March to Mexico.* College Station: Texas A&M University Press, 1995.

Davis, William C., ed. *The South Besieged: The Image of War, 1861–1865.* Garden City, N.J.: Doubleday & Co., 1983.

Debroise, Oliver. *Mexican Suite: A History of Photography in Mexico.* Austin: University of Texas Press, 1994.

Depredations on the Frontiers of Texas. 42nd Cong., 3rd sess., no. 39.

Dyer, Frederick H. *A Compendium of the War of the Rebellion.* Dayton: Morningside Bookshop, 1978.

Ford, John S. *Rip Ford's Texas.* Edited by Stephen B. Oates. Austin: University of Texas Press, 1963.

Freeman, Douglas Southall. *R. E. Lee: A Biography.* 3 vols. New York: Charles Scribner's Sons, 1934.

Fremantle, Arthur James Lyon. *The Fremantle Diary: Being the Journal of Lieutenant Colonel Arthur James Lyon Fremantle, Coldstream Guards, on his Three Months in the Southern States.* Edited by Walter Lord. London: Andre Deutsch, 1856.

Gallaway, B. P., ed. *Dark Corner of the Confederacy.* Dubuque, Iowa: Kendall-Hunt Publishing, 1972.

García, Genaro, ed. *Documentos inéditos o muy raros para la historia de México.* Mexico City: n.p., 1910.

Giese, William Royston. *The Confederate Military Forces in the Trans–Mississippi West, 1861–1865: A Study in Command.* Austin: University of Texas Press, 1974.

Glathaar, Joseph T. *Forged in Battle: The Civil War Alliance of Black Soldiers and White Officers.* New York: Meridian, 1991.

Horrocks, James. *My Dear Parents: The Civil War as Seen by an English Soldier.* New York: Harcourt Brace Jovanovich, 1982.

Haynes, David. *Catching Shadows: A Directory of Nineteenth-Century Texas Photographers.* Austin: Texas State Historical Association, 1993.

Hinojosa, Gilberto Miguel. *A Borderlands Town in Transition: Laredo, 1755–1870.* College Station: Texas A&M University Press, 1983.

Hughes, W. J. *Rebellious Ranger: Rip Ford and the Old Southwest.* Norman: University of Oklahoma Press, 1964.

Hunt, Jeffrey Wm. *The Last Battle of the Civil War: Palmetto Ranch.* Austin: University of Texas Press, 2002.

Hunter, John Warren. *Heel-Fly Time in Texas.* Bandera, Texas: Frontier Times, 1931.

Hutton, Paul Andrew. *Phil Sheridan and His Army.* Lincoln: University of Nebraska Press, 1985.

Hyde, H. Montgomery. *Mexican Empire: The History of Maximilian and Carlota of Mexico.* London: Macmillan and Company, 1946.

Irby, James. *Backdoor to Bagdad.* El Paso: Texas Western Press, 1977.

Kearney, Milo, and Anthony Knopp. *Boom and Bust: The Historical Cycles of Matamoros and Brownsville.* Austin: Eakin Press, 1991.

_____. *Border Cuates: A History of the U.S.–Mexican Twin Cities.* Austin: Eakin Press, 1995.

Kearney, Milo, ed. *Studies in Brownsville History.* Brownsville: Pan American University at Brownsville, 1986.

_____, ed. *More Studies in Brownsville History.* Brownsville: Pan American University at Brownsville, 1989.

_____, ed. *Still More Studies in Brownsville*

History. Brownsville: University of Texas at Brownsville, 1991.

Kelly, Pat. *River of Lost Dreams: Navigation on the Rio Grande*. Lincoln: University of Nebraska Press, 1986.

Kératry, Count Emile de. *The Rise and Fall of the Emperor Maximilian: A Narrative of the Mexican Empire, 1861–67 from Authentic Documents with the Imperial Correspondence*. London: Sampson Low, Son, and Marston, 1868.

Kerby, Robert L. *Kirby Smith's Confederacy: The Trans–Mississippi South, 1863–1865*. New York: Columbia University Press, 1972.

Lea, Tom. *The King Ranch*. 2 vols. Boston: Little, Brown and Co., 1957.

Leiker, James N. *Racial Borders: Black Soldiers along the Rio Grande*. College Station: Texas A&M University Press, 2002.

Lonn, Ella. *Foreigners in the Confederacy*. Gloucester, Mass.: Peter Smith, 1965.

_____. *Foreigners in the Union Army and Navy*. Baton Rouge: Louisiana State University Press, 1952.

Lott, Virgil N., and Mercurio Martinez. *The Kingdom of Zapata*. Austin: Eakin Press, 1983.

Lubbock, Francis R. *Six Decades in Texas: The Memoirs of Francis R. Lubbock, Confederate Governor of Texas*. Edited by C. W. Raines. Austin: Pemberton Press, 1968.

Lufkin, Edward B. *History of the Thirteenth Maine*. Bridgton, Maine: H. A. Shorey and Son, 1898.

McHatton-Ripley, Eliza Moore, *From Flag to Flag: A Woman's Adventures and Experiences in the South during the War, in Mexico, and in Cuba*. New York: D. Appleton, 1889.

Mahoney, Harry Thayer and Marjorie Locke. *Mexico and the Confederacy, 1860–1867*. San Francisco: Austin and Winfield, 1998.

Malsch, Brownson. *Indianola: The Mother of Western Texas*. Austin: State House Press, 1988.

Marten, James. *Texas Divided: Loyalty and Dissent in the Lone Star State, 1856–1874*. Lexington: University Press of Kentucky, 1990.

May, Robert E. *Manifest Destiny's Underworld: Filibustering in Antebellum America*. Chapel Hill: University of North Carolina Press, 2002.

Medrano, Arturo Gálvez. *Regionalismo y Gobierno General: El Caso de Nuevo León y Coahuila, 1855–1864*. Monterrey: Gobierno del Estado de Nuevo León, 1993.

Moneyhon, Carl, and Bobby Roberts. *Portraits of Conflict: A Photographic History of Texas in the Civil War*. Fayetteville: University of Arkansas Press, 1998.

Morsberger, Robert E., and Katherine M. Morsberger. *Lew Wallace, Militant Romantic: The Colorful Life of America's Foremost Literary Adventurer*. New York: McGraw Hill, 1980.

Newton, Alexander H. *Out of the Briars*. Ayer Publishers, 1910.

Oates, Stephen B. *Confederate Cavalry West of the River*. Austin: University of Texas Press, 1961.

Owsley, Frank Lawrence. *King Cotton Diplomacy: Foreign Relations of the Confederate States of America*. Chicago: University of Chicago Press, 1959.

Owen, Richard, and James Owen. *Generals at Rest: The Grave Sites of 425 Official Confederate Generals*. Shippensburg, Pa.: White Mane, 1997.

Palmquist, Peter E., Thomas R. Kailbourn, and Martha A. Sandweiss. *Pioneer Photographers of the Far West: A Biographical Dictionary, 1840–1865*. Palo Alto, Calif.: Stanford University Press, 2004.

Parisot, P. F. *Reminiscences of a Texas Missionary*. San Antonio: St. Mary's Church, 1899.

Parks, Joseph H. *General Edmund Kirby Smith, C.S.A.* Baton Rouge: Louisiana State University Press, 1992.

Pierce, Frank F. *A Brief History of the Lower Rio Grande Valley*. Menasha, Wisc.: George Banta Publishing Company, 1917.

Pitner, Ernst. *Maximilian's Lieutenant: A Personal History of the Mexican Campaign, 1864–7*. Translated and edited by Gordon Etherington-Smith. Albuquerque: University of New Mexico Press, 1993.

Rayburn, John C., and Virginia Kemp Rayburn, eds. *Century of Conflict, 1821–1913: Incidents in the Lives of William Neale and William A. Neale, Early Settlers in South Texas*. Waco: Texian Press, 1966.

Reports of the Mexican Committee of Investiga-

tion Sent in 1873 by the Mexican Government to the Frontier of Texas. New York: Baker & Godwin, 1875.

Richardson, James D., ed. *A Compilation of the Messages and Papers of the Confederacy.* 8 vols. Nashville: United States Publishing Company, 1906.

Richter, William L. *The Army in Texas during Reconstruction, 1865–1870.* College Station: Texas A&M University Press, 1987.

Rippy, Fred J. *The United States and Mexico.* New York: Alfred A. Knopf, 1926.

Roeder, Ralph. *Juárez and His Mexico.* New York: Viking Press, 1947.

Roel, Santiago. *Correspondencia Particular de D. Santiago Vidaurri, Gobernador de Nuevo León, (1855–1864), Tomo primero, Juárez–Vidaurri.* Monterrey: Impresora Monterrey, 1946.

Schoonover, Thomas, ed. *A Mexican View of American in the 1860s: A Foreign Diplomat Describes the Civil War and Reconstruction.* Rutherford: Fairleigh Dickinson University Press, 1991.

_____, ed. and trans. *Mexican Lobby: Matías Romero in Washington, 1861–1867.* Lexington: University Press of Kentucky, 1986.

Schuler, Louis J. *The Last Battle in the War Between the States, May 13, 1865.* Brownsville: Springman-King, 1960.

Smart, Charles Allen. *Viva Juárez: A Biography.* New York: J. B. Lippincott, 1964.

Smith, Margaret Denton, and Mary Louise Tucker. *Photography in New Orleans: The Early Years, 1840–1865.* Baton Rouge: Louisiana State University Press, 1982.

Smith, Thomas T. *The U.S. Army and the Texas Frontier Economy, 1845–1900.* College Station: Texas A&M University Press, 1999.

_____. *The Old Army in Texas: A Research Guide to the U.S. Army in Nineteenth-Century Texas.* Austin: Texas State Historical Association, 2000.

Stevens, Thomas N. *Dear Carrie.* Mount Pleasant, Mich.: Central Michigan University, 1984.

Stout, Joseph A. Jr. *Schemers and Dreamers: Filibustering in Mexico, 1848–1921.* Fort Worth: Texas Christian University Press, 2002.

Texas Frontier Troubles. 44th Cong., 1st sess., no. 343.

Thompson, Jerry. *Juan Cortina and the Texas–Mexico Frontier, 1859–1877.* El Paso: Texas Western Press, 1994.

_____. *Vaqueros in Blue and Gray.* Austin: State House Press, 2000.

_____. *Mexican Texans in the Union Army.* El Paso: Texas Western Press, 1986.

_____, ed. *Fifty Miles and a Fight: Major Samuel Peter Heintzelman's Journal of Texas and the Cortina War.* Austin: Texas State Historical Association, 1998.

_____. *Laredo: A Pictorial History.* Norfolk: Donning Company, 1986.

_____. *Warm Weather and Bad Whiskey.* El Paso: Texas Western Press, 1991.

_____. *A Wild and Vivid Land: An Illustrated History of the South Texas Border.* Austin: Texas State Historical Association, 1997.

_____, ed. *Texas and New Mexico on the Eve of the Civil War: The Mansfield and Johnston Inspections, 1859–1861.* Albuquerque: University of New Mexico Press, 2001.

Tilley, Nannie M., ed. *Federals on the Frontier: The Diary of Benjamin F. McIntyre, 1862–1864.* Austin: University of Texas Press, 1963.

Toral, Jesus de León, ed. *Historia Documental Militar de la Intgervencion Francesa en Mexico y El Denominado Segundo Imperio.* Mexico City: Secretaria de la Defensa Nacional, 1967.

Tucker, Phillip Thomas. *The Final Fury: Palmito Ranch, the Last Battle of the Civil War.* Mechanicsburg, Pa.: Stackpole Books, 2001.

Trudeau, Noah Andre. *Out of the Storm: The End of the Civil War, April–June 1865.* Baton Rouge: Louisiana State University Press, 1994.

_____. *Like Men of War: Black Troops in the Civil War, 1862–1865.* Boston: Little, Brown and Company, 1998.

Tyler, Ronnie C. *Santiago Vidaurri and the Southern Confederacy.* Austin: Texas State Historical Association, 1973.

Ron Tyler, Douglas E. Barnett, Roy R. Barkley, Penelope C. Anderson, and Mark F. Odintz, eds. *The New Handbook of Texas.* 6 vols.

Austin: Texas State Historical Association, 1996.

Underwood, Rodman L. *Death on the Nueces: German Texans, Treue der Union.* Austin: Eakin Press, 2000.

U.S. War Department. *The War of the Rebellion: A Compilation of the Official Records of the Union and Confederate Armies.* 128 vols. Washington: U.S. Government Printing Office, 1880–1901.

Wallace, Lew. *An Autobiography.* 2 vols. New York: Harper and Brothers, 1906.

Waller, John L. *Colossal Hamilton of Texas: A Biography of Andrew Jackson Hamilton, Militant Unionist and Reconstruction Governor.* El Paso: Texas Western Press, 1968.

Walraven, Bill. *Corpus Christi: The History of A Texas Seaport.* Woodland Hills, Calif.: Windsor Publications, 1982.

Warner, Ezra E. *Generals in Gray: Lives of the Confederate Commanders.* Baton Rouge: Louisiana State University Press, 1970

_____. *Generals in Blue: Lives of the Union Commanders.* Baton Rouge: Louisiana State University Press, 1972.

Watson, William. *Adventures of a Blockade Runner, Or, Trade in Time of War.* London: Unwin, 1892.

Webb, Walter Prescott. *The Texas Rangers: A Century of Frontier Defense.* Austin: University of Texas Press, 1970.

Williams, R. H. *With the Border Ruffians: Memories of the Far West, 1852–1868.* Edited by E. W. Williams. Lincoln: University of Nebraska Press, 1982.

Winsor, Bill. *Texas in the Confederacy: Military Installations, Economy, and People.* Hillsboro: Hill College Press, 1978.

Woodman, Lyman L. *Cortina, Rogue of the Rio Grande.* San Antonio: Naylor, 1950.

Wooldridge, Ruby A., and Robert B. Vezzetti. *Brownsville: A Pictorial History.* Norfolk: Donning Company, 1982.

Wooster, Ralph A. *Texas and Texans in the Civil War.* Austin: Eakin Press, 1995.

_____. *Lone Star Generals in Gray.* Austin: Eakin Press, 2000.

Wright, Marcus J., comp. *Texas in the War,* 1861–1865. Edited by Harold B. Simpson. Hillsboro: Hill College Press, 1965.

Yeary, Mamie. *Reminiscences of the Boys in Gray, 1861–1865.* Dayton, Ohio: Morningside, 1986.

Zorrilla, Juan Fidel. *Governadores, Obispos y Rectores.* Ciudad Victoria: Universidad Autónoma de Tamaulipas, 1979.

Articles and Other Published Materials

Ashcraft, Allan C. "The Union Occupation of the Lower Rio Grande Valley in the Civil War." *Texas Military History,* 8, no. 4 (1970).

_____. "Fort Brown, Texas, in 1861." *Texas Military History,* 3 (Spring, 1963).

Barr, Alwyn. "Texas Coastal Defense, 1861–1875." *Southwestern Historical Quarterly,* 65 (July, 1961).

Betts, Vicki. "'Private and Amateur Hangings': The Lynching of W. W. Montgomery, March 15, 1863." *Southwestern Historical Quarterly,* 88 (Oct., 1984).

Broussard, Ray F. "Vidaurri, Juárez, Comonfort's Return from Exile." *Hispanic American Historical Review,* 69 (May, 1969).

Brown, Russell. "An Old Woman with a Broomstick: General David E. Twiggs and the Surrender in Texas, 1861." *Military Affairs,* 48 (Apr., 1984).

Champion, A. A. "The Miller Hotel in the Antebellum Period." *More Studies in Brownsville History.* Edited by Milo Kearney. Brownsville: Pan American University at Brownsville, 1989.

Cheeseman, Bruce S. "'Let us have 500 good determined Texans': Richard King's Account of the Union Invasion of South Texas, November 12, 1863, to January 20, 1864." *Southwestern Historical Quarterly,* 101 (July, 1997).

Clampitt, Brad. "Camp Groce, Texas: A Confederate Prison." *Southwestern Historical Quarterly,* 104 (Jan., 2001).

Clendenen, Clarence C. "Mexican Unionists: A Forgotten Incident of the War Between the States." *New Mexico Historical Review,* 39, no. 34 (1964).

Cohen, Barry M. "The Texas–Mexico Border, 1858–1867." *Texana,* 6 (Summer, 1968).

Comtois, Pierre. "War's Last Battle." *America's Civil War*, 5 (July, 1992).

Davenport, Harbert. "General José María Jesús Carbajal." *Southwestern Historical Quarterly*, 55 (Apr., 1952).

De Planque, Louis. "A Photographer's Narrow Escape." *Philadelphia Photographer*, 12 (Dec., 1875).

Delaney, Robert W. "Matamoros: Port for Texas during the Civil War." *Southwestern Historical Quarterly*, 58 (Apr., 1955).

Delaney, Robert W. "Corpus Christi—The Vicksburg of Texas." *Civil War Times Illustrated*, 16 (July, 1977).

Elliott, Claude. "Union Sentiment in Texas, 1861–1865." *Southwestern Historical Quarterly*, 50 (Apr., 1947).

Ellis, L. Tuffly. "Maritime Commerce on the Far Western Gulf, 1861–1865." *Southwestern Historical Quarterly*, 77 (Oct., 1973).

Ewing, Floyd F. Jr. "Origins of Unionist Sentiment on the West Texas Frontier." *West Texas Historical Association Year Book*, 32 (Oct., 1857).

Fitzhugh, Lester N. "Saluria, Fort Esperanza, and Military Operations on the Texas Coast, 1861–1864." *Southwestern Historical Quarterly*, 61 (July, 1957).

Hager, William M. "The Nuecestown Raid of 1875: A Border Incident." *Arizona and the West*, 1 (Autumn, 1959).

[Haines, Lester]. "Tracing the Remains of Sheridan's Railroad Today." *Journal of Texas Shortline Railroads and Transportation* (Aug.–Oct., 1996).

Heidler, Jeanne T. "'Embarrassing Situation': David E. Twiggs and the Surrender of United States Forces in Texas, 1861." *Military History of the Southwest*, 21 (Fall, 1991).

Howell, Michael A. "Old Bayview—Not Just Another Cemetery." *Journal of South Texas*, 15 (Fall, 2002).

Kiel, Frank Wilson, ed. "'Wir waren unser 20 mann gegen 150' ('We were 20 men against 150'): The Battle of Las Rucias: A Civil War Letter from a German–Texan Soldier in the 1864 Union Invasion of the Lower Rio Grande Valley." *Southwestern Historical Quarterly*, 105 (Jan., 2002).

Larios, Avila. "Brownsville–Matamoros Lifeline." *Mid-America*, 60 (Apr., 1958).

Marshall, Bruce. "Santos Benavides: 'The Confederacy on the Rio Grande.'" *Civil War*, 3 (May–June, 1990).

Marten, James. "True to the Union: Texans in the U.S. Army." *North and South: The Magazine of the Civil War Conflict*, 3 (Nov., 1999).

Meiners, Fredericka. "The Texas Border Cotton Trade, 1862–1863." *Civil War History*, 23 (Dec., 1977).

Morris, Leopold. "The Mexican Raid of 1875 on Corpus Christi." *Quarterly of the Texas State Historical Association*, 4 (1900–1901).

Oates, Stephen B. "John S. 'Rip' Ford: Prudent Cavalryman, C.S.A." *Southwestern Historical Quarterly*, 64 (Jan., 1961).

_____. "Texas under the Secessionists." *Southwestern Historical Quarterly*, 67 (Oct., 1963).

Sansom, John W. "The Desperate Battle of the Nueces River, August 10, 186[2]." *Hunter's Magazine*, 1 (Sept., 1911).

Schoonover, Thomas. "Confederate Diplomacy and the Texas–Mexican Border, 1861–1865." *East Texas Historical Journal*, 11 (Spring, 1973).

Shearer, Ernest C. "The Carvajal Disturbances." *Southwestern Historical Quarterly*, 55 (Oct., 1951).

Shook, Robert W. "The Battle of the Nueces, August 10, 1862." *Southwestern Historical Quarterly*, 66 (July, 1962).

Sibley, Marilyn McAdams. "Charles Stillman: A Case Study of Enterpreneurship on the Rio Grande, 1861–1865." *Southwestern Historical Quarterly*, 77 (Oct., 1973).

Smith, Mitchell. "The 'Neutral' Matamoros Trade, 1861–1865." *Southwest Review*, 36 (Autumn, 1952).

Smyrl, Frank H. "Texans in the Union Army, 1861–1865." *Southwestern Historical Quarterly*, 65 (Oct., 1961).

_____. "Unionism in Texas, 1856–1861." *Southwestern Historical Quarterly*, 68 (Oct., 1964).

Thompson, Jerry. "A Stand Along the Border: Santos Benavides and the Battle for Laredo." *Civil*

War Times Illustrated, 26 (Aug., 1980).

_____. "Mutiny and Desertion on the Rio Grande: The Strange Saga of Captain Adrián J. Vidal." *Military History of Texas and the Southwest*, 11, no. 3 (1975).

_____. "Drama in the Desert: The Hunt for Henry Skillman in the Trans–Pecos, 1862–1864." *Password*, 3 (Fall, 1992).

_____. "Adrián J. Vidal: Soldier of Three Republics." *Hispanic Genealogical Journal*, 14 (1996).

Thompson, William G. "Letters from Commanding Officer in Area in 1863." *Port Isabel Press* (Mar. 31, 1881).

Trudeau, Noah Andre. "The Last Gun Had Been Fired." *Civil War Times Illustrated*, 29 (July–Aug., 1990).

Tyler, Ronnie C. "Cotton on the Border, 1861–1865." *Southwestern Historical Quarterly*, 73 (Apr., 1970).

_____. "Santiago Vidaurri and the Confederacy." *The Americas*, 26 (July, 1969).

Tyson, Carl Newton. "Texas: Men for War; Cotton for Economy." *Journal of the West*, 14 (Jan., 1975).

Weinert, Richard P. "Confederate Border Troubles with Mexico." *Civil War Times Illustrated*, 3 (Oct., 1964).

White, William W. "The Disintegration of an Army: Confederate Forces in Texas, April–June, 1865." *East Texas Historical Journal*, 26 (Fall, 1988).

Wilson, D. M. "The Last Battle of the War." *Confederate Veteran*, 18 (1910).

Wooster, Ralph A. "The Texas Gulf Coast in the Civil War." *Texas Gulf Historical and Biographical Record*, 1 (Nov., 1965).

Unpublished Material

Ash, Bette Gay Hunter. "The Mexican–Texans in the Civil War." M.A. thesis, East Texas State University, 1972.

Ball, Larry Durwood. "The United States Army on the Interwar Frontier, 1848–1861." Ph.D. diss., University of New Mexico, 1994.

Cowling, Annie. "The Confederate Cotton Trade with Mexico." M.A. thesis, University of Texas, 1926.

Crews, James Robert. "Reconstruction in Brownsville, Texas." M.A. thesis, Texas Tech University, 1969.

Dickeson, Sherrill L. "The Texas Cotton Trade during the Civil War." M.A. thesis, Texas Tech University, 1967.

Fielder, Bruce M. "The Mexican Connection: Confederate and Union Diplomacy on the Rio Grande, 1861–1865." M.A. thesis, North Texas State University, 1978.

Gallegos, J. J. "Santiago Vidaurri: Regional Power, Trade and Capital Formation in Northern Mexico." Author's files.

Graf, LeRoy P. "The Economic History of the Lower Rio Grande Valley, 1820–1875." Ph.D. diss., Harvard University, 1942.

Gray, Ronald Norman. "Edmund J. Davis: Radical Republican and Reconstruction Governor of Texas." Ph.D. diss., Texas Tech University, 1976.

Greer, Viola Ann. "Santiago Vidaurri, Cacique of Northern Mexico: His Relationship to Benito Juárez." M.A. thesis, University of Texas at Austin, 1949.

Hall, Ada Marie. "The Texas Germans in State and National Politics, 1850–1865." M.A. thesis, University of Texas at Austin, 1938.

Hildebrand, Walter W. "The History of Cameron County, Texas." M.A. thesis, North Texas State College, 1950.

Hunter, John Warren. "The Fall of Brownsville on the Rio Grande, November 1863." Center for American History, University of Texas at Austin.

Irby, James A. "Line of the Rio Grande: War and Trade on the Confederate Frontier, 1861–1865." Ph.D. diss., University of Georgia, 1969.

Kitchen, Carr P. "Mexican Depredations in the Lower Rio Grande Valley, 1835–1885." M.A. thesis, Baylor University, 1933.

Marcum Richard T. "Fort Brown, Texas: The History of a Border Post." Ph.D. diss., Texas Technological College, 1964.

"Reconstruction of Past Drought across the Coterminous United States from a Network of Climatically Sensitive Tree-Ring Data." National

Oceanic and Atmospheric Administration, Washington, D.C.

Riley, Denny. "Santos Benavides: His Influence on the Lower Rio Grande, 1823–1891." Ph.D. diss., Texas Christian University, 1976.

Townsend, Stephen A. "Steamboating on the Lower Rio Grande River." M.A. thesis, Texas A&I University, 1989.

Townsend, Stephen A. "The Rio Grande Expedition, 1863–1865." Ph.D. diss., University of North Texas, 2001.

Valerio-Jimenéz, Omar Santiago. "'Indios Barbaros,' Divorcees, and Flocks of Vampires: Identity and Nation on the Rio Grande, 1749–1894." Ph.D. diss., University of California at Los Angeles, 2001.

Webster, Michael G. "Texan Manifest Destiny and the Mexican Border Conflict, 1865–1880." Ph.D. diss., Indiana University, 1972.

INDEX

(Illustrations are indicated by a page number in **boldface**.)

COLOPHON

This book was set in Adobe Sabon with Diotima and Volta Script display type.
Printed at Toronto, Ontario by Schawk/Herzig Graphic Dimensions, Inc. on 100 lb. Lustro Dull Text.